WATERSTAINED LANDSCAPES

CENTER BOOKS ON
CONTEMPORARY
LANDSCAPE DESIGN

Frederick R. Steiner
Consulting Editor

George F. Thompson
Series Founder and Director

*Published in cooperation with
the Center for American Places,
Santa Fe, New Mexico,
& Harrisonburg, Virginia*

Seeing and Shaping Regionally Distinctive Places

waterstained landscapes

JOAN WOODWARD

Drawings by Kiku Kurahashi

The Johns Hopkins University Press Baltimore & London

© 2000 The Johns Hopkins University Press
All right reserved. Published 2000
Printed in the United States of America
on acid-free recycled paper
9 8 7 6 5 4 3 2 1

The Johns Hopkins University Press
2715 North Charles Street
Baltimore, Maryland 21218-4363
www.press.jhu.edu

Frontispiece: An S-shaped waterstain in Boulder County, Colorado.

Except where noted, all photographs are by the author.

Library of Congress Cataloging-in-Publication Data will be found at the end of this book.
A catalog record for this book is available from the British Library.

ISBN 0-8018-6200-0

FOR WARREN

contents

Foreword, *by Kenneth Helphand* xi

Acknowledgments xiii

ONE Settling Down 1

TWO Seeing the Waterstain 11

THREE Pattern Sources 31

FOUR Fingerprints of the Formative Processes 75

FIVE Patterns of Place 107

SIX The Stumbling-Forward Ache 141

SEVEN Planting Evidence 167

EIGHT There's No Home like Place 195

Appendix 205   References 211   Index 217

foreword

A MODERN AMERICAN tale familiar to most of us is about growing up in one place, moving to another, and moving again. We become packing experts and collectors of boxes. Moving becomes a habit with common questions. How do we settle in? How do we feel at home? How do we not feel like strangers? One way is to study the place, look, learn, ask questions, be eager, but take our time. It is smart to learn the lessons of others, but there is also satisfaction in the process of discovery. A fresh set of eyes sees things anew, and an enthusiast might ask new questions or seek answers to old ones that need revisiting. This is the story Joan Woodward tells, through her character Ann Crane. Ann's odyssey is commonplace; thus it is easy for us to identify with her. She recounts her story in a way that invites us along on her journey. We have all been there, even if we are among those who have rarely moved, or if we live far afield from the landscapes of the Denver region, the Front Range of the Rocky Mountains, or the arid West, which are at the heart of *Waterstained Landscapes*.

Waterstained Landscapes does not fit neatly into a single literary or professional genre. It is a journal but also a research report, workbook, notebook, sketchbook, textbook, historical fiction, and even garden advice column. At its core it is a professional and personal environmental autobiography, an intersection of person and place. We follow the narrator on her investigations, but she is actually leading, gently guiding us. Throughout, there is an infectious curiosity, the first and essential stage in learning about new places or ideas.

Ann Crane is motivated by a desire to learn new landscapes. Hers is the quest for a design language that speaks in the language of place. The ethic is clear: to conserve resources, tread lightly, be attentive to the sense of place. How do we understand, capture, and display the distinctiveness of a region? The entire book is a gentle polemic, a call to look carefully, listen to a place as it speaks, ask questions, suspend judgment, and then take informed action. Ann asks how we can be true to a place.

Embedded within places are discernible patterns. The question is how to interpret them. For designers, the question becomes how to embody that understanding in design. In the Front Range region of Colorado, it is through reading the waterstain, the key indicator, that this process is initiated. We follow Ann in seeking a strategy for this exploration and are privy to her findings. Her methods are diverse. They entail systematic seeing through searching for traces and methodical transects. Her eye is keen and her descriptions are rich; seeking regularity, she is also attuned to happenstance and anomaly. Like a skillful tracker she follows signs and learns to rely on instinct, but only after gaining all there is from those who have traversed the terrain before her.

A trajectory is followed, from curiosity to understanding to design and then to a proscription for the future. Working simultaneously at multiple scales, the keys are found in grand regional patterns and in telling details. Science and art are fused, natural process and cultural history are linked. The discovery, recognition, and identification of patterns does not in any way diminish the complexity and wonder of the landscape. Ann concludes with demonstrations and models. As a test case they include the most intimate and personal, her home garden, and the most impersonal, a highway interchange. Both accomplish the same objective, an informed connection to the nuances of the region. Finally, there are six exemplary case studies—models, in the many meanings of the term. They are something to emulate, they show off, and they are miniature versions of larger phenomena. Specific to one region, the lessons presented here are nonetheless applicable for all.

Woodward shows great respect for the world people have created without abdicating critical perspective or judgment. *Waterstained Landscapes* is both deeply humanistic and environmentalist, subversively working against the spurious—and dangerous—dichotomy of nature versus culture. This is a guide for a walk around the block, a drive to the store, or the view seen landing at Denver International Airport. *Waterstained Landscapes* is also a manual on how to redesign those experiences.

Kenneth Helphand, F.A.S.L.A.

acknowledgments

I AM GRATEFUL to many people for the birth, growth, and completion of this book. Colleagues and students played the strongest role in inspiring and helping with this study. Students in my graduate field-study course, "Interpreting the Landscape," at the University of Colorado, Denver, were the original excuse to get out there and look seriously at the region. Jeff Vogel invited me to speak at a Colorado Chapter of the American Society of Landscape Architects meeting, and preparing that talk solidified many of the ideas presented here. Stephen Humphrey, Devon Kohen, Lisa Langer, and Sharon Pulliam were hard-working research assistants; Kiku Kurahashi went beyond the call of duty to offer up innumerable Sundays and Friday afternoons to the cause. I am indebted to her creativity, tenacity, and sense of curiosity. I also appreciate the experiments performed by years of planting design students as we sought patterns and processes in the Los Angeles region, as well.

Caroline Etter, Kenneth Helphand, the late John Lyle, and Frederick Steiner constituted my advisory board for the book, and their comments and suggestions were enlightened and encouraging. David Buckner, David Fite, Joan Safford, Sue Scherner, Bob Scarfo, Ruth Yabes, and the book's numerous "interviewees" generously served as draft reviewers, and I appreciate their constructive comments.

The Landscape Architecture Foundation provided two grants in support of this work: the Ralph T. Hudson Environmental Scholarship and the AILA/Hope/Yamagami grant. California State Polytechnic University also provided a research, scholarship, and creative activity grant, which helped with the long-distance aspects of this study. Meléndrez Babalas Associates provided computer graphics equipment and time, and I appreciate their generous support.

I must acknowledge Ann Crane, who appeared one day on the page and wouldn't leave, despite some severe attempts at exorcism. I worried that a fictional character appearing in a landscape architecture design book would stymie the Dewey decimal system. Ann finally wore me down, along with a few critics, however, and stayed. Her presence seemed to derive from the inclusiveness of landscape architecture. She delves into science and uses art to express what she learns; she expresses both nature and culture in studies and design; she operates without a boundary between life and work; she moves and stays and moves; she describes place and finds she's describing herself; her story applies to both men and women—there are few boundaries here. There are also few boundaries between fiction and nonfiction in inspiring design, as one wise person, Denis Galvin, once told me when I described having to lock novels in my car to keep myself focused on my work. His observation freed me, in the nick of time for this book, to indulge in rereading the work of John Steinbeck and Wallace Stegner, both authors expert at describing the landscape's profound personal impact. Their fictional accounts instill a sense of caring. Design is inspired by profound personal impact and by such caring. It is my hope that Ann's story, more than another "how-to" landscape architecture book filed in the library's SB 472 section, can help others learn to care.

Author John Gardner once wrote that in all of literature there are only two stories: a person goes on a journey, or a stranger comes to town. With Ann's arrival and her subsequent journeys, both stories intertwine in this book. In my own life, which, admittedly, sometimes seems a bit like Ann's, a stranger came to town and changed everything for me; I thank my husband Warren for his good timing. He and our daughter became inextricably tangled up in the book's stories and fate.

Finally, I thank my editor, George F. Thompson, president of the Center for American Places, one of the earth's more intense and committed people, who agreed to take a chance that a book about waterstains might avoid being filed in the library's furniture-cleaning section. We can continue to hope, George.

WATERSTAINED LANDSCAPES

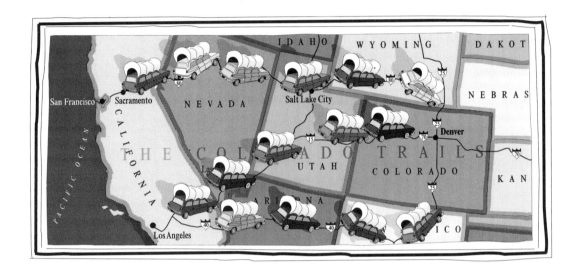

"Colorado, Here We Come!"
Illustration by Cindy Enright/Denver Post

chapter one
settling down

GRAVITY'S PULL Ann Crane's childhood nickname was "SP," short for "sturdy person." She was thick waisted, her thighs touched, and her dense hair was shoulder-length, so when she was backlit no light penetrated her shadow. This shadow would usually reveal a certain swelling along the outside of her lower torso, not from oversized hips but from pockets jammed with objects found along her frequent long walks through whatever neighborhood she happened to live in at the time.

An inventory of those objects served as a travelogue of her many moves as her family subdivided, reconfigured, and relocated. Fossilized crinoids from an Ohio streambed, which they called sharks' teeth, rattled in her jumper pockets; later, like a pack rat, she gathered and saved sweet, feral oat seeds from the vacant lot next to their new suburban ranchette in Indiana; brown, green, and blue broken glass pebbles, rounded from Lake Michigan's steady polishing, were her valued gemstones. Over time, Ann had placed these souvenirs in her treasure box, which also contained her mother's first wedding ring and a cigarette lighter stolen from her father. She believed in magic and was convinced, to no avail, that the right combination of stuff might bring this ill-matched pair back together again. Later, her expanded collection was housed in shoe boxes, along with letters from friends left behind after her family's various relocations. The objects she had later found, as an adult, reflected her trajectory west: a tiny, used-dental-floss hummingbird nest fallen from a Grand Tetons campground rest room; flaked subalpine fir bark riddled with woodpecker holes from Arizona's high mountains; lichen-crusted chunks of rock from Alaska's Chugach Mountains. These she had collected as she walked to the various cabins, trailers, and apartments she called home while working as a naturalist at numerous rural and urban parks. The collection was now artistically arranged in cosmetics boxes, offered free with the purchase of overpriced face cream, something she was using more and more of these days.

But not even thick applications of fancy ointment would help many of her senior co-workers, who had been naturalists longer than she. More, perhaps, than from the ravages of climate, their faces drooped with the effort of answering the same questions innumerable times. The rest rooms are to the right. No, female bighorn sheep—ewes—are pronounced "yous," not "eewees." No, crampons are climbing equipment, not feminine hygiene products. Ann was, indeed, sturdy, but even she could not bear to see the same down-turned lips in her own reflection. It was time for a career change.

This realization had struck her while she was working in Los Angeles. Like in a game of musical chairs, the music had stopped, and there was no familiar chair for her to fall into. Ann liked to be outside, but she did not want another park job. She loved science but wanted art in her daily life, too. Ann wanted to live in the arid West but found herself instead in saturated Los Angeles, dubbed "west of the West." She liked moving but wanted to pause. She boasted of her one carful of belongings and the speed with which she could pack and move, but she also found herself lusting after a handcrafted Arts and Crafts couch named the "Prairie Settle," which was so heavy she would have to stay put just to avoid moving it. And though she valued what she and her single friends dubbed "creative solitude," she had recently met and enjoyed the company of a warm-eyed, thoughtful man. She decided to stay in southern California a while longer.

"You're going back to graduate school? At your age?" her mother had asked. "To be a landscaper?" Thus began the first of many times Ann gently removed the "er" from "landscaper" and added "architect" to her aspirations. As a profession, landscape architecture seemed to knit together her various passions. She could collect objects as she walked design sites, interpret them, integrate them into artistic arrays—and be paid for this, no less. Her Faustian bargain was that were she to choose this enviable career she would be doomed to forever explain to family, neighbors, and fellow airline passengers that she did not in fact drive a truck with lawn equipment in the back.

Many of her classmates, also in their thirties, were fleeing previous lives as realtors, aerospace engineers, bankers, and even priests. Ann noted that those most successful could have been employee candidates for General Douglas MacArthur, who was said to have declared he would rather hire someone smart but lazy than dull but hardworking. Her first foray into the smart, lazy world had occurred in a planting design project for which the students had been asked to design two schemes, one for shade and one for sun. She felt that sunny and shaded areas should be expressively different; but she ran out of time and sheepishly designed just one scheme with plants that thrived in both sun and shade. The project earned her an A, much to her disdain. Toward the end of her third year in school, an observant professor had noted a common thread in all her landscape design concepts: they tend to be like an old jewel box, he said: sturdy and practical on the outside, needing little care, but intricate and valued on the inside, inspiring care. Just like her, Ann's new husband pointed out. Sheesh, she thought she had finally given that old nickname the slip.

After graduating, Ann was at a cusp: neither student nor worker bee, not yet pinned to place by a mortgage or children's needs. It was time at last to find a home and settle down. She liked the sound of that, "settle down." She had been told as a child to settle down, even as her family uprooted every second year, but it had then meant "be quiet." Her body was now settling down, the pull of gravity more evident every day. But like a leaf pile, she was rustling at the top, anxious to move, and she feared she would begin to compost if she stayed much longer. Her engineer husband was especially in need of rejuvenation. His daily commute to and from work was three hours long. One day she noticed that the hard plastic edge of his car's steering wheel had been picked away by idle thumbs while he languished in traffic. Almost a third of the wheel was missing. If ever there was a signal to find a new home, this was it. So was the tiny spot seen recently on an ultrasound screen, a human newt already three inches long. "Follow your bliss," mythologist Joseph Campbell wrote. "Do what you love and the money will follow," the popular self-help books proclaimed. "Just Do It," advertisers advised.

EAST TO THE "WEST" The Cranes packed their household items into a U-Haul; the weight of the Prairie Settle splayed the tires somewhat as they bumped onto rural roads, into café parking lots and national park campgrounds. They were seeking a new home, and, judging from the bookstore shelves crowded with books dispensing advice on how to find a new home or crowing about having found one, they were not alone.

As they met others on similar sojourns, the Cranes recognized that they were part of a popular movement toward areas where more land, more value, more sense of home would be possible. Geographer D. W. Meinig names this activity "westering" and notes that it is a major national phenomenon: "The image of the West as new country where one might embark upon a new life in more congenial circumstances has persisted as a powerful attraction."[1] The Cranes realized they would have to move east from California to begin the process of westering. Walter Prescott Webb, in *The Great Plains* (1931), records anecdotes about the direction of migrations in the 1870s. "It is possible to tell which way the emigrant is going by the remains around his camp fire. If he is going west, the camp is surrounded by tin cans and paper sacks; if he is going east, it is littered with field-lark feathers and rabbit fur.'"[2] During their migration the Cranes could easily distinguish east from west, because almost all the moving vans they saw were traveling east, from California toward the Rockies.

As in all migrations, the participants shared a common motive. According to economist James Davidson, "When opportunity is cut off in one direction, peo-

1. Meinig 1972, 174.
2. Webb 1931, 320.

ple will move in another. Where there is freedom to move, the process is practically as automatic as that which inclines a plant toward sunshine."[3] Ann fondly recalled a previous summer spent in a canyon community along Denver's Front Range. She, her husband, and their newborn son started leaning toward the sunshine there.

The Cranes joined more than one hundred thousand other Californians who, since the early 1990s, had retraced the 1849 gold rush trails to move to the region where the Rockies meet the Great Plains. They left behind not temporary camps that would be erased by winds but the legacy of suburban subdivisions built in an oasis civilization, propped up by imported Colorado River water. Like returning anadromous fish, Californians were following the flow of their watershed back to the source.

Their welcome in Colorado was not exactly a warm one. In fact, their California license plates often prevented them from merging in traffic and invited irate gestures and honks. To many in the growing Denver region, the arrival of Californians signified the almost certain loss of what character remained in the Denver region. In a *Time* article on Denver's boom, former Colorado governor Richard Lamm worried that Denver would become the "Los Angeles of tomorrow."[4] Other recent newspaper articles issued forth such titles as "Yuppie-ai-ay," "California, Here We Go," and "Colorado, Here We Come." A billboard near downtown Denver asked, "Are we becoming L.A.?" Ann had seen a history museum exhibit that invited Denver residents to place an adhesive dot on a map of the United States indicating where they had lived before moving to Denver. She was not surprised to see the mountain range of dots forming over Los Angeles. A friend of hers joked about the correlation between Los Angeles earthquakes and immediate jumps in Denver property values. Nonetheless, despite the scarlet "L.A." affixed to their breasts, they determinedly continued their assessment of this potential homeplace.

They sought a place of safety and community; a place in contact with its landscape; a place where they might find responsible work; a place to host the possibility of clarity and joy. In many areas within the Denver region they found what they sought, evidenced by graffiti oriented toward love rather than male territorial sprays, walls erected as property definitions rather than property

3. Davidson and Rees-Moog 1991, 430.
4. Dawson, Donohoe, and Jackson 1993, 25-26.

defense, and dogs kept primarily as pets rather than alarm systems. They saw ample evidence of accessible community life: mixtures of denominations, people walking or sitting outside, old people interacting with babies and fathers with sons, women and children talking and playing in a neighborhood park, teenage activities accommodated and respected, opportunities in the form of classes, concerts, and commerce offered and taken. They sought and found access to landscape: trail systems, parks, nearby nature, and nearby countryside. Along the region's river ran a walking and biking path, which invited exercise, learning, art, and gathering and afforded protection of water and species. And as for joy, the stage was set here. Ann found the great hinge between the West and the East invigorating and accessible through views reaching toward distant horizons. She liked the region's location on the time zone, favoring early light and cloudless mornings. A sense of history was present in these mountains and plains, from geological to paleontological to archeological to historical. Many historical artifacts had been preserved and interpreted, thanks to persistent and dedicated history aficionados as well as the economic benefits of heritage shopping areas. Yet, many relics in the plains had not been sanitized or gentrified. Ann could still see outlines of old homestead buildings and persistent vegetation surviving long after buildings were gone, promising the pleasure of discovery.

As for work, there was much to be done here in landscape planning and design. In fact, the very elements satisfying her homeplace requirements were in most danger of being lost. In her homeplace search, Ann represented thousands of other people looking to meet similar requirements—expressed more straightforwardly, jobs, affordable housing, good schools, and a healthy environment. Population changes and new construction to accommodate growing demands for housing, transportation, and water all accompanied these desires and ran the risk of canceling out the beneficial sense of home. As Lewis Mumford had presciently written in 1925, "We may either permit it [the migration] to crystallize in a formation quite as bad as those of our earlier migrations, or we may turn it to better account by leading it to new channels."[5]

5. Mumford [1925] 1976, 64.

SCALES OF PLANNING AND DESIGN Landscape planning and landscape design, Ann mused, operating on a variety of scales, were vehicles to lead this migration toward new channels. She reviewed these scales as she targeted her search for employment. At the largest scale, regional planning serves to provide overall data and policy guidance for regions linked by a common homogeneous characteristic, which can be shared culture, an extent of urbanized land, or a geographic feature, such as a watershed. General frameworks for guiding growth and development are created at this scale, using information about regional landscape patterns and trends. The regional planning needs of Denver's Front Range are served by a group known by the wizardly sounding cronym, "Doctor Cog" (the Denver Regional Council of Governments, or DRCOG). This group provides smaller governmental units with data and forecasts, such as projected population growth, as well as visions for the region. Recent regional plans forecast the addition of 280,000 households and 355,000 jobs between 1995 and 2015, with a 35 percent increase in the number of car trips per day.[6] Developing a preferred growth scenario to adapt to this swelling population was one of the regional consortium's priorities. Working at this scale appealed to Ann and would satisfy her itch to see how macroscale systems work together.

City comprehensive plans are required by law for each incorporated city within the region. The plans, which state specific goals and objectives to be reached within each community and outline approaches to reach these objectives, are revealing markers of the current community ethos. For example, the Denver Comprehensive Plan of 1989 reinforces the importance of an imageable city: "Beautify the city and preserve its history" is the second goal, after "Stimulate the economy."[7] The plan designates many areas within the city for growth and investment. And sure enough, in traveling to these designated areas, which fifteen years earlier had been homes to industry and an occasional artist's loft, Ann saw evidence of districts shining as if anointed by the Good Economic Witch of the West. Banners proclaimed special events, bands played, shoppers spent money and searched for parking spaces. Planning paired with investment had wrought tangible change in this region.

At a smaller scale, site design involves drawing from goals, data, and a pro-

6. Denver Regional Council of Governments 1995, 4.

7. City and County of Denver 1989, 1.

gram and arranging the physical and natural elements of a site. In Denver, design of specific land parcels, funded by bond issues and private capital, was observable on a daily basis. In fact, it was a heady time for design firms, whose projects included planning the Denver International Airport, rejuvenating parks and parkways, expanding libraries, rebuilding amusement parks, ball fields, and an aquarium, and creating entrance sequences into the city. New population and job growth, coupled with the public's self-funded goal of beautifying the city, made this a remarkable time to shape the landscape. To do this in a manner that maintained long-term resource quality and quantity was a challenge Ann would enjoy.

One part of site design is planting design, which uses the medium of plants to create beneficial site function and human response. Ann's practice was to create designs that satisfied people's desires for comfort, image, beauty, safety, and free movement and also fitted with natural flows of water, energy, species, nutrients, and so on. When plants are selected on the basis of minimal watering, pruning, and fertilizing requirements, landscapes can achieve maximum functioning with minimal maintenance. This saves money on materials and labor, conserves valuable resources, and conveys a sense of long-term commitment to land. In landscape interpretation circles, this practice is dubbed the "least effort principle"—the same principle that General MacArthur admired in his lazy but smart employees. Such designs give the appearance of continuity, of history—as if created by people who had settled down. Ann inhaled a ticklish breath of desire; maybe it was at last time for her to have her own garden and begin to live these ideas for herself.

CARING Work at all these scales requires an ability to see and understand a place and to design in a way that allows a place's own skeleton, its functions, its past, and its future, to emerge. And the Cranes, having rented an apartment, decided that this was now their place. They had sampled many other communities across the West and assessed compatibility with their needs, and they were ready to make the leap. Ann had read enough western literature to gain insight into the alignment between her motivations and what historians William H. and William N. Goetzmann call "the West of the imagination."[8] Her need for

8. Goetzmann and Goetzmann 1986.

landscape contact, responsible work, and joy seemed to be a current translation of the mythic sense of freedom, heroism, and individuality that had always lured people to the West.

With their West quest now satisfied, they joined thousands of other people bumping up against each other for jobs, jostling for a space on the freeway at rush hour, demanding good water from the tap, hoping their children would be able to enjoy the occasional pause of development in the countryside. Here, they saw honest evidence of what they needed; they trusted that the magnetism of being at this great energetic hinge, the clarity of the skies, the occasion to see a backyard deer, and the laughter they heard ringing off front porches would help them overcome the dulled restlessness they had felt in Los Angeles. They intended to be alert to what they regarded as a major contributor to their Los Angeles ennui: disorientation resulting from places unquestioningly designed to look like somewhere else, covering up or removing evidence of the place, ignoring change, squandering resources. Ann vowed to apply the care and fear that she now felt to her professional activities. Armed with a deliberately selected place in which to settle down and that mysteriously potent human force, caring, the Cranes stepped out into the region to learn to see and understand and create what John Steinbeck called "the stumbling-forward ache": beneficial change.[9]

9. Steinbeck 1939, 164.

Substantial change is imminent along the Denver Front Range.
Photo by Debb Smith and Cynthia Owens

chapter two
seeing the waterstain

WATERSTAINS Ann got out of the car, drawn toward the edge of mountain and plains like metal filings to a magnet. Strains of Sons of the Pioneers songs from the car stereo floated through the open door. At first, only the For Sale sign drew her attention to the property; but when she noticed the adjacent public park, she drove to the park overlook and gazed eastward over the last tremors of rock and the great Rocky Mountain range before it smoothed out for a thousand miles of plains.

Ann looked toward the plains, the drama of uplifted, iron-laden red rock slabs acting out behind her (figure 2.1). In the foreground, yellowed grasses flowed downward, suddenly greening at a slight juncture in the slope. A fence line ran perpendicular to the grassy slope, shrubs marking the fence posts. Brown soil patches and taller, branching plants crowded the area within the fence. The far edge of the fence divided these plants from tall, verdant-canopied, veiny-trunked trees, which paralleled the distant road. From the

2.1 View from Red Rocks State Park overlook provides much information to those who look.

road, the slope suddenly rose again, with clear stripes of grasses, then dark and yellow-blooming shrubs and, beyond, yellowish, rounded evergreens clattering around in rock outcrops. In the distance, grasses again flowed east until interrupted by the dark green vegetative nests for thousands of constructed white boxes.

Ann looked with a child's eyes at the dizzying complexity unfolding before her and strained to find the thread that would help her better understand the fabric. Being a relative newcomer, she was not yet aware of the Jurassic flood that had trapped dinosaurs just over the ridge, leaving their footprints intact. She did not know the names of the birds depositing seeds along the fence posts or of the yellow grasses. But in the distant foothills she could see the face of one slope consistently cloaked with dark green trees, the rest uniformly covered with grasses: north, she read, where the cooler climate supported plants requiring more water. She could predict from the stripes of different rock types in the road cut that soil shifts and the difference in water availability were responsible for determining whether trees, shrubs, or grasses would thrive on the slope. She could see that the ditch running alongside the road contained enough water to support trees. She could see the pulse of the irrigated urban forest, deciduous tree heights stepping down at regular intervals as the newer subdivisions succeeded west toward her.

Her lips dried out from the sun and the wind; Ann thought about water. Most people would argue that what was missing from her view was water. All these browns, reds, grays. The occupants of the scattered houses adjacent to the park seemed to agree—irrigated lawns ringed their houses like green doilies. If Wallace Stegner were standing beside her, she thought, he would explain that these residents had not learned to appreciate the beauty of the West, which requires that we "get over the color green."[1] Yes, she nodded in this imagined conversation, as her eye moved toward the houses. Get over it. To herself, though, she whispered: But where it does occur, pay close attention.

Green is loaded with information. Green, and the densely textured reminders of it in other seasons, indicates where water is or once was, leaving a green stain in a land where umbers, ochres, sepias, warm grays, and tans prevail. Where water concentrates, plants respond. Ann experimented with her eyes' new lenses and looked for these water concentrations, these waterstains. They read like the semiarid West's signature inscribed on this land. Sometimes the pen scribbled with meandering cottonwood ink. Sometimes it boldly underlined, especially at the edge of impermeable surfaces like roadsides, where green weeds pronounced extra runoff. The waterstain spilled like ink, drenching cooler north-facing slopes, soaking the distant subdivisions, defying gravity, and moving up slopes via irrigation systems.

Ann's new lenses helped her detect numerous repeated arrangements of plants, or plant patterns. She began to test herself, spinning around and repeatedly determining north, whether she peered at slopes in the distance, at the mountain mahogany slope in front of her in contrast with the opposite juniper-dotted grassy slope, or at the pockets of deciduous trees clustered on northern red rock exposures. She was learning to read the landscape. Naturalist Aldo Leopold urges his readers to "[think] like a mountain."[2] Ann was thinking like a mountain mahogany.

Bob Nolan's voice from her car stereo penetrated the birdsong: "Dan can't you see that big green tree where the river's flowin' free and it's waitin' there for you and me? Water. Cool. Clear. Water."[3]

1. Stegner 1992, 45.
2. Leopold 1949, 137.
3. Nolan 1945.

Ann mused that *waterstain* was the word that seemed to best describe what she saw. Usually, she thought, "water stains" are something we regret seeing: the telltale ring on the bedside table, the Iowa-shaped mark on the basement apartment's ceiling, the rain-smeared ink in the field notebook. She later consulted the dictionary. The verb *to stain* is defined as "to taint, tarnish, corrupt, . . . discolor, soil, spot."[4] As a noun, *stain* fares even worse: "A blemish upon one's character, personality, or reputation; a stigma; . . . a spot or smudge of foreign matter." A stain of water, then, is an anomaly, something found in a normally dry environment. It stands out as a "smudge of foreign matter." To Ann, the word *waterstain* was satisfyingly unvarnished: it represented a rather blunt report of water's former or hidden presence. The more elegant word, *watermark,* summoned up for her images of classic laid bond paper inscribed with a hidden insignia. She pictured the many new green lawns planted in self-promoting business parks and subdivisions. Sandwiched between soil and turf lay the hidden insignia of irrigation pipes, making the lush image possible. No, she thought, we have too many landscapes with a watermark sensibility as it is.

LEGIBILITY Waterstain legibility depends on the aesthetic principle of contrast: the contrast between wet and dry locations, wet and dry seasons. In this landscape, there was more dry than wet in both location and duration. As a result, dry was the matrix, or ground, and wet was the patch, or figure, a view dependent on scale. Earlier that day, Ann had stopped to examine a roadside wetland. Surrounded by spiky cattails, blackbird calls, humidity, and humic smells, it seemed like all-encompassing lushness. But if she could hover high above this wetland and look down from an aerial perspective, the isolated wetland would protrude as a tiny raisin in the dough of aridity. Elwood Mead wrote in 1909, "The problems of Western irrigation grow largely out of the fact that there is more land than water. If every drop of water which falls on the mountain summits could be utilized, it is not likely that more than 10 percent of the total area of the arid West could be irrigated, and it is certain that, because of the physical obstacles, it will never be possible to get water to even this small percentage."[5]

Although large areas within the Denver region were currently irrigated, giv-

4. Unless stated otherwise, word definitions are from *The American Heritage Dictionary of the English Language*, ed. William Morris (Boston: Houghton Mifflin, 1976).
5. Mead 1909, 5.

2.2
The precise plaid pattern created by lawn mowers expresses this business park's image at a small scale.

2.3
Aerial scale reveals the business park's semiarid context.

ing the impression of lushness, Ann hypothesized that if she could step back far enough and see the region on a grander scale, the true nature of nature would return. She remembered a persistently watered swath of green turf, mowed to a perfect plaid, lining one side of a freeway corridor she had driven that day, announcing the presence of a Scottish-themed business park (figure 2.2). The pacing of mowers and arcing shafts of sprinkler-dispensed water attempted to convince her and thousands of commuters that they had been transported to another more tasteful, successful world of exceedingly good landlordship. At the aerial scale, however, where browned, late-summer ranchlands pressed along three edges of the park, the emerald image became simply a strip of conspicuous resource consumption (figure 2.3). It reminded her of the inverse deception she had experienced when driving in the Pacific Northwest where logging companies had left an almost-convincing, old-growth tree fringe adjacent to the roadway, known as a "beauty strip." Every so often, she would catch a glimpse of the stumps and scattered slash that had not been successfully camouflaged. An aerial view would have exposed the sham immediately. Similarly, semiarid landscapes require observation at a variety of scales to appreciate their legibility.

Like Goldilocks, Ann had to choose a single chair, but in her case, none were comfortable by themselves. She needed aerial-scale, driving-scale, and walking-scale views to gain an appropriate perspective from which to read the region's signatures. Remembering how she regularly annoyed fellow airplane passengers by refusing to lower her window shade during the in-flight movie, she acted upon an urge to hire a small plane and pilot to fly over the region. The green golf-course stripes, turf rectangles, and ditch traceries she saw enlarged her growing collection of waterstain patterns.

Only when Ann leaned her head and camera out the small plane's window did she realize that hers was no mild case of piqued curiosity about a new home. She felt the crooked finger of an academic investigation beckoning. Her interests were rapidly growing into a study that she could not seem to keep herself from doing. Not only was the landscape becoming more legible, her future was as well. Back on the ground, she paid the pilot and returned home. She was plagued by questions: How can we characterize the distinctiveness of a region?

How can those elements that make a region distinctive be applied toward design? Why should we bother to learn to read our region and then apply this learning to design? And how can such region-based design both use resources appropriately and be enjoyed by the inhabitants? She found herself procrastinating for weeks about buying appropriate shoes to accompany her interviewing outfit and put off finishing her resumé and portfolio. Yet when she saw an advertisement for a grant that supported study in landscape architecture, she snapped at it and successfully funded part of her project.

The first steps of her official study were to designate the region she would come to know very well and to develop a system for studying it. The steps that followed would develop somewhat like a Polaroid photo: she could detect the rough outline, focusing on plants and planting design, but the picture awaited full color and detail.

DEFINING THE REGION A region is a slippery concept to define, as Ann soon found after again consulting her dictionary. The definitions—"any large, usually continuous segment of a surface or space; an area; . . . a large and indefinite portion of the earth's surface," lacked specificity but did free her to create her own definition of what composed that "continuous segment." She designated as her study area the land between Boulder and Brighton to the north, Buckley Air Force Base to the east, Highlands Ranch to the south, and foothills communities such as Morrison, Golden, and Eldorado Springs to the west, an area roughly thirty miles wide by thirty-six miles long (figure 2.4). Ann recognized that her selected study area was not a watershed, as it did not include the headwaters of the South Platte River and other stream sources. It was not a single physiographic region, as defined by a single dominant vegetation type: it included plains, foothills, and mountains. It was, however, representative of (although not identical to) the region studied and worried over by the Denver Regional Council of Governments and mapped by the United States Geological Survey (USGS) in its map series on the Front Range urban corridor. This area appears repeatedly on promotional maps of the region and roughly, for the present, was where the bulk of urbanized and urbanizing land appeared. Meteorologists also cite this precise area as being within the "urban heat

2.4
Location of Denver
Front Range region
and study area.

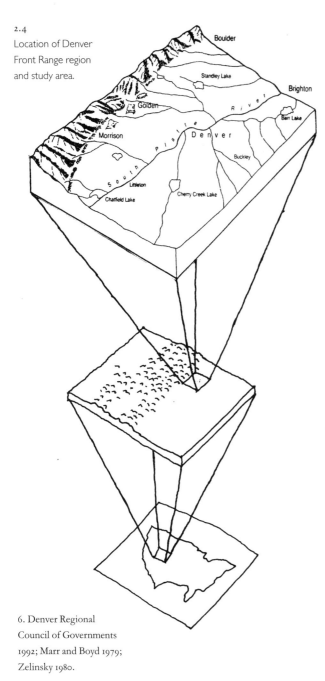

6. Denver Regional
Council of Governments
1992; Marr and Boyd 1979;
Zelinsky 1980.

island." Cultural geographer Wilbur Zelinsky defines a region as whatever the masses of people perceive it to be.[6] Ann therefore followed the lead of the masses and decision makers before her in defining the Denver Front Range area in this way, with an emphasis on a semipolitical, urbanized features rather than purely physiographic or watershed ones. Others grappling to understand their own regions may choose other definitions that are equally valid.

STUDYING REGIONAL PATTERNS

Ann then sought a system for systematic seeing. She was interested in seeing the plants that characterized the region and the way these plants are arranged. It was easy to gain anecdotal information: she asked new friends (who were already learning to humor her) what immediately came to mind when they thought of plants in the Denver region. Many stories emerged: some friends acknowledged deliberately choosing to drive along the slower parkways rather than the faster, wider streets because they enjoyed the trees and flower displays; some immediately described the golden drying grasses of the foothills contrasted with the dark conifers rising up mountain slopes. Some acquaintances mentioned the trim neighborhood gardens with floral displays at key spots; others described backyard vegetable gardens. Anecdotal information gave her a start in understanding what plant groupings people value. She then wanted to know whether these plant arrangements appear repeatedly throughout the region, so that she could begin to see the patterns that characterize the Denver region. Discerning patterns would help her shift from simply seeing plants to reading and learning and predicting the factors contributing to the appearance (or disappearance) of these plants.

Ann felt that she would be closer to understanding the region's distinctiveness if she had a technique to prevent her from being too subjective. Thus, she rolled out a U.S. Geological Survey map of the Greater Denver Area, Front Range Urban Corridor, Colorado, and drew a large X on the map (figure 2.5). She then drove along this X, stopping regularly at three- and five-mile intervals to look carefully. Thanks to Thomas Jefferson's cardinal grid, this was a challenge entailing hundreds of left and right turns. (Coming from Los Angeles, she thought, and having a high capacity for intense driving experiences provided good qualifications for doing this study.) At these stopping points, she walked, talked to people, sketched, and squinted, looking for repeated arrangements of plants as indicators of place. Vegetation patterns were abundantly evident along these transects, and she discovered ironic and charming surprises: the riparian-choking and ornamentally beautiful tamarisk shrub gracing the planter in front of the Federal Center's Bureau of Reclamation headquarters and the dainty petunias at Buffalo Bill's Grave were among her favorites (figures 2.6 and 2.7).

She began the northwest leg of her exploration in South Boulder, where ponderosa pine savannah scooted down mesas to infiltrate grasslands (figure 2.8).

2.5
Transects form an X over the region, showing stops made along the way.

SEEING THE WATERSTAIN 19

2.6
A tamarisk shrub makes an entry statement at the Bureau of Reclamation building.

2.7
Petunias and a sign direct visitors to Buffalo Bill's grave.

She proceeded southeast for five miles to the northern grassland edge of Rocky Flats, then five more miles to the weedy edge of Standley Lake. Her route passed the Two Ponds National Wildlife Refuge, a welcome surprise of wetland preservation in the urbanizing area. The next stop was along the Colorado and Southern Railroad tracks at the edge of Arvada. Her route flowed near several well-loved Denver city parks as she continued southeast along the transect. She ventured a side trip to Inspiration Point, which had been revegetated with dryland plant species to emphasize Denver landscape architect Saco DeBoer's inspired ponderosa pine allée (figure 2.9). Walking along the unpaved, fragrant allée Ann noted how DeBoer's design effectively linked the park's formal gardens to dramatic views of the mountains to the west. The park, she soon discovered, was also a type of lover's lane, and she quickly returned to her car after making a few missteps to investigate nearby shrub plantings.

As Ann continued on her way, her transect bisected a path between Berkeley Park and Rocky Mountain Park, with DeBoer's eighty-year-old zigzagging double row of honey locust street trees still visible along the Forty-sixth Avenue Parkway. The legs of the X crossed neatly near the new Gateway—two obelisks inscribed with the plan for Denver's street grid—that marks the entrance to Denver's lower downtown from Speer Boulevard (figure 2.10). Five miles from there her route brought her close to Four-Mile House Historic Park, where the historic stagecoach stop into Denver has been preserved and interpreted for the heyday period between 1859 and 1872 (figure 2.11). Continuing south, she intersected the mowed and trimmed edges of Interstate 225, between the Interstate 25 confluence and Cherry Creek Reservoir ("Cherry Creek Lake," according to the road map.) Landscape tidiness continued at her next stop, a country club. The last two stops on this forty-mile leg were in open montane rural residential areas, where shrubs once again crowded north-facing slopes and yuccas hung heavy along slope edges (figure 2.12). A diverse region, indeed, she concluded.

The next day, as Ann tackled the second transect, she was reminded of her favorite refrigerator-door quote, attributed to Spanish explorer Juan Francisco de la Bodega y Quadra: "I pressed on, taking fresh trouble for granted." She stopped at three-mile intervals on this shorter route. The southwest leg began at Red Rocks State Park, where she had dallied at the overlook when she first

2.8
South Boulder open space is the first stop along the transect.

2.9
DeBoer's ponderosa pine allée leads Inspiration Park visitors to a notable vista.

moved to the region. A new geological exhibit was under construction, along with a new interpretive trail to help spark constructive learning and behavior in the park. Her next stop brought her to the undeveloped southern slopes of Green Mountain, where northern slopes were darkened by shrubs (figure 2.13). She progressed to the Federal Center, a national aggregate of federal buildings built after World War II; snagging such an employment center had been a coup for the growing city.

Ann had logged many hours in the U.S. Geological Survey library, where original diaries, drawings, and photos of the earliest western explorations are archived. The next stop found her in the Lakewood suburbs, where rural properties were larger and more densely vegetated, with tall trees and a conspicuous shrub layer. Mile High Stadium and older neighborhoods greeted her at her next stop, where store signs were scribed in Spanish and productive gardens were visible, interspersed with vacant lots and intensely detailed Victorian style buildings. Her X shuttled her forward past residences and on to the still pungent stockyards along the banks of the South Platte River (figures 2.14 and 2.15). She stopped for a beer in the cool Stockyard Inn and Saloon and perused old photographs that captured the stockyard's vital role in Denver's history. Her route nicked the Mile High Kennel Club and Racetrack, then the blooming prairie of the Rocky Mountain Arsenal National Wildlife Refuge for the next two stops. An informative refuge manager gave her a cross-country tour of one transect point on the wildlife refuge property, the site of former homesteads and small farms prior to condemnation of the area by the United States Army (figure 2.16). The second point she was able to see only in aerial photos: it was still polluted

opposite

2.10
The transect legs cross near Denver's obelisk gateway.

2.11
Four-Mile House is a former stagecoach stop.

this page

2.12
Shrubs mark greater moisture availability in southeast portions of the region.

2.13
Green Mountain's north-facing slopes are evident.

SEEING THE WATERSTAIN 23

by chemical insecticide, weapons, and rocket fuel production fallout, and access to this Superfund site was restricted. Real estate signs greeted her at her last stop, in the vicinity of the Denver International Airport. Short-grass prairie ranches and former dryland farmlands now sported commercial zoning announcements, tempting prospective buyers.

Her transect completed, Ann found herself near enough to Brighton to search out a recommended Mexican restaurant. Her green-chile-burrito radar took her by a farmer's field raked by opalescent white-faced ibis near Barr Lake, repetitive subdivisions outside of Brighton, and a Buddhist temple, one sign of Brighton's vibrant Japanese population. As she settled into a booth, she considered the images collected along her trip and felt she had seen an impressive cross-section of the region's cultural and natural wealth. She needed more information about what she had witnessed, however; thus, as her study expanded in spatial scale, it also needed to expand in time. Chiles dripping onto her plate, Ann decided she wanted to know more about the region's past, present, and future.

That summer found her poring over indicators of time, so apparent in the

Denver region, to find out more about plant patterns. She ducked out of the summer heat by repeatedly visiting history libraries, historical societies, botanic garden libraries, archives, and manuscript collections. She examined homey, informative Colorado Cooperative Extension Service annual reports incongruously housed in the Petroleum Building skyscraper downtown. She interviewed long-term residents, historians, photographers, ecologists, commercial growers, planners, and designers.

WHY BOTHER? Although she found many intact, legible, humorous patterns throughout the region, Ann also saw the rapidity with which waterstain legibility was disappearing. The For Sale sign that had caught her eye near Red Rocks Park was one of many proliferating in the region. One way she marked the rate of development was to peruse revised copies of individual U.S. Geological Survey seven-and-one-half-minute quadrangle maps and trace the color purple, which the USGS uses to indicate recently revised residential development. At first glance, it seemed that the cartographer carelessly spilled the purple ink bottle over formerly prominent features like Old Indian Head or Pine Gulch. At second glance, though, she realized that these names had most likely been incorporated into the signs at subdivision entrances. Another approach used to measure the rate of development over the same period of time was to examine aerial photos taken at various intervals throughout the 1900s. The rapidity and thoroughness of development in many locations was startling.

As people move to semiarid urban areas, they enlarge the sense of oasis. As a result, Ann saw much the same plants growing in lawns and gardens that one would expect to find in temperate areas with much higher rainfall. Irrigation systems allowed large, lush plants to grow on hot, dry slopes. On one hand, she was deeply impressed by people's persistent desire for green, considering the evaporative, gravitational, and entropic forces working against such semiarid denial. On the other hand, and this was probably a habit bred from thinking about landscapes drowned by western reservoirs, she wondered which instructive patterns were masked by this green cover. In looking at any one of many urban highway embankments, irrigated to produce perfectly matching north- and south-facing slopes, she mentally stripped away the green carpeting to see

opposite

2.14
Denver resident proudly displays her backyard along the transect route.
Photo by Kiku Kurahashi

2.15
Stockyards illustrate Denver's regional ranching importance.

2.16
The Army's tree corridors line field edges at the Rocky Mountain Arsenal National Wildlife Refuge.

what could be there, given enough time, in the absence of irrigation. Would yuccas cling to the slope edge, as they always do here, taking advantage of this precarious niche? Would there be a stripe of green at the toe of the slope? Would the north side of this slope be greener or more densely populated with plants? Could she stand back and know which way is north, simply by examining this slope? Rolling the sod back in place, she mused that people like green as a symbol of orderliness and care. She realized that most semiarid cities look alike, leaving people dulled by homogeneity, and imported water was not yet expensive enough to counteract this desire. The French author Honoré de Balzac once said that behind every fortune is a crime. Ann felt that behind every flippantly installed bluegrass sod lawn in a semiarid landscape was a crime of undervaluing water.

Ann saw the greater impact, beyond the loss of the ability to see the inherent legible patterns of the region, a lost act of joy in and of itself. With increasing development comes a greater need for imported resources in semiarid landscapes, especially water. In 1990, when the Environmental Protection Agency denied the permit to build the Two Forks dam in Colorado, for example, Denver was considered to have only twenty years' worth of identifiable water remaining.[7] And although new reservoirs have slaked this particular shortage, within the urbanized Denver Front Range corridor served by Denver Water, total water usage is increasing. Power usage has also increased; gravel is being mined at an increasing rate; and more organic soil is imported to compensate for the region's poorly developed soils. Increased development will continue to hasten this importation of materials unless resource-conserving alternatives are accepted on a wider basis.

Ann felt a sense of urgency. New transportation routes, acting as dispersal corridors for residential, commercial, and industrial development, were being developed rapidly within the region. Popular and mass-produced artifacts were daily replacing ever more vestiges of hard-earned responses to this challenging climate and location. Already, as equipment bit into the slope, Ann watched the clear line between shrubs and grasses along the foothills near Golden being erased, to be replaced a month later with smooth green grass lawns (figure 2.17). She saw a windrow of trees knocked down by bulldozers to make way for a new

7. Dawson, Donohoe, and Jackson 1993, 26.

2.17
New development gilds Golden.

freeway extension. Such instant change at the bulldozer line triggered enormous emotional response in her. At one point, watching stockpiled topsoil blow off a newly graded construction site before revegetation could begin, she broke down and cried. Sheesh, she thought, I haven't done this since my father died. She scrutinized her motives and did not feel she was clinging nostalgically to relics of days gone by. Rather, she was deeply troubled by the loss of orientation and identity she had already observed in this region. Ann missed the cues and information remnant tree populations could tell about water and survival. She was offended by the exploitative borrowings of regional character, such as the subdivision names recalling, for marketing purposes, the landscapes just obliterated. As Laurie Olin asserts, "The ubiquitous homogenization of culture and environment, the rapacious consumption of the products of art and heritage, the proliferation and rapid debasing of the accumulation of works of architecture and art through mass industry, marketing, and consumption, and the substitution of images and simulacra for real objects or places of historic achievement that are ideologically or aesthetically laden with meaning for particular societies has led to revulsion for such facile and exploitative devices on the part of many practitioners and academics in design."[8]

8. Olin 1995, 268.

But though her father's death had been wrenching, it was inevitable. Ann eventually adjusted to the change, and she carried his influence into the world. How could the heritage of this place be carried forward in the face of such change?

THE GAP   As she looked for guidance on how to design with a sense of regional distinctiveness, Ann found mostly mixed messages. On a positive note, she repeatedly encountered authors emphasizing the importance of regionalism and distinct, legible places. Eighteenth-century English poet Alexander Pope admonished designers centuries ago to "consult the genius of the place in all." Landscape architect Michael Hough writes convincingly in *Out of Place* that design suited to the regional context is imperative to our well-being. The writings of city planner Kevin Lynch assure us that we are dependent on legible places to be well oriented and positively affected by our environment. Architect Kenneth Frampton reminds us that regionalism is no longer an inevitable response between people and place—we must self-consciously cultivate it. Geographer Josiah Royce emphasizes the need for the "vigorous development of a highly organized provincial life to offset dead national conformity that tends to crush us as an individual." Unless such regional emphasis arises, in Royce's view, the nation is "in danger of becoming an incomprehensible monster, in whose presence the individual loses his rights, his self-consciousness, and his dignity."[9]

Sufficiently revved up, Ann looked in Denver's largest bookstore for guidance on applying a regional sensibility to landscape design. She found dozens of green-backed books on creating Victorian gardens, perennial borders, butterfly gardens, all-white gardens, edible gardens, and shade gardens but none on how to create a "context" garden: a garden based on a region's legible plant patterns.

The bookstore's clerk directed her to the landscape architecture section and to a large collection of books addressing water-conserving landscape design, also known as Xeriscape. This widely demonstrated, and increasingly ordinanced, concept originated in Denver in 1981, following a series of dry years. According to an early Xeriscape Colorado! newsletter, "The goal of the

9. Pope 1731; Hough 1990; Lynch 1960; Frampton 1987; Royce 1969, 1070, 1083-84.

Xeriscape movement is to promote the 'greening' of Colorado while encouraging water conservation via the use of diverse plant materials and practical landscaping guidelines."[10] Ann found a listing of twenty public Xeriscape demonstration gardens throughout the West and realized she had visited many of them. These gardens serve to educate and convince the public that water-conserving gardens can be lush and beautiful. They all demonstrate Xeriscape principles, the seven steps that focus on appropriately zoning plants for microclimate control, reducing turf areas, and reducing evapotranspiration through efficient use of mulches and irrigation. The steps are purposefully generic and apply to many design styles. Yet by being so generic, they provided her with no guidance in creating regionally distinctive landscapes. Gardens inspired by English countryside themes, but substituting drought-tolerant plants, seem to be favored models in these demonstration gardens. As a result, inherent, orienting patterns of semiarid regions are repeatedly obscured by temperate climate patterns even in model demonstration gardens. She remembered the surge of pleasure in seeing the waterstain patterns at Red Rocks. What a missed opportunity, she thought—the gap between what we designers say and what we do still loomed.

Alright, then. Here we go, she decided, inadvertently speaking aloud and drawing the clerk's attention. It was time to build on Xeriscape's useful resource-conserving foundation and resurrect a region's underlying relationship between plants, people, landforms, and drainage as expressed through its plant patterns. Such an approach may not stop the bulldozer line, but it might influence the line's shape and location. The Polaroid photo of her study was becoming more vivid as it developed. She would start by better understanding the region's relationships, then move toward determining patterns resulting from these relationships.

The clerk peered at her over his reading glasses, smiled, and wished her luck.

10. Bonand 1992, 2. Note that *Xeriscape* is a registered trademark held by the National Xeriscape Council.

View of the Hogback in winter, near Morrison, Colorado.

chapter three
pattern sources

FORMATIVE PROCESSES Ann drove to the outer edges of her study area and concentrated on what she saw. Well, she thought, this is about the fifth time I've seen young cottonwoods growing like a military sword salute along road cuts (figure 3.1). What's up? And so her investigation began.

For Ann, seeing a pattern was always a satisfying first step in understanding a place. Patterns sparked curiosity, invited investigation, and helped her sort everyday chaos. In fact, she craved patterns, to such an extent that she sometimes jumped to conclusions before adequate information was collected. Ann looked to natural historian Diane Ackerman to keep her honest with this definition of pattern: "Once is an instance. Twice may be an accident. But three or more times makes a pattern."[1] This definition of *pattern* has to do with understanding repetition. A second definition refers to a pattern as a "model, prototype." Both of these definitions apply to planting design.

1. Ackerman 1993, 11.

3.1
Trees colonize a road cut, taking advantage of a water source.

In school, Ann had been taught that when undertaking a design project she should carefully inventory site characteristics: what plants are present, soil types and depths, water quality and quantity, structures present, and so on. This information guides appropriate placement of new structures and plants. As her personal investigation into design methods grew, she discovered designers who called for taking an additional step: looking to the larger region for repeated arrangements of plants for design inspiration and incorporation. For example, one designer notes the presence of groves of birch trees within meadows in the high mountains above a northeastern U.S. town where he worked.[2] He advocates using this pattern of random vertical elements along a meandering path to create an entrance and transition between a "natural"-appearing house and lawn. The repeatedly seen "pattern" (first definition) was used as a "pattern" (second definition) for the new design. To translate the first definition of *pattern* into the second—that is, to move from identifying a raw inventory of repeated objects to creating a model—more information is necessary. Why do those birch trees flourish in the mountains but not in the existing suburbs? What creates the distinctive edge between forest and meadow? Are there parallel soil and

2. Dube 1994.

microclimate conditions between the suburban and mountain sites? Will a cribbed mountain pattern survive in the suburbs? Ann felt that pursuing these questions would help the author—and her—to understand the larger context within which these plants flourished: understanding the pattern's context keeps designers from disconnecting patterns from the forces that shape them.

She remembered making train models when she and her brothers were young. They used sparkly plastic bits for grass and broccoli for the forests. They lathered on the glue and sifted plastic grass liberally up and down slopes and throughout the downtown areas. They thrust pins through the broccoli stems and arranged the vegetables in clumps and lines to complement the green slopes and fields. Adults still accomplished much of their planting designs in this way, she feared.

As geomorphologist William Marsh has written, "When we describe the forms and features of a landscape, we are actually observing the artifacts and fingerprints of the formative processes."[3] She clearly remembered her brother spilling soda on the model, right next to a railroad trestle: the green plastic grass that had been carefully sprinkled evenly over the slopes became unglued in the bubbly flash flood and coagulated at the base of the slope. Gravity and precipitation were suddenly stronger formative processes than their small yet divine model-making hands had been. In order to understand the formative processes shaping vegetation patterns in her home region, she followed plant ecologist John Miles' suggestion that we look at the geomorphic, climatic, and biotic processes shaping vegetation presence and change.[4]

Ann unpacked her undergraduate science texts, marveling at the contrast between the listlessness with which she had earlier approached them, under duress, and the attention with which she now read them, from her own motivation. She reviewed these formative processes: Geomorphology is a branch of geology dealing with the earth's surface landforms. Geomorphic processes are those activities that determine underlying parent material and landforms within an area—specifically, material deposition and uplift, soil erosion by water or gravity, redeposition of material by wind or water, and changes in soil stability owing to frost action. Climatic processes are investigated to identify dominant influences on vegetation. Precipitation, wind speeds, solar radiation, tempera-

3. Marsh 1991, 43.
4. Miles 1979.

tures, evaporation rates, and overall periods of climate change are examples of climatic processes. Biotic processes affecting vegetation patterns include the effects of other plants, animals, and plant diseases. To keep her focus on reading and off lunch, Ann occasionally stopped to remind herself why she was studying these processes. She knew she was restless to learn about the conditions resulting from these activities that to a large degree determined vegetation responses and their resultant patterns. But, more so, she anticipated the potential pleasure awaiting her, according to another favorite refrigerator-door quote from Virgil's *Georgics:* "Happy is the person who has been able to discover the causes of things."

Miles classifies human influences as biotic forces. He acknowledges humankind's usually deliberate yet sometimes unconscious need to change landscapes—and its far-reaching consequences—but groups them with the influences of locusts and cattle on vegetation patterns. After her earlier flight over the region, Ann agreed with geographer Donald W. Meinig's emphatic version of landscape as "comprehensive and cultural"; thus, she veered from the ecologist's lumping of all biotic influences together and split humans into their own category as agents of change in the landscape.[5] Based on her reading, she narrowed to three the driving human forces creating, shaping, and affecting different vegetation patterns: the need for protection, production, and pleasure. Protective efforts include the use of plants to provide relief from sun, wind, cold temperatures, fire, and intruders. Productive strategies such as cultivation and ranching involve efficiency, domestication, and technology and create distinct vegetation forms. Following the lead of others, Ann interpreted *pleasure* broadly to include the human need for faith, power, order, cultural and personal expression, and healing.[6] Political tools such as taxation, ordinances, and plans institutionalize protection, productivity, and pleasure and ultimately reinforce or change prominent vegetation patterns.

As often as Ann saw the distinctions between these processes, she also saw their interactions and intersections; a line demarcating one from the other was artificially drawn when describing plant patterns. Geomorphic processes of erosion and climatic processes of precipitation are inextricably linked in shaping vegetation responses, such as trees crowding the rim of a foothills stream.

5. Meinig 1990, xv.
6. See Francis and Hester 1990.

Similarly, high solar radiation rates and human need for shade interact to result in recognizable plant patterns, such as trees lining roads or marking the southwest corner of a house. Usually one or two formative processes dominate the others, but all are inevitably present and to some degree manifest themselves in the arrangement of plants.

Collecting and recording plant patterns without understanding the forces shaping them, it struck Ann, was like going to the deli and buying a ready-made dinner and drawing a blank when asked for the recipe. Reproducing plant patterns as models or prototypes without understanding the formative processes reminded her of building that model railroad landscape. It may look good, but the broccoli will wither without roots, the grass will plunge to the base of the slope when mice nibble at the glue, mold will colonize the slopes, kids will grow up and lose interest in maintaining their control over this miniature world. The law of entropy always works against this type of design.

Ann turned to the experts to understand the formative processes of the Denver Front Range region. They helped her to understand the place, from past to present, from large scale to small. She knew all too well from her training that the process of collecting and digesting this type of information should precede design, both on a regional scale and at smaller scales, in the Denver region as elsewhere.

GEOMORPHIC PROCESSES Ann had studied geology while living in Indiana. There, it seemed more an act of faith than here in Denver, where landscape development was dramatically legible in the region and attracted professional and amateur geologists worldwide. Visiting the Interstate 70 road cut near Morrison, she experienced the "immense journey" sensation best described by naturalist Loren Eisley as he crawled into a plains crevice that exposed ten million years of geological history: "I had projected myself across a dimension I was not fitted to traverse in the flesh."[7] The I-70 road cut related a fast-forward story of change in the bedded layers of rock: Precambrian granitic intrusions; oceans advancing and retreating; reptiles captured by floods and released two hundred million years later by erosion and paleontologists; soils deposited by oceans, uplifted, eroded, uplifted, eroded again, uplifted again,

7. Eisely 1959, 11.

eroded yet again, creating different alignments, colors, textures, depths, pockets, permeability, personalities—all seen as a blur by most people driving past at sixty miles an hour.

Processes of mountain building, glaciation, and erosion create soils and slopes that plants respond to and people often try to change with mulches and grading. Ann grimaced, recalling all the landscape-elucidating naturalist hikes and brochures with lead-ins like, "This landscape was once a vast inland sea." But indeed this was the starting point for the story of slopes and soils in the region (figure 3.2). The advance or retreat of that sea determined whether fine-grained silts and sediments filtered out or sand dunes and sandy bluffs formed.

While walking in the foothills with a park ranger and his attentive audience, Ann noted how he used his hands to explain the rest of the story. He held his hands in front of him, palms down, fingertips touching, the whole unstable chunk of continent, 325 million years ago, between Kansas and Utah, represented by those hands. By slowly bending his knuckles on both hands upward, he formed the Ancestral Rockies, flanked on both sides by the ocean's solidified but crumbling sediments. The knuckles slowly flattened down again as the ancient mountains eroded, streams and wind depositing layer upon layer of gravely, sometimes iron-rich conglomerate materials atop fine-grained sediments. Lush vegetation and reptiles from the humid Jurassic period were caught in the layers forming in this flattening landscape. Then, the ranger's fingertips rose as if in prayer, their upward motion representing ten million to twenty million years. The igneous Rockies lifted, granite pushed upward, adjacent sedimentary basins sagged. His A-frame fingers

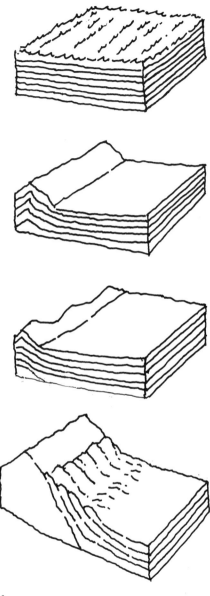

3.2
Evolution of landforms over time.
Illustration by Devon Kohen

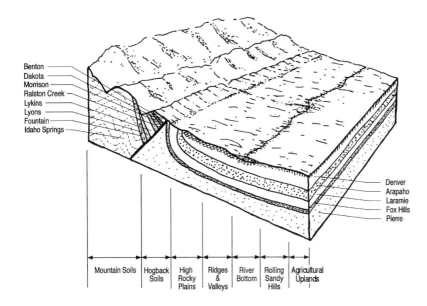

3.3
Soil sources and rock types. *Based on data from Chronic 1980, Robson 1987, and Wenk 1978*

then spread, allowing glaciers and outwash streams to wear down the steep slopes. Weathered rock was transported to the plains by wind and water, thickening the sagging basins. Resistant rock, such as the iron-rich redbed formations, lay on the slopes like red dishes drying in a drainer or impressively flanked the mountain edge like the Great Wall of China. This latter formation somehow was unceremoniously called "The Hogback."

The ranger dropped his hands when describing the origin of the soils found in the mountains, foothills, and plains. Then he gesticulated, animatedly providing facts. He invited the audience to imagine drawing a representative line from mountains to plains. Elevations range from more than fourteen thousand feet to five thousand feet; most slopes face east until the South Platte River drainage is crossed, then they are west-facing, with occasional slopes trending north-to-south. Ann sketched as the ranger described regional soil formation along this west-to-east transect and later supplemented his description with information from other sources (figure 3.3). The mountain and hogback area soils were primarily formed on site from more resistant rock. These soils are therefore more sorted, and shifts between rock types are evident through soil type changes and vegetation responses to these soils. In sandstone areas, soils

PATTERN SOURCES 37

tend to be thin and well drained, with rocks forming reservoirs of water protected from evaporative forces.

The ranger then described the high, rocky plains stepping down from the mountains. These were old river or alluvial terraces, raised by bedrock uplift, cut by streams and glacial melt. The rocky alluvium over the thin-grained sedimentary layers capped the terraces, slowing erasing erosion. Where the rocky cap contacted the less permeable sedimentary soils, a distinct line formed, frequently designated by trees and shrubs responding to available water storage. Aha, Ann thought. The line of cottonwoods appears where the road cuts through these terraces.

Much of the region's underlying drama is evident in the Morrison area. Here the underlying formations rise vertically to breach the surface, as if pinned tightly together near the hogback, and then relax and sag as they gain bulk in depth and flow underneath the surface. Where the fine-grained clay and siltstone Denver formation surfaces, soils shrink and swell with rainfall—a well-known fact to home owners confronting shifting basements and foundations in these areas. The contact between Denver and Arapahoe formations often forms unconfined aquifers, with verdant vegetation responding to the additional water.[8]

Proceeding east, the ranger described how the original surface of the High Plains had eroded, depositing silts and alluvium, creating rolling topography. Notable mesas dotted this landscape, capped by volcanic flows and protecting soft bedrock from wearing away. Golden's North and South Table Mountains, along with Denver's Inspiration Point, Boulder's redundantly named Table Mesa (*mesa* translates as "table" in Spanish), and others give a sphinxlike presence to this landscape.

Ann found herself drifting from the talk's content in pursuit of her own thoughts. She remembered Branson and Shown's study of Lakewood's Green Mountain, describing the contrast between north- and south-facing slopes[9] (figure 3.4). North-facing slopes are steeper than those facing south owing to differing slope erosion rates: warmer soil temperatures, increased evaporation, sparser vegetation, and increased runoff contribute to faster eroding, and therefore shallower, slopes on the south face. Between two slopes, drainage

8. Hillier, Schneider, and Hutchinson 1983.
9. Branson and Shown 1989.

courses are often asymmetric in shape and are located closer to the toe of the north-facing side, owing to the south face's debris fill. As a student, Ann had once been asked to sketch her preconceptions; for example, she was asked to quickly draw a house: invariably she drew a square with two windows, centered door, and curled-smoke chimney. When visiting Branson and Shown's Green Mountain study area the first time, she prodded herself to quickly draw a section view of a drainage area in front of her. Invariably, the stream was neatly centered within its banks. Once she had studied the geologists' observations, the asymmetrical features were suddenly visible.

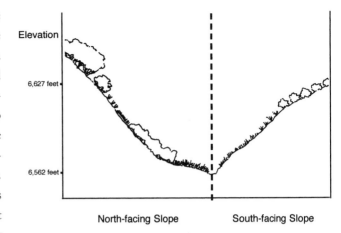

3.4 Differences in north- and south-facing slope vegetation area are apparent at Green Mountain. *Based on data from Branson and Shown 1989*

Water shaped and was shaped by landforms along this transect. Ann felt her preconceptions again crumble when she drew her first cross-section across the study area. This time she was surprised to find that, because of continuous erosional surfaces dropping from the mountain front, the South Platte River did not flow due east. Instead, the South Platte flowed north, its once wide, meandering path carving channels and distributing gravel and fertile alluvium throughout the region's bottomlands.

She tuned back in to the ranger's ongoing talk as he described the South Platte River, originally named by French trappers for its uninspiring, dominant characteristic: its flatness.[10] The ranger then asked his audience, "Do you think the South Platte River now has greater or less stream flow than it did two hundred years ago?" More than half the group wrongly guessed less. Once an intermittent, milewide stream, the river was described by an old adage as being "too thick to drink, too thin to plow, too wide to shoot a rifle across, and too narrow to sail." Farmers brought groundwater up to the surface through windmills and wells and applied this water to new croplands. Water percolated through the sandy, loamy soils, and the South Platte basin water table rose, now sustaining a permanent, year-round flow[11] (figure 3.5). Several other modifications changed

10. Whitney 1983.
11. Knopf 1986.

PATTERN SOURCES 39

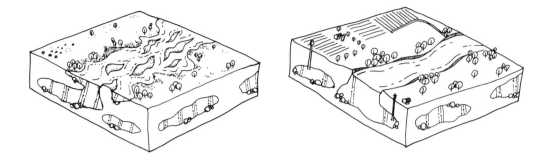

3.5
The South Platte River has changed from an intermittent to a perennial stream following the introduction of irrigation.

Illustration by Devon Kohen

the form and function of the river as well. Channelization of streambanks for flooding and erosion control have shrunk the stream margin in some places to one-twentieth of its historical width. Dams regulated water quantity to reduce flooding potential. Urban development's concrete, asphalt, and roof surfaces increased runoff heading toward the river. As a result, the South Platte River is now a more stable corridor than previously, but the loss of flooding and shifting regimes has curtailed riparian forests from colonizing its banks and diamond bars.

Moving east into the High Plains, the ranger continued, streams change character. Whereas streams generally flow directly and energetically through the foothills, High Plains streams to the east dawdle on their way toward the South Platte River, often eroding less permeable soils, watering and nutrifying them, resulting in riparian wetland systems. In many areas, these streams cut through rolling, sandy, wind-deposited uplands, which do not offer strict stream guidance. Streams, unless channelized, scribble through the plains. Stapleton Airport was built on these sand deposits. During the summer shifting sands sometimes blow across runways, mimicking winter's snow drifts, according to one report. Rolling hills in the southeast corner of the study site reflect the higher elevation by the invasion of shrubs into the grasslands. Agricultural uplands of different pockets of wind-deposited soils overlie shale and sandstones. The ranger finished his talk, thanked his audience for joining him, and left them with an appreciation of the ongoing dynamic power embodied in these seemingly frozen forms towering above them at the mountain edge.

As she returned home to inevitable chores, Ann considered the ranger's talk and some of the missing pieces in a discussion of the Front Range's geomorphic processes—particularly those that shaped landforms. Ann was aware of the hazard of separating processes into categories: precipitation is a climatic process; yet water above and below the ground shapes, and its paths are shaped by, landforms. Some visualization of the relation between water, landform, and water's availability to plants was needed to explain the plant patterns she was beginning to collect. How did groundwater and surface water become available to plants in this region?

Ann pondered this as she stacked clean dishes, and as she nested successively smaller bowls in her kitchen cupboard, she found the image she was looking for to describe the Denver groundwater basin. This sixty-seven-hundred-square-mile area extends west to the Front Range west of Golden, north to Greeley, east to Limon, and south to Colorado Springs.[12] Her study area was primarily on the northwest margin of the raisin-shaped basin. The outer bowl, the deepest bedrock aquifer, is the Laramie–Fox Hills aquifer, which underlays the next bowl, the more permeable Arapahoe aquifer, then the Denver bowl, and finally the Dawson aquifer bowl, which is exposed to the surface toward the southern end of the basin (figure 3.6). Almost all of the basin's stored groundwater is found in these dense, water-laden layers of conglomerate, sandstone, and shale. In the 1880s the potential for tapping bedrock to supply wells near downtown Denver was discovered, leading to a rapid increase in the number of excavated wells as well as the first hydrological studies.[13] Early Denver was dependent on these water sources: they were unpolluted and, for a time, plentiful.

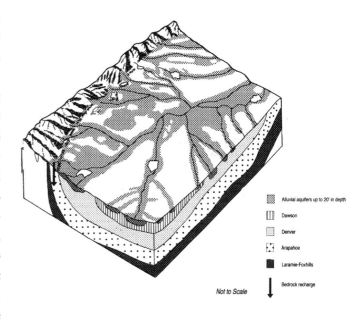

3.6
Denver region bedrock and alluvial aquifers. Based on data from Robson 1987, Hillier et al. 1983.

12. Robson 1987, 8.

13. Colorado Scientific Society 1884.

PATTERN SOURCES 41

Finishing her chores, Ann returned to the stacks of reports collecting in her office. She read in several hydrological reports that plenty of water stained this land: 5,000,000 acre-feet of water per year fell onto the basin from the mean annual precipitation of fourteen inches per year. She held her hands a foot apart and tried to picture this amount of water spread over five million acres. Difficult to imagine. For reference, she found that in an average year the South Platte River carries about 250,000 acre-feet past the Denver area.[14] Most of this water was lost to evaporation, transpiration, and runoff; less than 1 percent recharged bedrock aquifers.[15] Yet, 9 percent of the stored bedrock water was pumped to supply the region's agricultural, industrial, and domestic needs. This led to a water-level decline of five hundred feet in locally pumped areas and two hundred feet in a broader 240-square-mile area to the north, east, and south of Denver.[16] Ann wondered how bedrock aquifers could possibly meet what must be greatly increasing demand as more people inhabited the region. Clearly, water departments must hijack water from one watershed and transport it to this one, an act she was familiar with from having lived in Los Angeles. In fact, water had been transported from the Western Slope to the Front Range through systems of tunnels, pipelines, and reservoirs since the first large-scale project was completed in 1936.

Ann studied diagrams and continued reading these reports. Alluvial aquifers flow across the rims of the four bedrock aquifers. These fingery, stream-hugging basins are composed of water-laden gravel, sand, and clay. They contain 3 percent of the basin's stored groundwater, and 91 percent of this water is pumped and used. Alluvial aquifers are ten times as transmissive as bedrock aquifers, meaning that these aquifers transmit water much more readily than bedrock. Yields also are larger. The next most transmissive aquifer is located south of Littleton in the Laramie–Fox Hills and Arapahoe aquifers. Wells located here offer the greatest potential for developing new groundwater sources and potential groundwater injection areas. Water withdrawal from the Arapahoe aquifer has led to as much as eight inches of subsidence in land surface.[17] As of 1994, Denver Water, the independent agency responsible for supplying water to the city and the outlying area, had reduced pumping since the peak in 1981, thus also reducing the potential for further subsidence. With rapid

14. Whitney 1983.
15. Robson 1987, 2.
16. Ibid.
17. Ibid., 66.

population increases and greater demands on water, pumping figures are now creeping upward again. Construction of a new Western Slope reservoir and plans to reuse water should alleviate subsidence and the overwithdrawal of groundwater.[18]

Delving into geomorphic processes of land formation, erosion, deposition, and soil formation helped Ann understand the region's dynamic vertical and horizontal landscape checkerboard. She ventured beyond the ranger's story and contemplated contemporary forces shaping today's landforms. More recent evidence of landform change is the appearance of mesalike road, rail, and reservoir embankments prominent throughout the region and appearing with increasing rapidity. Concentrated, imported limestone and crushed rock form the walls of reservoir dams, reminiscent of the hogback. Lavalike linear flows cap miles and miles of previously erodible silts, clays, and sands, using reconstituted Jurassic wetland plants for asphalt. Wood, brick, metal, pressed board, and occasionally stone outcroppings, ten- to twenty-feet high, are erected in regular intervals over the foothills and plains surfaces, creating symmetrical north- and south-facing slopes. Occasionally, these outcroppings attain heights more than four hundred feet in certain key pockets and are surfaced with erosion-resistant metamorphic quartz, heated to become glass. Square and rectangular stone blocks, layered as vertical surfaces without mortar or other accreting devices, have recently proliferated along these linear asphalt flows, announcing intersections and concentrations of structures. Artesian-well-like water sources spring to the surface throughout the region, sometimes on cue. Their outputs temporarily flow through surface layers of coarse organic debris, hit an impermeable plastic layer, then flow horizontally to hard concrete surfaces, metallic tubes, and streams. The erosive quality of the water is undetected on a daily basis.

Geomorphic processes are in full effect today, right now in the Denver region, Ann concluded. Recognizing the power of gravity, sediment-laden water, and wind-blown sand on stone inspired her to add the other formative processes to her understanding.

18. Denver Water 1994.

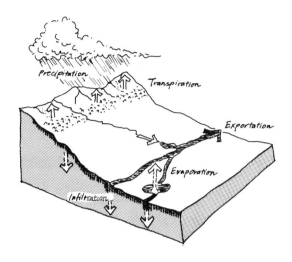

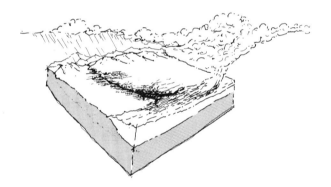

3.7
Hydrological cycle shows water's transformations.

3.8
Hydrological cycle as interpreted in *Finnegans Wake*.

19. Joyce [1939] 1960. See also Campbell and Robinson 1944.

CLIMATIC PROCESSES One of Ann's favorite malapropisms was the description of a disappointing event as "anticlimatic." When she saw pop-up irrigation heads hosing slopes in the middle of a thunderstorm, she supposed there should be such a word. Climatic processes responsible for shaping vegetation are difficult to separate from geomorphic processes, because a semiarid climate affects rates of erosion, and wind and stream flow determine deposition. Elevation influences temperatures, and landforms affect rain and wind patterns. These elements are inextricably connected. Yet studying climatic processes of flows of air, water, and energy promised to help Ann understand plant patterns, as well as the area's attraction for her. Many people are drawn to this region because of climate. What are we inviting upon ourselves?, she wondered, and she flipped through a few of her texts for clues.

Climate! The most dramatic, magnetic, ecstatic component defining the Denver region was often described, she found, through the dullest, most repeated diagrams: the hydrologic cycle (figure 3.7). The typical diagram illustrates the forces interacting in this region: seasonal precipitation, infiltration, exportation through streams, evaporation, and then a repetition of the same cycle. Yet, what Ann found most interesting is that the hydrologic cycle served as an apt metaphor for many things. Ann doodled as she remembered James Joyce's description of a woman in *Finnegans Wake*.[19] Joyce's woman is young like a mountain stream. Like the stream passing through agricultural land, she grows mature and fertile. Then the infirmities and breakdowns of old age settle in, as the stream moving through urban and industrial portions becomes soiled and tattered. She passes to the Ocean father, and the sun evaporates her, until convective clouds lead to the new precipitation over the mountains. Old and new water commingle, becoming rejuvenated, refreshed. The older woman smiles with the glee of the girl. The girl witnesses the tragedy of a spider's death with adult, mournful eyes. We are surrounded by all stages of this cycle. It is in us. We design in cycles. We like to think life is linear, but looking at soil or sea can convince us otherwise. Perhaps the hydrologic cycle diagram does indeed tell us this, Ann thought, glancing at her new doodled diagram (figure 3.8).

Ann's task for that day was to summarize much of the information she had gathered on climate within the region. She glimpsed the spotless blue sky, breathed in the fresh morning air, and packed her things for a bicycle trip to the library, to fill gaps in her study.

Ann soon found a few truths emerging from her reading. One understated generalization applicable to the Denver region was that climate is constantly variable. She looked backward in time for evidence. A detailed record of climatic conditions since the last full glacial period (eighteen thousand years ago) has been interpreted from pollen preserved in lake and bog sediments.[20] The region's climate was cold and dry, with treeline thought to have crept at least fifteen hundred feet lower than it is today. This means that the mountains appeared bald-headed, with tundra to about ten thousand feet. Four thousand years later, humidity increased, but temperatures stayed low, with pine, spruce, and fir forests thriving in the winter-dominated precipitation, pushing far out into the plains. Warming and drying conditions occurred between six thousand and nine thousand years ago, stranding cooler climate plants in isolated north-facing slopes, canyons, and caves. She imagined a camera taking time-lapse snapshots of the Front Range: glaciers melting, trees advancing, climate drying, trees retreating, leaving just a few stalwart relicts behind in protected places. Tree ring analyses further fleshed out the climate picture and substantiated extended periods of drought throughout the West.

Ann found evidence of climate variability on shorter time spans in the Front

20. Thompson et al. 1993.

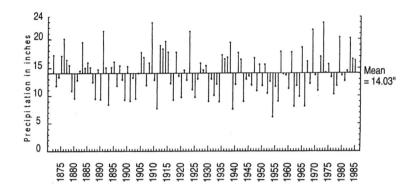

3.9 Long-term climate variability for Denver, precipitation records from 1872 to 1985. *Based on data from Noel, Mahoney, and Stevens 1994*

Range as well. Denver precipitation data dating back to 1872 showed striking variability in rainfall levels[21] (figure 3.9). Analyses of long-term weather data indicate that past winters were wetter in the Rockies, with much drier springs than at present. An even larger study of almost half a million weather stations in eleven western states indicates that spring precipitation has been declining, with summer rainfall increasing.[22] A clap of thunder startled Ann from her reading and confirmed the likelihood of short-term variation in weather: heavy afternoon rain obscured her view out the library window.

The second most reliable description of the region's current climate, she found, was that it is semiarid. On a global scale, this region is sometimes termed "middle-latitude steppe," linking the Front Range to similar climatic conditions in the Russian steppes. The term *semiarid* was once thought to be an objectionable term. For example, Major John Wesley Powell's maps employed the term *sub-humid*, "to keep from offending those who object to the terms 'semi-arid' and arid.'" According to Walter Prescott Webb, "Even the scientist has to apologize for designating certain regions as arid or semi-arid, and some of them have used the term 'sub-humid' in order to shield themselves from the local critics. . . . The inhabitant of the Great Plains likes to read that his country is a land of sunshine, of hospitality, of honesty, of promise and prosperity . . .

21. Noel, Mahoney, and Stevens 1994.
22. Bradley, Barry, and Kiladis 1982.

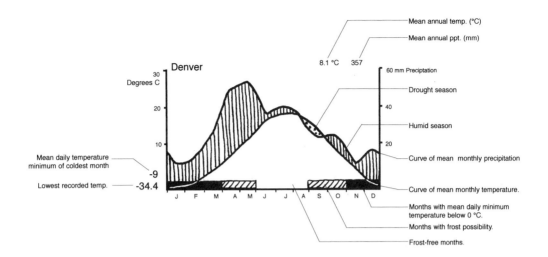

3.10
Denver climate summary.
Based on data from Walter, Harnickell, and Mueller-Dombois 1975

but he often prefers that hot winds, sand storms, droughts, hard water, and dry rivers be left unmentioned."[23]

Ann found two sources of diagrams that served as useful illustrative tools for these often unseen but vividly felt climatic elements. She worked back and forth between them, sketching her own versions. In the first, she found the Wal-Mart of climate diagrams, devised by botanist Heinrich Walter and summarized in the thin tome, *Vegetation of the Earth,* and accompanying maps[24] (figure 3.10). This one-stop-shopping diagram impressed her with its information density. Working back and forth between the diagram and its key, she gained information about average temperatures throughout the year. She saw that January is typically the coldest month, with mean low temperatures hovering around freezing, and July the warmest, with mean temperatures in the low seventies. She gleaned precipitation data from the diagram, which showed that roughly half of the region's annual precipitation falls in the form of snow, mostly in late winter and spring.

From the second source on climatography of the Front Range, she learned that mean precipitation within the region varies between 18.6 inches in Boulder and Golden and 13.3 inches at Cherry Creek reservoir and in Brighton[25] (figure 3.11). The lowest mean precipitation rates are for downtown Denver, at 12.9

23. Webb 1931, 321-22, including quote from Powell.
24. Walter 1985; Walter, Harnickell, and Mueller-Dombois 1975.
25. Hansen, Chronic, and Matelock 1978.

PATTERN SOURCES 47

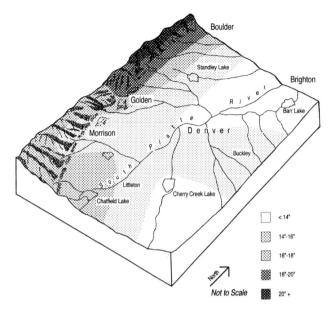

3.11
Mean annual precipitation.
Based on data from Hansen, Chronic, and Matelock 1978

opposite
3.12
Mean date of last spring frost.
Based on data from Hansen, Chronic, and Matelock 1978

3.13
Mean date of first fall frost.
Based on data from Hansen, Chronic, and Matelock 1978

26. Obmascik 1996, sec. 1A, 1 and 22.

inches. These numbers belie the great variability of the region, however. At one extreme, historic storms of June 1965 dropped fourteen inches of rain over the greater Denver area in only three hours. At the other, Denver could receive less than seven inches of precipitation in a drought year. Walter's diagram shows Denver's predilection for drought even in an average year. In looking at the overlay between temperature and precipitation, Ann observed that in the Denver area, when winter temperatures dip, precipitation increases, leading to a water surplus, shown downpouring as vertical lines in the diagram. In the summer, however, precipitation drops and temperatures increase; the diagram shows a parched, spotty pattern, indicating the periods of drought to which plants and people must adapt. For this reason, Denver is considered semiarid, because evaporation is at times greater than precipitation.

Walter's diagram offers still more. Frost-free periods are illustrated, showing the relatively short growing season from late May to October. During these months, snow melts, largely dictating stream and reservoir water levels. Releases of dissolved nutrients from the snowpack also occur at this time. The average date of the last spring frost is important for gardeners to know, because success of new plants depends on frost-free conditions. The urban-heat-island effect from heat-absorbent and heat-radiant materials covering Denver soils results in an earlier planting date in the city than in less urbanized portions in the area (figure 3.12). In fact, meteorologists have recorded in the city an increase of two to three degrees Fahrenheit in the summer and up to eight degrees of increase in the winter over nearby suburban fringe areas.[26] In downtown Denver, tender plantings are now generally safe from frost after May 3. In his 1948 book, *Around the Seasons in Denver's Parks and Gardens,* the landscape architect Saco DeBoer records that he swore by the sacrosanct May 20 planting date in the early 1900s. Old-timers advised him of the wisdom of waiting until this date; and he learned to respect tradition the hard way, after planting geraniums and other bedding plants on Denver's parkways before this date. They promptly froze. Boulderites have six additional days to wait before the last mean frost date. Golden and Morrison residents should usually wait until May 15 to trust that winter is over. Garden tools should be packed up by early October for most of the region, leaving a frost-free season of four to five months (figure 3.13). Ann, an impatient gardener in the spring and a reluctant harvester in the fall, saw that she was well suited to the relative warmth of Denver and Boulder.

Three types of storm path are typical within the Front Range. By knowing the season and time of day, she learned, one can generally predict which type of system is about to move through the region (figure 3.14). In the winter, moisture-laden air masses from the Pacific move eastward over the Rockies, falling as snow on happy skiers. In spring and fall, moist air masses from the Gulf of Mexico tangle with the Front Range's east slope, drenching foothills and plains. On a shorter time scale, daily air masses, warmed by the land, rise and generate convection storms during most summer afternoons. These are frequently

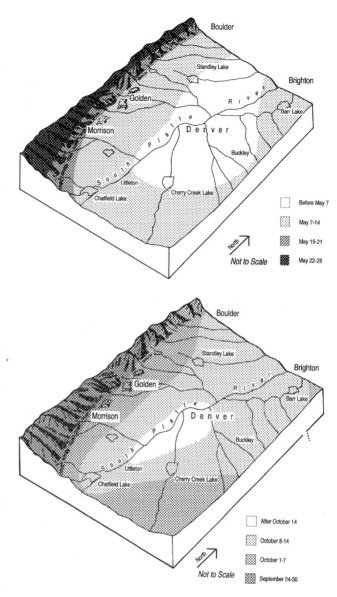

PATTERN SOURCES 49

accompanied by severe hail storms, lightning, and occasionally tornadoes. Today's storm was no exception, Ann thought, distracted by the dramatic view of the deepening storm from the library window.

Wind on the Front Range is remarkable. The mountains are slightly bowed toward the west, forming an enormous wind tunnel that channels winds down valleys, canyons, and over the hogbacks and flatirons. Wind pulses between 40 and 80 miles an hour are common through the winter months and during late afternoon summer thunderstorms. Ann had climbed a young ponderosa pine during one summer pulse, expecting the tree to rock back and forth as the wind pushed down from the west. Instead, the tree wound and rewound, like an automatic top, dizzying her as she tightly wrapped the flaky barked trunk with her arms and legs. Lightning convinced her to disembark (so to speak). Residents become accustomed to fetching trash cans, newspapers, and hats in downwind collection areas during Chinook wind storms. Ann recalled a story told to her by a friend: He had just replaced his home's carpeting, which had been ruined by basement flooding. He dragged the sodden roll outside his house and left it in the driveway. During the night, the heavy roll was escorted by a Chinook wind down the driveway into the street, where it turned left at the corner, continued down another street, turned right, went up another driveway, and then unfurled over a Subaru station wagon. It took four people and a truck to haul the heavy, wet roll back to his house.

Winds as strong as 135 miles an hour have blown in Boulder, removing roofs, desiccating succulence, warming the winter temperature by fifty degrees within a few hours. Prevailing winds in Denver are generally southerlies, with a westerly component, blowing pollutants generated in Denver toward Brighton.[27] Other locations within the diverse Front Range, such as Rocky Flats south of Boulder, show remarkable constancy of wind direction at high speeds, from the west. On a smaller-scale cycle, valley winds create distinct wind patterns of draining cool air down valley during early morning and draining warmed air up valley in the evenings. In cool air drainages above Boulder and Golden, cottonwood trees notably lean downwind in response to gentle prevailing down-valley winds.

Residents particularly enjoy the region's abundant sunshine and often stop to bask, lizard-like, on a sun-drenched rock. Days are generally clear, with an average of only one cloudy day in six along the Front Range (figure 3.15). A plume of cloudier weather occurs northeast of Denver and near Chatfield Reservoir in the southwest, with fewer than 30 percent clear days per year in the area from Commerce City to Brighton. This contrasts with the 60 percent clear days in a rainshadow trough between Wheatridge and Longmont. Between the wind, sun exposure, high summer temperatures, and low humidity, standing water disappears quickly. In fact, evaporation for most of the region totals between fifty and sixty inches per year, meaning that as much as five feet of water per year evaporates from reservoirs, ponds, and puddles, exceeding natural replenishment rates. Ann now had a surplus of cosmetic boxes in which to place her collection of found objects, resulting from her more frequent face cream purchases to counteract the effects of this "sub-humid" climate.

Ann, who enjoyed drama, was never disappointed by the Front Range's weather. On an extreme but not uncommon basis, temperatures could drop seventy degrees within an hour from Chinook winter conditions, bringing

opposite

3.14
Common storm patterns in the Denver region. (A) Precipitation from Pacific air masses moves eastward over the Rockies, falling as snow over the mountains in wintertime; (B) Moist air masses from the Gulf of Mexico circulate upslope, bringing precipitation to the Front Range during spring and fall; (C) Summer afternoon storms are prevalent as rising air is warmed by land surfaces, generating convective storms.

27. Hansen, Chronic, and Matelock 1978, 54.

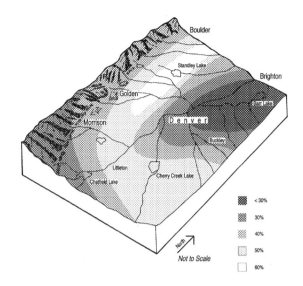

3.15
Mean annual percentage of clear days.
Based on data from Hansen, Chronic, and Matelock 1978

balmy, breezy weather to a cyclonic, sleety, freezing conclusion. Rainbows frequently dazzled summer viewers; in fact, a recent newspaper clipping had noted three accidents on Denver area roads in a single day caused by motorists distracted by rainbows. Ann tried to be home each evening in time to watch the sunset with her young son. One evening they witnessed a thunderstorm of mythic proportions throw lightning bolts and hail beneath the anvil clouds. Rotating to the west, they saw the sun dip below the mountains, lighting up sheepy cottonball clouds with neon red. The moon loomed large over the plains to the east, highlighting the clear cerulean blue sky. Well, at least she witnessed it: her son's attention had been absorbed by a moth. Front Range weather, Ann decided, was seldom anticlimactic. Sunlit rain on the library window was now refracting rainbows onto her hands and papers as she finished her reading, reinforcing her conclusion.

Climatic processes of water, air, and energy flow have a significant effect on the look of this landscape and the adaptations that life must make to thrive. Cottonwoods cling to the road-cut edge because there they find water and soil to support their needs. Their roots tap into an aquifer, protected from the evaporative forces of this semiarid climate. Planting these same trees on fine-grained plains soils, with only atmospheric precipitation to sustain them, would kill the tree. Feeding them an irrigation IV would sustain them but would also change the region's water budget by distributing stored water in a highly evaporative condition. Even if the water were applied by means of underground systems, these soils could also be expansive and shrink, then swell with the additional water input. You could never do just one thing. Knowing the forces at work and adapting to them would enable planting designers to create fitting

52 WATERSTAINED LANDSCAPES

designs requiring less maintenance and stirring up fewer problems down the road.

Right now Ann's down-the-road problem was dodging puddles and traffic as she rode her bicycle home. The rain had stopped an hour ago, sunlight glistened on wet broad-leaved trees, and she simultaneously felt like James Joyce's gleeful girl, purposefully splashing in the remaining puddles, and his curmudgeonly old woman, cursing the line of muck spinning off her back tire onto her white shirt.

BIOTIC PROCESSES   Ann's walk the next day took her through an untrailed section of the South Boulder open space, an area where she had not yet wandered that summer. When she had previously lived in the region, this had been a favorite spot; in fact, after almost two years of looking, she and her husband were still house hunting in the nearby neighborhood because of its proximity to this beautiful juncture of mountains and plains. In the open space, Ann used to find many familiar and unusual species of tall grasses and wildflowers, and now she anticipated what she would find. Because she had brought along her two-year-old son, the going was slow, giving her a chance to really look. Ann was reminded of a hike she had taken with an entomologist who specialized in ants: they took a half-hour to cross over a bridge, because every ant required their attention.

Between answering her toddler's "What's that?" and "Why?" questions, Ann took note of the many familiar prairie species present, but she was astonished by the seemingly increased numbers of certain plants: more sages than she remembered now glinted gray in the grasslands. Gumweed seemed more plentiful than before, its sticky flower heads uncomfortably brushing against her legs. Scratchy knapweed and thistle colonized areas where she was certain tall grasses had earlier grown, and she steered her son around the patches. She was, as always, surprised by the variability of plants from year to year. She sought causes and later, speaking with range management specialists, learned about this year's drought conditions and also that increasing numbers of enthusiastic hikers had inadvertently compacted ever-widening trails and spread weed seed.

With her study of formative processes still fresh in her mind, it seemed to Ann that most of the vegetation change she noticed was caused by geomorphic, climatic, and cultural processes. Biotic processes on plants—the effects of other plants, animals, insects, and microorganisms—are less obvious in arid and semiarid climates. Her son, rapturously poking a grass culm into a mushroom-sprouting cow pie, seemed to have the knack and the right height for such investigations. After their walk, she decided, she would set the stage for understanding biotic processes at work in vegetation mosaics by investigating vegetation change, also known as plant succession.

SUCCESSION Describing vegetation is like describing your own child, Ann concluded from her reading later that afternoon: one description rarely fits for long because the child grows and changes so rapidly, and vegetation patterns change no less dramatically. They may not change by such orderly means as ecologist F. E. Clements first described in his early 1900s studies of vegetation changes in fallow fields over time, by which colonizers are shaded and successively replaced by the next best adapted species until a "climax" community of great stability is reached.[28] Ecologists now reject this idea: long-term stability in vegetation is the exception, and episodic disturbance the rule, according to ecologist John Miles.[29] In other words, the neat, orderly world of constant change toward the "climax" community is subject to constant interruption. In fact, many plant communities undergo such frequent disturbance, such as flooding or fire, that no ultimate stage beyond the earliest successional stages ever appears. However, Ann found many aspects of Clements's descriptions of succession, or vegetation change, useful for study. Succession must be initiated by formative processes; species must be able to immigrate to places conducive for growth. Plants must become established; they must compete successfully for resources; they must adapt to changing environmental conditions; and they may exhibit some aspect of stability, such as persistence in time. Ann explored each one of these descriptions of succession through the lens of this region.

Initiation. The vegetation patterns Ann saw as being relatively stable are, in fact, always in flux. Hiking along a Front Range mesa, she was once present for

28. Clements [1916] 1928.
29. Miles 1979.

a sudden rockfall where igneous rocks broke along a fracture and catapulted downslope to bury a patch of grasses at the mesa base. An event like this destroys the grasses but also provides a new surface for shrubs to become established in newly formed rock reservoirs — thus geomorphic processes are at play in initiating succession. Extended periods of drought also initiate vegetation changes. Upland streambank species no longer able to tap into a drying intermittent stream wither and blow away during a drought year — climatic processes affording new species a colonization spot as long as too much of the soil does not blow away with the plant. Plants die of old age, leaving gaps in a community that are filled by others — biotic processes in effect. The scar left by bulldozers is quickly populated by sunflowers and other rapidly growing annuals, a cultural process affecting vegetation change.

Immigration. Once the stage is set, plants must disperse themselves to the new opportune location. A good rule of thumb, Ann read, is that the closer the seed or plant source is to the disturbed area, the more successful colonization will be. Thus smaller disturbance areas are generally colonized more thoroughly and quickly than large disturbance areas. Grasses tend to spread most effectively by underground rhizomes; most plant dispersal over longer distances, however, is by seed. But seed production can vary widely from year to year because of climate, hungry animals, or disease; therefore, colonization by surrounding plants is difficult to predict.

Establishment. Once seeds touch down in their new promised land, they must pass through a vulnerable phase: that of becoming established. If they have landed in a "safe site," as defined by the seed's needs, they will germinate. For example, ethnobotanist Gary Nabhan describes the particularity of lotus seeds germinated by scientists after lying dormant for more than four hundred years. "Unless abraded by scouring or scarified by acidic organics slowly accumulating on a lake bed, the tough shell of the lotus seed will remain fairly impermeable."[30] Domesticated beans, however, must find a "safe site" and germinate immediately or they will deteriorate. In fact, the odds are stacked against germination success, with drought, disease, sun scorch, insect herbivory, and ani-

30. Nabhan 1989, xviii.

mal hooves serving as distinct obstacles to success. Small gaps in established vegetation caused by plants dying or by burrowing animals or by being blown into rock crevices may offer the best chances for self-sown seedling success.

Competition. All is still not necessarily well, once seedlings have germinated. Competition between species for basic needs such as light, water, and minerals can be fierce. Like competing beaus, plants gain advantage by developing certain attributes to utilize resources to the detriment of rivals. In the semiarid West, water is scarce and plants must adapt to the shortage to survive. To be drought-adapted, plants have a number of options: they can become drought avoiders—opportunists that take advantage of every drop of water at key wet times of year; or they can become ascetic—resistant to the ravages of drought by requiring little water at key dry times of year.

The appropriately named cheatgrass, for example, is a love-'em-and-leave-'em kind of plant (figure 3.16). Cheatgrass is a winter annual capable of germinating in the fall, maintaining ground-hugging leaves over the winter, and then growing rapidly in late winter and spring, once temperatures warm and abundant moisture from snowmelt becomes available. One February Ann had kicked a patch of snow from a pasture, to find green cheatgrass already at work. After snows melt, overgrazed pastures turn uniformly green with an abundance of these annuals, which soon set seed, much earlier than their competitors. Just as suddenly these pastures turn uniformly yellow once cheatgrass seeds have matured and plants have died. Seeds hitchhike, with the help of animals, wind, and socks, to greener pastures during summer droughts; and after the summer's heat, the next generation is off to a successful start. So if you were cheatgrass, you would literally make hay while the sun shone. You would leave—in fact, you would die—when things got tough. You would survive only in the best of times. Ah, Ann thought, I certainly have known men like this. She was not surprised that plants named "lovegrass" and "stinkgrass" also fell into the drought-avoider category.

Now if you were resistant to drought, an ascetic, you might be more like, say, buffalo grass (figure 3.17). This grey-green, curly matted grass is found on the plains in the driest places. Leaves are paper-thin and curl low to the ground to reduce the evaporative wind's pull. Flowers are tiny—nothing showy—and oriented perpendicular to the wind. Pale-colored leaves reflect light, reducing heat and evaporation. Runners spread densely, forming a mat if not overly disturbed. You can walk all over buffalo grass; it likes it. Too much water drowns it, and aggressive irrigated grasses like bluegrass march right over it. Buffalo grass is not a good competitor for the choice spots but very tenacious in marginal locations where the juicy grasses dare not tread. We know this type, Ann thought. Hard-shelled, impervious, tough. Yet, abuse it and it dies, and the soil blows away with it. The other grasses flash and muscle each other for the best locations and seasons, but buffalo grass stays low, dependable. You can read the West all over its appearance. It comes to a party wearing a clean work shirt and jeans, with just a little manure on its boots. If the party gets too crowded, it leaves. Or waits.

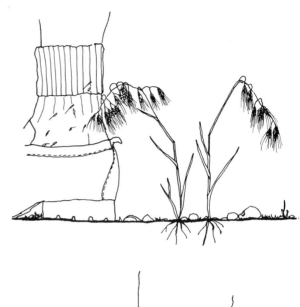

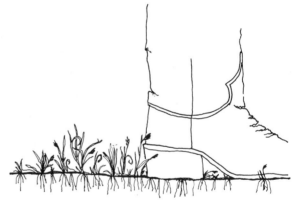

And when the water is just right, the sun bright and shining, the animals depositing enough nutrients and trampling it a little now and then, this grass flourishes. Ann had married a guy like this, she realized. But she bet he would prefer to be compared to, say, wolftail or maybe wild rye than buffalo grass. If he complained, she would remind him that she could have compared him to, say, bastard-toadflax.

Ann reined her straying focus back to her studies on plant competition strategies that helped determine plant patterns. Other plants utilize sabotage to their

3.16
Cheatgrass is a drought-avoider.
Illustration by the author

3.17
Buffalograss is a drought-resister.
Illustration by the author

3.18 Russian olives are attractive trees, but threaten riparian habitat diversity throughout the West.

competitive advantage by exuding toxins, smothering neighboring plants with leaf litter, or impacting shared soil. Tamarisk is an example of a plant taking advantage of the latter two strategies. An escapee from cultivation, tamarisk easily colonizes the incompletely developed riparian forest niche along western bottomlands and sandbars. These attractive, wispy shrubs send roots directly to the water table and are so efficient in tapping the water supply that they lower groundwater levels to a significant degree. Their deep roots also extract salts from deep layers of soil and deposit them through salt-excreting glands in harvestable quantities at the soil surface. Less salt-tolerant riparian plants such as willows and cottonwoods cannot compete in such hostile soil conditions and are declining in numbers. Ann recalled the irony of seeing tamarisk in the planter at the entrance to the Federal Center's Bureau of Reclamation building.

The introduced Russian olive also cuts its swath through the plains' undercolonized riparian forests, Ann read (figure 3.18). These grey-green trees from the Russian steppe fill the currently unoccupied midcanopy layer between the tall cottonwood canopy and low shrubland vegetation. Ann had witnessed their success in colonizing this niche in streams across Colorado. Like tamarisk, the Russian olive flourishes where dams provide consistent flows in arid stream courses.

In response to the streamside invasion of Russian olive, City of Boulder

Open Space managers declared war on this biotic process and attempted to cut out rapidly expanding weed trees before cottonwood and shrub habitat was decimated. Ann read the following remarks in a public information brochure: "Throughout the West, an intruder invades our grasslands and riparian areas along rivers, streams, and ditches, forever changing the plants and animals found there. The intruder? The Russian olive (*Eleagnus angustifolia*). This seemingly innocent tree is actually an aggressive Eurasian invader engaging in a subtle takeover!"[31] One photo showed a flamethrower being used to control a Russian olive tree stand. This would be a good time to learn to make Russian olive furniture or paper, Ann thought.

Today's dilemma regarding species colonization and adaptation is this: If trees were not part of the riparian ecosystem as recently as one hundred years ago, should we work so hard now to protect them from the next colonizer? The argument for intensive management states that bird and other wildlife species, including invertebrates, are rapidly being driven out of other habitat areas such as wetlands suffering from draining and the removal by pumping of underground aquifers. These riparian ribbons stretching across the plains are lifelines of national and international importance as bird species move between north and south during annual migrations. Riparian plant communities dominated by cottonwoods and willows provide versatile habitat—good insect breeding for warblers and other insect-feeding species, good cavity formation for cavity dwellers like bluebirds, good nest sites for herons, ibis, and other wading birds, shade for fish species, and understory woody and herbaceous plants. Cottonwoods and willows generally greatly add to species diversity in a semiarid region. And according to conservation biologists, diversity is good.

Russian olive wood, on the other hand, is so hard that cavity nesters cannot build in it. It harbors few insects, and it provides good parasitizing cowbird habitat. The trees lurk in the shadows of cottonwoods and willows; once the native trees have died, the Russian olives monopolize all habitat, reducing the likelihood of other natives establishing themselves. Monocultures are bad, Ann read.

Other site modifications by established plants are not as hostile to other plants as those described. Asters colonizing an exposed site change the micro-

31. City of Boulder Open Space Department n.d.

climate by shading the soil with their leaves. Legumes fix nitrogen and nutrify the soil, allowing plants less tolerant of nutrient-poor soils to become established. Clements felt that this modification process by plants was largely responsible for the successional change in species, but this has been rejected by ecologists who see geomorphic processes as having more influence on successional change than biotic processes.[32]

Adaptation and stability. Once a plant community becomes established, it needs to compete successfully with other species and adapt to changing site conditions if it is to meet its life cycle needs and remain stable in this location. Explaining plant communities in terms of stability is complex and highly interpretable, Ann learned. Clements thought that a community is stable if it persists in time. Thus, bristlecone forests of the Sierras, whose members live more than four thousand years, are highly stable communities. But plant community stability is more dynamic than this. One ecologist, H. S. Horn, defines *stability* in terms of the speed with which a community returns to equilibrium following a disturbance. "Disturb early succession and it becomes early succession. Disturb a climax community and it becomes an early successional stage that takes a long time to return to climax."[33] Early successional communities, such as aspen recolonizing a previously occupied site after a fire, return to equilibrium much more quickly than a late successional community, such as an old growth spruce-fir forest.

Other ecologists define stability in terms of flows, such as energy, mineral nutrients, and water. Early successional communities then tend to be less stable than late successional communities, which slow site flows and have more developed layers of vegetation and accompanying insects and wildlife. Thus, the dispute over the relative stability of the plants seen on a daily basis has implications for land managers: if flows are managed carefully for early successional forests, their productivity can be maintained. Expecting the rapid return of stability found in disturbed old-growth forests is futile.

Implications. So what?, Ann prodded. How does this affect home owners and decision makers in the Front Range? She recalled that several years ago, Boulder

32. Miles 1979.
33. Horn 1974, 32.

open-space rangers tagged ponderosa pine trees for removal from the tall grass prairie remnants, in response to the concern that succession from a grassland to a pine savannah would remove these last relicts of Pleistocene prairie, a unique ecosystem. Fire processes had been suppressed long ago, with the advent of homes creeping onto the edges of the protected area, and the pines were flourishing. Controlled burning was not an option for adjacent home owners, they let it be known. Nor was timbering, as it turned out. Adjacent landowners sent out a cry when the first trees were cut—they did not want stumps. So managers acquiesced to the inevitable fact that succession will succeed.

Ann wondered what this open-space parcel would look like in the future. Small areas of tall grass patches would be maintained mechanically, but pines would eventually replace many of the midgrass areas, filling the grasslands—and increasing the fire hazard. Several U.S. Forest Service ecologists she interviewed believe that someday the Front Range will be home to one of the more cataclysmic fire events known in the nation.[34] No large fires have burned for many decades. First and second homes are creeping into forested areas, many built with fashionable log timber construction kits. Long driveways isolate the homesites from adjacent roads on which firetrucks can pass. Dead standing timber from beetle-killed logs abound. Forests are advancing onto sites previously supporting grasslands. The stage is set for a serious fire disaster.

RELATIONSHIPS BETWEEN PLANTS, ANIMALS, INSECTS, AND MICROORGANISMS Ann's brief review of plant succession helped her understand some of the basic effects plants had upon each other, primarily through competition and site modification. Following her walk earlier that day, she cleaned her socks of cheatgrass seeds and beggar's ticks and thought about the impact of animals upon plants. Animals enable seeds and plant parts to reach more distant and sometimes more advantageous colonization sites, ensuring better survival. The appearance of duckweed in newly established wetlands attests to the mobility of plants under the influence of duck feet. Many seeds cannot become established without the help of digestive systems that break down seed-coat growth inhibitors; thus the reliable presence of edible plants where birds perch.

34. Carl Edminster and Merrill Kaufmann, U.S. Department of Agriculture Forest Service ecologists, personal communication, Fort Collins, Colo., 22 July 1994.

3.19 Deer sculpt junipers into vase shapes.

Plant health and survival are affected by relationships with animals. Buffalo wallows and prairie dog towns once kept plant communities in these locations in a state of early succession; the plants historically colonizing these frequently disturbed locations would be useful, Ann suspected, in creating a seed mix for newly exposed construction sites: maybe they would give the weeds a run for their money. Beaver frustrate the efforts of many good restoration projects by felling the well-intended tree plantings along a stream corridor, the designers of the South Platte River Greenway discovered. Beaver-proof plantings consisting of chickenwire-wrapped trunks were now being installed in vulnerable locations. Browsing deer greatly affect the form and sometimes survival of many garden plants: most gardeners find that the more heavily watered and fertilized a plant, the more palatable it is to deer. However, native plants are not immune to deer diners. Many of the junipers in Boulder's highly deer-populated open-space valleys have been trimmed to a vase shape, with a spray of greenery frothing just out of deer-shot (figure 3.19). Grazing by domestic animals also significantly affects plant health and survival by selectively removing plants and by compacting the soil and abetting erosion.

Insects shape the presence and condition of Front Range plants as well. They serve as pollinators and predators, bringing life and death to the vegetation mosaic. Forests in the mountains and piedmont show the effects of insect damage. When insect outbreaks are limited, they provide forest openings and needed snags for cavity-nesting animals. However, large-scale insect outbreaks can have significant impact on forest regeneration and wildlife. Thorough logging in the mid-to-late 1800s caused regrowth of even-aged forests in many Front Range areas. These trees reached insect-susceptible ages as fire suppression policies took effect. The "thinning" effect of fire, whereby weak and standing dead trees are burned, making way for new, upwardly mobile seedlings, was interrupted. As a result, forest researchers K. S. Hadley and T. T. Veblen have determined, infestations of the Douglas fir bark beetle between 1984 and the present and spruce budworm outbreaks from 1974 to 1985 constitute the single largest and most severe disturbance in Rocky Mountain National Park since the late 1800s.[35] Ann noted that Front Range forests now appear as a herringbone pattern, with a dominant gray thread woven into the forested fabric where standing dead trees are interspersed among the live ones. The abundance of standing fuel from insect kills and fallen timber from wind is impressive; Ann successfully resisted all seductive mountain property advertisements simply by looking up at those attentive, patient matchsticks.

Insects have been used to advantage in this region. Klamath weed is a European species that infests the Rocky Flats area and other undeveloped areas in the northwestern portion of the study area. When eaten by animals with white hides, such as sheep and cows, the plant sensitizes them to light in this bright climate. Animals are blinded and usually die of starvation. To combat the impact from this plant, a beetle that feeds solely on Klamath weed has been introduced to control the plant's spread. Now as she hiked through the grasslands, Ann occasionally saw the plant but also usually found its accomplice beetle keeping the plant in check.

Microorganisms play a beneficial role as well in affecting plant health. *Rhizobium* is a genus of nitrogen-fixing bacteria that occupies sometimes-visible nodules on the roots of legumes such as clover and beans. The eventual death and decomposition of the nodules is responsible for enriching soils with usable

35. Hadley and Veblen 1993.

nitrogen. Ann recalled one of her favorite stories, related by ethnobotanist Gary Nabhan: He and author Wendell Berry had stopped along an Arizona road to investigate a surreal wheat field marked by a perfect, deep-green circle of tall wheat, about twenty feet in circumference, much taller than the wheat in the rest of the field.[36] They sought out the farmer to confirm their suspicions regarding the cause. Sure enough, the farmer had cut down a leguminous mesquite tree from that spot; the perfect circle was the tracery of the canopy where roots, leaves, and pods had littered the ground with nitrogen-rich remains for many years—a mesquite ghost haunting the wheat field with *Rhizobium*. Many other plants in the semiarid grasslands extend their ability to absorb water and nutrients through the symbiotic help of mycorrhizal fungi. These fungi grow into or between the cortical areas of host rootlets and out into the surrounding soil. Nutrients and water are absorbed by the host, and food derived from photosynthesis is used by the fungi. Plants able to host these fungi, such as skunkbrush, prickly pear, snowberry, sage, and juniper, have a competitive advantage over others. When we import plants into our gardens, Ann concluded, we should also import soil inoculated with these fungi.

Ann tried to envision the process by which these tiny bacteria and truffles make the difference between a plant succeeding or failing in this challenging environment. Scientists remind us that 85 percent of total plant biomass in North American grasslands is underground, yet we often forget or ignore the complex necessity of subsoil interactions. She appreciated novelist and ecologist Barbara Kingsolver's poetic link between the role of rhizobia assisting a wisteria plant and a single woman depending on a host of friends to help her raise a child alone: "The wisteria vines on their own would just barely get by . . . but put them together with rhizobia and they make miracles."[37] These relationships are necessary and mutually beneficial.

The interrelationships between plants, insects, animals, and microorganisms are important to consider when learning about a region and how it functions. Ann now noticed starlings gleaning corn crops for insects that might otherwise damage plants. She imagined insects and microorganisms breaking down animal excrement into vital nutrients available to plants. Ann appreciated that plants provide shelter and food for wildlife species stressed by fragmented

36. Nabhan 1985, 72.
37. Kingsolver 1988, 228.

urban development. Biotic processes do indeed affect vegetation patterns, and vice versa.

CULTURAL PROCESSES Ann surveyed the landscape from her car window as she continued house hunting. She saw pines invading grasslands, beetle-killed trees, tall grasses forming open-space corridors, and green weeds growing along the edges of hard-packed trails. In the foreground, she saw trimmed lawns, mature trees, colorful planter boxes. The entire view showed varying degrees of human intention and attention.

What forces drive us to manipulate plants as we do? What urges us to select, plant, trim, mow, harvest, irrigate, excavate, save, taste, touch, listen to, breathe in, view, derive meaning from, and attach significance to plants? Seeking to answer this question, Ann looked first to Darwin's fundamental motivation: survival. To survive as animals, we first need food and water; second, we need a place suitable for raising families in safety. To achieve these goals, we use plants for two purposes: production and protection.

PRODUCTION Production needs include growing plants for food, supporting production of other species, such as grazing cattle, and manufacturing goods. Since Native Americans first selected plants and grew food-bearing cultivars, the role of productive landscapes has grown from helping individuals survive to supporting the economic goal of obtaining from the landscape the highest yield of marketable products possible. Early successional plants cultivated for food, fiber, and building materials were favored in productive landscapes. These were harvested at the peak of their growth and seldom allowed to reach maturity. Since many plantings are monocultures of single, highly productive species, little is left to protect the landscape from uncertainties such as harsh weather, disease, or insect strikes. Energy, water, and nutrient inputs were also high in these early successional landscapes. For humans to survive on more than this tenuous limb of production, protective landscapes were required as well.

PROTECTION   In this suburban landscape, Ann found that protective forces are fairly well represented. Plants shade rooflines and slow strong winds. Conifers block views from neighboring houses. Groves of trees sift leaves and needles over time to create a thick, root-protective mulch. Compost heaps even appear in a few yards, exhibiting faith that today's pulled weeds and vegetable peelings will become a valuable source of future stored nutrients. Grasses slow flows of water from patios, terraces, and driveways, reducing erosion. Diversity and nutrient storage characterize protective landscapes, and the suburbanites fill the role as unwitting accomplices in providing this hedge, so to speak, against unfavorable times.

PLEASURE   Yet these two motives alone do not explain our urge to visit and shape gardens, Ann realized. Geographer Jay Appleton sees Darwinian roots in these actions. His "habitat theory" suggests that once we have found productive and protective places, we continue to explore and change them, because this helps us efficiently use all the opportunities latent in the chosen site. Appleton uses the term "pleasure" to account for this tendency of animals to explore their surroundings: "We do all these things on which our survival depends *because we want to.*"[38] We are drawn to hazards to test our skills in danger recognition, we want to see and not be seen, we naturally want to be predators and not prey. Thus, according to Appleton's theory, we seek places of prospect for views and refuge for safety to provide our habitat needs; and these needs, in turn, shape our aesthetic preferences. He concludes that pleasure is a driving principle of aesthetics.

The biological basis for landscape preference further blurs the line many people believe exists between nature and culture; it also serves as a foundation for understanding what people in this region do to achieve pleasure and meaning through the landscape. Looking again at residents' gardens, Ann saw upper-story decks swathed with pots of bright annuals, with perfect prospect views of mountains and people below. She saw a man reading a paperback on a cozy bench hedged on either side with small flowering shrubs in a small pocket garden—a reading refuge. Garden after garden was oriented toward the slabby mountains, "hazard symbols" in Appleton's jargon, with views of oncoming

38. Appleton 1994, 200.

ominous storms and brilliant skies. Pleasure in prospect, refuge, and views of hazards abounded, as she saw exemplified by children climbing toward their treehouse. Ecologist Gordon Orians, well known for his ornithological research, is intrigued by Appleton's links between pleasure and survival. He has built a strong case for further research into human behavior ecology, especially that which addresses fundamental questions such as why people are attracted to flowers.[39] The study of biological roots for pleasure continues, Ann thought; stay tuned. Thus, she added pleasure to production and protection as three fundamental cultural motivations.

Referring again to her dictionary, Ann found that *pleasure* is broadly defined as "a state of happiness or personal satisfaction; one's preference, wish, choice." One group of designers exploring the question found that we create gardens as expressions of faith, power, order, cultural and personal touchstones, and healing.[40] We choose to design for these purposes, and the process and results often bring us personal satisfaction. Ann looked to design literature for general examples of these five motivations and then sorted signs of their presence in Denver.

Faith. Gardens designed to express faith often use plants as symbols. These can be literal or figurative. Ann remembered seeing the carcass of a saguaro cactus outside an Arizona church, its arms outstretched as if poised on a cross. At the Denver Botanic Gardens, botanist Gayle Weinstein and others have created a scripture garden, featuring plants mentioned in the Bible. Less literal symbols included a grove of redwood trees gracing the entrance to the AIDS Memorial Grove in San Francisco's Golden Gate Park. Here, ashes of AIDS victims have been placed; mourners are instinctively drawn to the grove's solace and gravity, a place to address the inexplicable, the unknown, the spiritual. Redwoods as symbols are appropriate: if cut, they vigorously resprout; life springs from death. John Muir once wrote, "They tell us that plants are not like man, but are perishable, soul-less. I think that this is something that we know exactly nothing about."[41] Pleasure is derived from connecting the meaning of plants with deeply felt human experience.

39. Orians 1998.
40. See Francis and Hester 1990.
41. Quoted in Rodis and Odell 1992, 221.

Power. Plants express power in numerous ways. Landscape architect Kenneth Helphand writes of "defiant gardens": those gardens created under adverse situations, such as in concentration camps, in the French trenches of World War I, in prisoner-of-war camps, and so on. These gardens reflect their importance as a psychological outlet in high-stress environments, whether its creators are the oppressed or the oppressors.[42]

Power symbols, like other features of the landscape, are visible at a variety of scales. Large-scale social decisions, such as zoning and environmental regulations, involve conscious political action. These determine the juxtaposition of landscapes from suburban to industrial to commercial to rural, regionwide treatment of drainage, management of pollutants, transportation corridors, presence of habitat areas for species preservation, and removal of weeds from a neighbor's property. Larger-scaled service institutions like extension services, soil conservation services, water boards, Xeriscape boards, and so on offer advice in the Denver region and reflect current priorities and best management practices.

Respect—or lack thereof—for boundaries and rights affects many aspects of how the landscape looks: for example, the new plantings Ann saw along a Denver freeway embankment greatly contrasted with graffiti marking the wall behind them (figure 3.20). It was likely that the freeway did not respect the neighborhood's boundaries just as much as the graffiti artists were not respecting the Department of Transportation's territory. Cultivated purple loosestrife has been under siege in the Denver region because of the rapidity with which it spreads through riparian corridors. Ann learned of a Big Brother-like hotline where one could report neighbors planting these invasive ornamental plants. Cottonwoods and olive trees are prohibited in some cities because many people are allergic to their pollen. When developing land, water must be retained on site and not disrupt a neighbor's drainage patterns. Regulations like these reflect society's current priorities and are powerful motivators in shaping the land.

Order. The diversity and irregular pattern of natural vegetation is difficult for most people to appreciate in urban settings. Plants are used deliberately to

42. Helphand 1997.

3.20
Graffiti marks a new highway overpass in a Denver residential neighborhood.

derive order from chaos. "Uncovering the order is a key to the meaning of the garden," according to Mark Francis and Randolph Hester.[43] A desire for order motivates us to design with dominant themes, and designers need not just "know-how" but also "know-why." Why, the designer might ask, are deciduous trees and annual flowers used in a particular garden? To provide a sense of the seasons, might be the answer. A sense of order can be derived from using aesthetic building blocks such as form, line, color, texture along with formal principles of balance, rhythm, harmony, and so on. The stately elms lining Denver's older neighborhood streets provide unified form, color, texture, and strong visual lines (figure 3.21). These helped to create a strong sense of unity in a neighborhood—until the elms began to die. Sometimes order is short-lived.

Sometimes, too, it is unexpected. A friend introduced Ann to a favorite commercial garden where adventive Siberian elms growing from a building foundation were being trained into an orderly hedge (figure 3.22). Order can be provided by restoring native plant communities, as was planned for portions of the Rocky Mountain Arsenal and the former Stapleton Airport site, for example, although many people cannot see the order inherent in self-sorting, competing,

43. Francis and Hester 1990, 12.

PATTERN SOURCES   69

3.21
Elms create a sense of order and unity along Denver streets.

3.22
Adventive Siberian elms are trained into orderly forms.

44. Duncan 1992, 40.

changing grassland communities: such arrangements appear too irregular and diverse. In learning to discern water concentrations and predict plant responses to moisture availability, Ann felt she was beginning to unravel the mystery of such diverse landscapes. The waterstain, in fact, is an ordering tool.

Cultural and personal expressions. Plants are also used to express cultural and personal interests. James Duncan has observed that landscapes encode conventional signs of group membership and social status. Landscapes allow people to tell "stories" about themselves and society's social structure and are a major repository of cultural symbols: "Landscape care is a primary vehicle through which the integrity of the group is maintained."[44]

Ann could attest to this truth from her days in California. She and her husband had been fortunate to rent a home in a desirable Los Angeles suburb, but they had stretched their budget to do so. In addition, Ann had been working late hours on her graduate thesis and her husband had an arduous daily commute, leaving them little time for regular yard maintenance in this trim neighborhood. Luckily, the property was dominated by groundcovers instead of lawn. Ann wrote her thesis at home and noted the daily neighborhood tides. In the morning the houses emptied of owners and schoolchildren and filled with domestic workers: nannies, maids, personal assistants. The yards were patrolled by groups of men and their machines, pacing green lawn surfaces and poking hoses in every corner for errant leaves, reminding her of clownfish prodding anemone tendrils for morsels. By evening, the Datsun trucks and Ford Pintos had left the streets, replaced again by Explorers and Suburbans. The tide had swept every leaf away—except in their yard, which had a pleasant, easygoing feel to it, Ann thought: leaves eddied and composted, moles set up permanent residence, bunchgrasses actually flowered, and hummingbirds fed from her flowers when the neighbors forgot to refill their feeders. One Saturday a neighbor delivered a rebuke: why didn't they park an old pickup truck out front to complement their yard? Ann and her husband were caught off guard by their differences in perception. Clearly, they were threatening the "integrity" of the neighborhood that depended on paying others (who parked pickups in front of these manicured yards) to maintain a certain acceptable, though sterile, standard. Thus, she learned, we can read neighborhood landscapes to find out about social attitudes of the times.

Duncan also suggests that social class can be determined by evident landscape design decisions. For example, lower-middle-class landscape designs feature property boundary definition and symmetry more than other classes. Upper-middle-class landscapes feature asymmetrical tree patches and staggered entrance walkways. Upper-class landscapes, especially with "old money," frequently obscure views of the property. Anglophilia is a common legible theme in American residences, betraying a belief in "Englishness as the most prestigious ethnic identity."[45] Ann was reminded of this while perusing a Denver developer's sales brochure, offering to sell a tract home with one of three exterior finishes, one being a "Tudor" design with strips of wood affixed to the facade.

At a smaller scale, personal expressions in planting design range from using favorite plants in honored places in the garden, such as Ann's pampered gardenia moved to the front door stoop or entrance hallway whenever she expected guests, to the expulsion of disliked plants, such as a friend's tirade against mint. A study of gardeners performed by Rachel and Steve Kaplan found that inexperienced gardeners tend to emphasize the tangible benefits of growing plants, such as having fresh vegetables. But as gardeners grow more experienced, they increasingly stress the intangible personal benefits, such as a garden's ability to fascinate and to sustain interest.[46]

45. Ibid., 41.
46. Kaplan and Kaplan 1990, 239.

Healing. The healing benefits of plants have been well documented. Much has been written about the benefits to physical and psychological health accrued by the gardener, and sometimes these are difficult to separate. "Weeding keeps your waistline trim," Ann's cheery grandmother always said. Many gardeners garden because of physical health benefits, both from eating healthy vegetables and from physical exertion. People interested in horticulture therapy have tracked gardening benefits to disabled people and have a successful program at the Denver Botanic Gardens. It has been discovered that hospital patients with garden views require less medication and leave hospitals sooner than other patients. Gardening activities and views of gardens have substantially aided AIDS and Alzheimer's patients. A flurry of studies and gardens are being designed to explore and promote the powerful connection between health, gardens, and plants. As Charles Lewis has written, "Plants exhibit life-enhancing qualities that encourage people to respond to them. In a world of constant judgment, plants are nonthreatening and nondiscriminating. They respond to the care that is given to them, not to race, intellect, or physical capacities of the garden. The garden is a benevolent setting in which a person can take the first steps toward self-confidence."[47] Thus, the pleasure derived from the healing properties of plants and gardens is another factor behind cultural shaping of the land.

The forces motivating people to shape the landscape as they do are quite legible on the landscape of the Denver Front Range. At the fringes of her transects, Ann saw expressions of power: fences marking the boundaries of public open-space, zoning change signs, and "Coming Soon!" signs marking the conversion of ranches to more profitable short-term ventures. Productive landscapes still flourish where water is more plentiful along the stream corridors. Protective gestures, such as planted hedgerows, are apparent. Industrial zones reflect an order of sorts—landowners are less concerned, apparently, with neatness and thus plants form their own unchecked order. As a result, many of these areas support relatively rich habitat and wildlife diversity. Spanking new suburban areas reflect power of profit and cultural expression—many new developments sport a token tree, lawn, and irrigation system provided by the contractor as the cheapest landscape treatment acceptable to both city and prospective

47. Lewis 1990, 248.

buyers. Suburbs in different parts of the city reflect Duncan's landscape statements of status. Older suburban landscapes have matured to reflect personal expressions and the desire for healing, as Ann saw in a number of community gardens in public places and as she peered through alley fences into private pocket gardens. Symbolic plantings are scattered throughout the region: plants memorializing loved ones in cemeteries and parks and DeBoer's ponderosa pine plantation at Inspiration Point symbolizing the link between city and wildland. How these forces have intertwined over time in Denver's gardens needs further exploration, she felt.

THE WEST AS PROCESS Through these descriptions of the four formative processes Ann's vivified appreciation of the forces at play in this region, originally so confusing and chaotic to her, grew. Mountains rise and erode. Rain pummels the ground, at times causing floods. Drought often leaves a parched crunchiness to the grasses. Plants, animals, insects, and microorganisms affect each other constantly by competing, shading, eating, dying, working in concert. Myriad human needs are satisfied through plants and the act of gardening. Through her study of the region's processes, Ann felt a heightened sense of understanding. The landscape shifted from black and white to full color; it extended from two to four dimensions, breaking free from her previous static view and becoming fluid in time. She saw in this region Gertrude Stein's struggle to describe America in a single sentence: "Conceive a space that is filled with moving."[48] Wallace Stegner, as usual, had long before discovered the essential ingredients of western landscapes and summed up her new discovery thus: "The West is less a place than a process."[49]

Nonetheless, with an understanding of process under her belt, Ann still had to come to grips with the region as place, as well as the other part of Stegner's statement: "The Westerner is less a person than a continuing adaptation." To this task she now turned.

48. Stein, quoted in Stegner 1992, 72.
49. Ibid., 55.

Plants delineate the additional water available at the roadside edge.

chapter four
fingerprints of the formative processes

THE LOOK OF THE LANDSCAPE   Ann was hungry and rummaged through the kitchen. Her hands pulled bread and butter from drawers. She sliced a thick piece of bread; crumbs fell. She unwrapped the butter and spread it in dense swaths across the bread. Simple pleasures, she thought, ignoring the voice telling her to scrape some of that butter off. Her teeth made crescent-shaped channels through the bread.

Food reliably inspired analogies for her, and her thoughts turned back to her project. She had studied the impressive rock and soil base of the region, like bread that once rose, was kneaded, and rose again. Similar to a baker's hands, climate and living things had shaped the resulting forms. These forms were Marsh's "fingerprints of the formative processes." Plants, people, insects, visible water, soil, and manufactured products spread over the landscape like thick butter over this bread. What did the landscape look like? She pushed crumbs away and pulled paper and pen forward.

As always, scale was an issue in understanding the "look" of a region's vegetation. Because the land contains relicts of past phenomena imbedded in the present forms, it was necessary to move back in time to set the stage. Because events at the large scale affect small-scale appearances, Ann began with large-scale descriptions of the landscape context and then tailored the region into smaller representative views.

OVERALL LANDSCAPE CONTEXT: NATURAL VEGETATION Pollen records and pack rat middens perform double duty: not only do they yield information about climate change, but they also help botanists reconstruct past vegetation information. Through pollen samples, midden remains, and evidence of relict species, botanists have learned that the vegetation of the Front Range region has changed as dramatically as the climate. As Ann had read earlier, cooler and moister climate conditions of the glaciated Pleistocene, or Ice Age, provided habitat in the Front Range for plants that are now associated with higher elevations or more northerly distribution. Spleenwort ferns in cool sandstone enclaves at White Rocks in Boulder are widely separated from other oceanic climate populations and are thought to be relicts from this time. Paperbark birch trees in Boulder's Gregory Canyon are hundreds of miles disjunct from the next southernmost population; these are also considered relicts from Pleistocene times. Cool, north-facing enclaves at Red Rocks near Morrison host aspen, Douglas fir, and Colorado blue spruce located several hundred feet lower than other populations adapted to today's climate. Woodlands colonize the plains through streamside dispersal corridors.[1]

By the end of the Pleistocene, horse ancestors, camels, and mammoths were extinct, probably owing to overhunting and the relatively abruptly warming, drying climate. Vegetation is thought to have developed into the distinct forest-grassland complex we see today as a result of the removal of large herbivores and the drying climate. Eventually, Plains Indians may have used fire to drive game out onto the plains, but the frequency of fires caused by humans and the effect of fire on vegetation patterns has not been fully documented.

Periodic scarcity of game may have sparked domestication of animals for food and development of food-producing wild plants around campsites to fill

1. Covich et al. 1994; Knopf 1986.

the nutritional gap. Edgar Anderson speculates that these may have been the first gardens, which eventually led to the development of food-bearing, genetically distinct cultivars.[2] Were any of these native plants selected for beauty, Ann wondered? for protection from the sun? for their pleasing aromas? to ward off or invite spirits?

Descriptions of vegetation from trappers and early explorers record differences from today as well. John C. Frémont described his inability to see the Rocky Mountains when approaching the great range from the east, because of obfuscating smoke from intense plains fires. Stephen Long, in his 1819-20 expedition along the Platte River, noted huge buffalo herds grazing the "verdant plain." He also described the state of vegetation in the plains in his journal: "Intermixed in the narrow fringe of timber, which marks the course of the river, are numerous trees, killed by the action of the beaver or by the effects of old age."[3] Other journal accounts, photos, and diagrams recording vegetation prior to the advent of irrigation note the absence of woody vegetation along the intermittent South Platte River and other plains streams. Several explanations of this absence focus on influences of intermittent stream flow, fire, buffalo trampling, and beaver predation.

With the climate well established, the region developed flora similar to that of other semiarid locations in the world. Where temperatures and rainfall are relatively similar, large, easily recognizable units with relatively uniform "climax" vegetation and soils are notable, known as *biomes*. Heinrich Walter refers to these as *zonobiomes,* because they are based on nine climate zones.[4] Denver is within the "arid-temperate with a cold winter" (continental) zonobiome and characterized by steppe vegetation (figure 4.1). This zone sweeps through the entire Midwest, from southern Canada to the Gulf of Mexico. In Eurasia, the zone stretches from the mouth of the Danube across much of eastern Europe and Asia, to the Yellow Sea. In South America, the famed Pampa grasslands of Argentina are also in this zone, as are the grasslands of New Zealand's South Island. Ann had traveled to many of these grasslands, not knowing they are considered relatives of the Front Range landscape. No wonder their beauty had tugged at her in a familiar way, she thought.

Numerous plants from these climates similar to the Great Plains–Rocky

2. Anderson 1956.
3. Quoted in Covich et al. 1994, 34-35.
4. Walter 1985, 3.

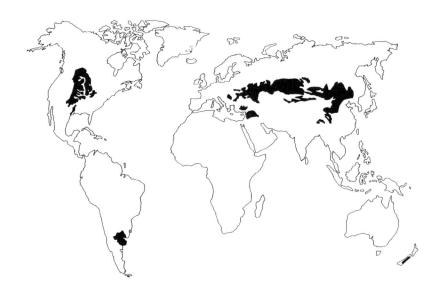

4.1
Zonobiome diagram shows areas with climate similar to Denver's.
Based on data from Walter 1985

5. The account that follows is based on a personal interview with Panayoti Kelaidis, Denver Botanic Gardens, Denver, Colo., 12 August 1994; also see Kelaidis 1990, 1995.

Mountain interface arrived here and thrived. The expert on these plants is Panayoti Kelaidis, curator of the Denver Botanic Gardens' Rock Alpine Garden.[5] Ann made an appointment to learn more about Kelaidis's perspective on regional plants and patterns in the Front Range. From cues and signals collected from a variety of sources — his refined voice on the phone, his reputation in rock gardening and plant introductions, and enthused reports from former students — she was curious to meet Kelaidis at the Denver Botanic Gardens for their scheduled appointment. She was delighted to find that the very accessible man in a T-shirt and work gloves hauling a wheelbarrow along a pathway whom she asked for directions was indeed Kelaidis himself. They found chairs in a potting room. Ann asked him what constituted a regional perspective on planting design in the Denver region. Her pencil blurred as she recorded the rapid ignition of this man's response.

Kelaidis presented a global perspective on what composes regional plants and patterns. He animatedly described Soviet botanist M. G. Popov's observations, in the 1930s, of the many parallels between plants of the arid and semiarid American Southwest, the Mediterranean Basin, and the western and central

4.2
Hardy pink ice plant is now a popular Denver garden plant.

Asian steppes. Popov hypothesized that plants from these regions, now greatly separated by oceans and mountains, once grew along the coast of an immense sea, which he dubbed the Tethyan Sea. These plants share many similar characteristics: silvery, reflective, thick foliage that reduces evaporation and a longer flowering season to aid reproduction. Some steppe and inland Mediterranean areas share aspects of climate as well in that they have cool to cold winters with ample precipitation and hot, dry summers. By examining plants associated with similar climates in other parts of the world, horticulturists can expand significantly the number of species available for Denver Front Range gardens. Kelaidis has played an important role in introducing several species from Mediterranean climates to fill important horticultural niches in the Denver Front Range. For example, hardy pink ice plant, a long-lived, nubby-leaved South African succulent with shocking pink flowers, was not available in the United States until 1985 (figure 4.2). In 1986, Kelaidis imported the plant from a botanical garden and grew two thousand cuttings as an experiment to see if it could survive Denver's challenging climate. One by one, he dispersed these to local nurseries. Within two years, K-Mart garden centers were offering hardy pink ice plant, and Paulino's Nursery in Denver had sold twenty thousand of the hardy perennial plants. "It was a plant of a lifetime," Kelaidis concluded. Somehow, Ann suspected there would be more such plants of a lifetime for him.

Kelaidis believes we have not begun to tap plants from steppe and Mediterranean climates for their potential use in regional gardens. He feels that the future lies in developing unirrigated landscapes and that these adapted plants must infiltrate nurseries to replace temperate climate plants so inappropriately prevalent today. Furthermore, many of the imported steppe plants are insect free, adding to their longevity. For example, *Salvia* is a steppe- and Mediterranean-climate genus with a thousand species in the world, none endemic to the Front Range (although blue sage is native to the eastern plains). *Salvia* are well adapted to the semiarid climate yet inflicted with weevils in their native lands. Because there are no natural predators here, they should thrive in controlled circumstances. One might argue that Russian olive is also a steppe plant without natural predators that is dangerously reducing habitat for native species. Yet, Kelaidis feels, we cannot freeze flora to a single point in time. Russian olives are amazingly adaptable because of their ability to thrive in both wet and dry soils. Because imported temperate plants can fail under both inundated and drought conditions, the value of surviving trees for habitat, shading, and soil-erosion protection is great enough for us to tolerate and accept nonendemics into our own steppe flora. Kelaidis sees an important future role for these largely unknown, carefully selected species as water sources become more limited. His intent at the Denver Botanic Gardens was to present them in attractive ways to increase their acceptability. Kelaidis is the ultimate "steppe-parent."

Numerous ecologists in this century have provided a more local yet regional perspective on the Colorado Front Range's plant communities. Ann reviewed many of these ecologists' publications, including Francis Ramaley's 1907 article, "Plant zones in the Rocky Mountains of Colorado," John Marr's seminal 1961 *Ecosystems of the East Slope of the Front Range in Colorado,* and Robert Peet's 1981 article, "Forest Vegetation of the Colorado Front Range." Three methods of diagramming regional vegetation emerged from these sources; and each could be useful, Ann thought, in giving travelers and residents a way of ordering the complexity around them. The first method, courtesy of Ramaley, Marr, and others, usefully describes Front Range vegetation in sectional view (figure 4.3). For example, if Ann were to drive a straight line from the plains through the foothills to the mountains and back down again, she would note distinct vegetation change. This diagram is easily interpretable, yet the representation is not very precise. If fire or logging has disturbed a location, for example, plants will not conform to the diagram, as it sometimes takes up to five hundred years for the canopy to return to the diagrammed configuration.[6]

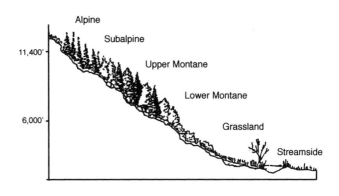

4.3
Front Range vegetation cross-section.
Based on data from Marr 1961

The second approach describes communities in plan view, as if looking down upon the region from an aerial perspective. John Marr and William Boyd's 1979 version, entitled *Vegetation Map of the Greater Denver Area, Front Range Urban Corridor, Colorado,* shows four dominant regional ecosystems: grassland, montane forest, streamside shrubland and forest, and cultural vegetation (figure 4.4). When Ann stood back from the map posted on her wall at home and squinted, the knife-slice of north-south-trending foothills and mountain vegetation contrasting with the plains grassland was most dramatic. Vying for attention, however, was the splat of urbanized ecosystems, laying like a dropped egg on the agricultural lands and grasslands. Streamside communities ringed reservoirs in evenly spaced locations throughout the thirsty region. Data for this map were gathered in 1976, and Ann imagined that twenty years of further urbanizing had isolated grasslands into patches and undoubtedly speckled the montane areas as well. Although the plan view located vegetation more precisely than the section view, it was not easy to interpret from it the relationship between vegetation and site conditions. For example, the map portrayed scattered shrublands in the southeast portion of her study area, but only through her own familiarity and through reading the accompanying text would she know about the effect of the direction of slope face on vegetation.

6. Peet 1981, 13.

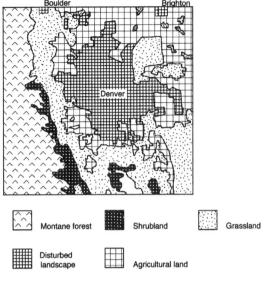

4.4
Plan view of vegetation of the Denver Front Range. *Based on data from Marr and Boyd 1979*

7. Peet 1981.
8. Ibid. See 34-35 for diagrams of shrub and herbaceous layer mosaics.

Robert Peet employs a third method of diagramming Colorado Front Range vegetation.[7] Using an *x*-axis of elevation, a *y*-axis of moisture and related topography, and a *z*-axis of vegetation descriptions, Peet has diagrammed canopy, shrub, and grass layers for a section of the Front Range north of Denver near Estes Park (figure 4.5). Looking somewhat like a crazed stained-glass window, the illustration shows plant community types: those groupings of plants that tend to grow together under similar circumstances where the climax species might not be evident. Understory diagrams are included for several reasons, among them the belief, supported by many botanical studies, that herbaceous species, with more than five hundred species represented within Peet's study area, are better indicators of site conditions than the twelve tree species.[8] This three-dimensional approach addresses many of the problems inherent in the two previous approaches.

Focusing on Peet's plant community mosaic diagram, Ann concentrated her attention on describing community types up to an elevation of eight thousand feet, the upper extent of her study area. At first, reading the diagram was as confusing to her as reading the landscape was to a newcomer. But digging deeper to understand it proved worth the effort: it provided a blueprint for site analysis and planting design using native plants. It spelled out the conditions in which these key plants grew best. Transport the plants to different conditions, and they need help adapting. This usually means more than providing tender loving care: it means also expending money and resources such as water and imported soil.

From wet to dry, and from lower elevations to higher, she reviewed her notes and envisioned the plant communities that the diagram and her other collected information represented:

Cottonwood forest. Ann could almost smell this perfumed plant community as she read about it. Dominated almost exclusively by plains cottonwood, crack willow, and a number of shrub species—hawthorn, currant, wild rose, snowberry—this is the most waterstained community described by Peet. It is still developing, as she had learned earlier, and is being replaced by a mixed community type increasingly dominated by Russian olive, Siberian elm, box elder, and green ash. Cottonwood-clad streams finger into the mountains as slopes rise, with plains cottonwood and Russian olive replaced by a hybrid between plains and narrowleaf cottonwood, and then narrowleaf cottonwood.

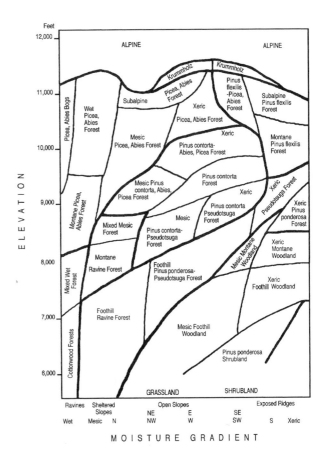

4.5
Plant community diagram of the northern Colorado Front Range, showing distribution of plants relative to gradients and topographic moisture.
Based on data from Peet 1981

Mixed wet forest. Eventually, around the seventy-two-hundred-foot elevation, these give way to mixed wet forest, notable for the tall fish-bone-branched Colorado blue spruce along the floodplains and Douglas fir, river birch, alders, and aspen in ravines and wet pockets. This type has high species diversity in the Front Range and includes the colorful perennial flowers many visitors make special sightseeing trips for: roses, geraniums, golden banner, horsetail, arnica, black-eyed Susan. Peet points out that homesick easterners would feel most at home within this type, as it has the greatest affinity with eastern flora. Ann felt that suburbanites should make regular, mandatory trips up to these eight-thousand-foot-elevation ravines throughout summer to get their hit of temperate climate plant aesthetics instead of cultivating them in the semiarid steppes. Perhaps this trip should be the eighth Xeriscape step.

Foothills ravine forest. Ann considered how cold air drainage, shade, and resulting low evaporation in the cool ravines of north-facing foothills slopes sometimes saved her a lot of driving. Instead of driving far into the mountains on hot days, she headed for areas above Clear Creek, in Eldorado Canyon, or Turkey Creek Canyon. The conditions there provided an ideal low-elevation setting for forest species typically seen at higher elevations. Trees included shade-tolerant Douglas fir and, to a lesser extent, ponderosa pine. On such trips, she could predict where fire was still a regular presence in the region, because ponderosa would likely be present to a greater extent in response to the greater sunlight levels in newly burned areas. The shrub layer was also shade tolerant and included common juniper, kinnikinnick, and waxflower.

Montane ravine forest. When tempted by a beautiful day to drive to higher elevations, Ann would note that the foothills ravine forest gave way to montane ravine forest, which also sustains high species diversity, especially in shrubs. Here she looked for, and found, abundant roses, ninebark, waxflower, junipers, snowberry, and currants.

Grasslands. Grassland community types vary according to precipitation, which decreases from eighteen inches per year along the western edge of the region to thirteen inches per year along the eastern edge. In the wetter, narrow band between mountains and plains, grasses are quite variable, because of small-scale changes in soil parent materials, topography, and elevation; aspect does not play a significant role here. In certain cobbly areas with clay and sandy soils, tallgrass prairie species, remnants from wetter climates, are dominated by big bluestem, switch grass, and Indian grass. She recalled the irresistible urge to run seed heads from these species through her fingers as she walked through the prairie patches. Ann was of medium height, and most of these grasses bloomed just at fingertip height. In moderately moist areas, she would have to bend at the waist to sample the midgrass species of western wheatgrass, Junegrass, Canada bluegrass, little bluestem, needle-and-thread and others. Further east on the drier plains where shallower and loamy soils dominate, she would have to kneel to collect seeds of grasses primarily composed of buffalo grass and blue grama, hence the name, short-grass prairie. It was troubling to Ann to note that photographs of the same plots of land taken in 1900s and again in the 1940s and 1980s reveal that bunchgrasses such as little bluestem have declined dramatically in the short-grass prairie, perhaps because of droughts and abusive grazing. Sandhills grassland communities are present in the eastern portions of the region, dominated by bunchgrasses if undisturbed. If disturbed, sand sagebrush dramatically takes over, as revealed by long-term photographs.[9]

Mesic foothills woodland. At lower elevations and within a central moisture range, neither wet nor extremely dry, mesic foothills woodland scatters across the foothills-mountain edge, arising from the grasslands from six thousand to eight thousand feet in drier areas. The pines grade into cottonwoods along streams; Douglas fir along cool, north-facing ravines; grasses on lower, fine-grained-soil sites; and shrublands on rockier sites. The forests are open, with scattered shrubs such as currants, bitterbrush, and occasional juniper. These, too, are aromatic woodlands. Ann had been known to step off a busy hiking trail to clasp a large ponderosa pine, imbed her nose in the orange-furrowed bark, and inhale its intoxicating vanilla scent. Her husband had at first been surprised but then pulled her away by the hand, admonishing the tree, "Hey. She's with me!"

Foothills ponderosa–Douglas fir forest. At about sixty-five hundred feet on moister open slopes, the mesic foothills woodland grades into foothills ponderosa–Douglas fir forest. This community type contains more shade and closed canopy; consequently, shrubs and grasses play a less important role in the understory.

Mesic montane woodlands. At about seventy-eight hundred feet on drier open slopes, open ponderosa woods become more populated with Douglas fir and

9. McGinnies 1991.

are typically encountered on finer-grained soils. Peet dubbed these locations mesic montane woodlands.

Shrublands. Shrublands are important communities throughout the southern portion of the study area, where scrub oak chaparral reaches its northern limit along the Front Range. William McGinnies calls this area "foothills thicket vegetation" and notes that shrubs such as scrub oak, mountain mahogany, skunkbrush, and scattered junipers follow drainages and gullies far out into the plains. The impressive diversity of shrubs, succulents, grasses, and other herbaceous plants often give the impression of invasion and instability, according to McGinnies, but eighty years of photographs taken at repeated intervals in the same areas show great stability and longevity. Some of the shrubs appear in the photos year after year, still going strong after eighty years. In fact, scrub oak populations are so stable that they do not appear to enlarge patch size or invade other areas as they reseed. The only changes noted are areas where they have been removed for development. Care should be taken when impacting these old oak stands, Ann noted, as they are very difficult to replace.[10]

Ponderosa pine shrubland. Above elevations of six thousand to seventy-two hundred feet on exposed ridges, ponderosa pine shrubland dominates. Understory shrubs and grasses constitute well over half of all vegetation, indicating the relatively minor role of canopy pines. Cheatgrass, skunkbrush, and mountain mahogany are dominant species, along with the pines.

Xeric foothills woodland. At higher elevations, from sixty-eight hundred to eight thousand feet, xeric foothills woodland communities come into their own on south-facing slopes and exposed ridges. Here, ponderosa pine canopy dominates, though it is sparse. Red cedar attains its highest importance here, especially on rocky sites. Peet indicates that south of Denver, this habitat area is occupied by pinyon pine–juniper woodlands. Shrubs such as currants, Boulder raspberry, and mountain mahogany compete with grasses in the understory. Cracks and seeps feature water-loving plants such as the colorful monkey-flower.

Ann examined Peet's diagrams for usefulness in planting design. They certainly assisted designers in knowing what plants to expect at various elevations and in various topographic situations. They provided information about what species to replace, particularly the shrub and herbaceous layer, following construction. The detailed moisture analysis of different site exposures was most beneficial to landscape architects, Ann felt. She looked at the apartment complex where she and her family were renting until they found a house to purchase. With Peet's diagrams in mind, she noted that a ditchline catching roof runoff from the north side of the building functioned somewhat like Peet's cool ravines. The shaded north-facing house wall provided moisture availability similar to that of a sheltered slope. The sunny, south-facing second-story deck, where potted plants struggled, was like an exposed ridgeline, the driest exposure.

Ann could bring this diagram along with her to clients' properties and use it to gauge the moisture gradient on the site, from wet and protected to xeric and exposed. Then she could evaluate whether the plants present were well located according to this gradient. If so, little water supplementation would be necessary. If not, modifications could be made in soil or sun exposure, irrigation, or drainage to better suit the plants. Most of the plants in the apartment complex's shrub and perennial borders were well adapted to mountain areas but not well placed in the low-elevation, exposed suburban site. That explained the early demise of the aspen trees, sticky with oystershell and cottonwood scale, and the frequent replacement of perennials. Some plants thrived, however, such as an adaptable Colorado blue spruce and numerous Pfitzer junipers, their forty-five-degree saluting branches sheared back to allow light to penetrate into apartment windows. Most plants needed more of something than the site offered, however: more water, more organic soil, more trimming, more mowing. Someday, she thought, there will be a charge for excesses. It could be called a "more-gage."

Ann did not think that only plants described by Peet's community types were permissible in Front Range gardens; she suspected that sites could be modified to provide appropriate conditions for many ornamental plants. She simply felt that Peet's diagrams helped her and others see how Front Range vegetation responded to site conditions in a way that plan and section views could not.

Thus far in her studies of the Front Range, Ann had addressed the plant community structure, the formative processes as functions, and how both changed over time. This approach was aligned with how landscape ecologists examine a region: they look at how landscapes are structured, how they function, and how they change. One piece missing from her study, a landscape ecologist might chide her, was a look at the region from a connectivity perspective. In evaluating the region for the roles vegetation plays, the ability of plant communities to support wildlife feeding, breeding, and movement also needs to be considered. As the Denver Front Range has urbanized, wildlife habitats have been reduced to fragmented patches, causing animals such as deer, coyotes, and other mammals to breed in smaller areas, to come into conflict with home owners, to be reduced in population size, or to migrate out, when possible. Birds utilizing the South Platte River flyway must search for patches in which to land and possibly feed and breed. Although some argue that increasing suburbanization increases species diversity through plantings, these new gardens tend to favor certain species that can tolerate the high density of urban pets that accompanies development.

In *Wildlife Survivors,* author John Quinn postulates that at current rates of habitat transformation, we are favoring a number of highly adaptable, successful wildlife species that will eventually dominate and make up most of the species we see, hear, and experience, while other species dwindle.[11] As she listened to cats yowling and hissing outside her window one night, Ann pictured a world where crows, ravens, jays, English sparrows, house finches, and cowbirds fully replaced the warblers, wrens, chickadees, nuthatches, neon bluebirds, and spiral-voiced thrushes she enjoyed hearing and seeing during her walks. Often in the morning she saw the fallout from the high suburban cat population: mangled young robins and, most recently, a vireo — never English sparrows. Yes, it's the call of the wild for cats to kill birds, but these cats were subsidized with Friskies and Science Diet, she thought bitterly; the birds were not. Skunks, raccoons, opossums, and coyotes had already proved their omnivorous adaptability. She remembered once camping under the stars at an urban

11. Quinn 1994.

campground, only to find her head unfortunately resting smack in the middle of a nocturnal skunk corridor. Skunks, along with their memorable odors, greeted her whenever she opened her eyes during that long night. She hoped for better wildlife interactions for her children.

But what could be done? Many excellent references describe maintaining wildlife habitat in urbanizing areas through the creation of greenways and vegetated corridors to connect habitat patches. As she prepared to dig into the repeated patterns seen along her transects, Ann made a note to remember the overall, larger picture of the region, where maintaining such vital lifelines for migratory and resident species was crucial to preserving a region's wildlife diversity.

DESIGNED LANDSCAPE CONTEXT Gardens are fingerprints of formative processes and tend to favor cultural processes. These processes of production, protection, and pleasure are quite legible in spots throughout the Denver region, but it was more difficult for Ann to sort and understand their jumbled appearance as she toured the region along her transect. Where she saw trees invading grasslands, she could predict the eventual successional pattern if the land was left undisturbed. Yet when she saw a railroad-tie planter filled with junipers in one yard next to a garden with star-shaped planters and symmetrically placed poplars, she had difficulty discerning which garden was constructed first; we do not tend to carve dates into our gardens as we do onto building edifices. However, she suspected that these fingerprints would eventually yield revealing information to a detective willing to dust and examine them.

One of Ann's favorite natural history authors, Mae Theilgaard Watts, writes in *Reading the Landscape of America* that there is a legible succession of styles in residential gardens.[12] Watts traces this succession by recording the development of the garden of a single house as it passes from one owner to the next from 1856 to present. Her approach deftly communicates dominant design philosophies of the time. Watts's work sparked Ann's curiosity in assessing neighborhoods and discovering when they were constructed, a thought that does not occur to many to do. Tracking neighborhoods over time also reinforces the idea that landscapes are dynamic records of all landscape processes.

12. Watts 1975.

If we were to unravel dominant landscape styles in Denver, Ann mused, what would they look like? Following historian Lyle Dorsett's lead in breaking Denver's history into manageable partitions, she saw characteristic landscape design eras emerge.[13] The first era, sketchy and speculative, would be the years prior to white settlement. A survival era would follow, spanning the years 1858 to 1867, from the discovery of gold in Cherry Creek to the arrival of the first water delivery system, City Ditch. This would be the time when plants were placed in their most critical locations, for their most important purposes. Transporting plants from the East Coast by stagecoach or later by train and watering them by hauling buckets from the well or stream meant strong intent and purpose. Following easier access to irrigation, an era of promotion began, from 1867 to 1904, during which many Denver area subdivisions were created, streets were lined with trees, and the City Beautiful movement caught fire. The period between 1904 and World War II was a time of enhancing earlier commitments to a city beautiful. The war sparked a show of patriotism through Victory Gardens. From the post–World War II years until the 1960s, the construction boom changed the face of Denver. New housing developments appeared within weeks. Lawns were perfected to show good citizenship and neighborliness. Junipers were planted, property boundaries designated. From the 1960s through the 1980s, change in the way Denverites consider their property occurred again, with increasing recognition of resources needed to maintain a garden, but no dominant design philosophy guided landscape development. Residences reflected a confusing array of styles and materials, from mass-produced, developer-driven turf-and-tree designs to pastoral Xeriscape designs. Finally, a new era was presently emerging, based upon a recognition of resources and place; this she hopefully dubbed the "Context Era."

What would it have been like to make landscape decisions during representative eras in Denver's history? What would have influenced her choices of plants and patterns? What might the landscape of this place look like over time, as fashions and philosophies changed? Through her reading, talking, listening, and sifting through many sources from these different eras, Ann sought a vehicle to answer these questions and settled upon the representational voices of fictional characters. After studying historical records, archived drawings, and

13. Dorsett (1977) describes community leaders and quality of life during five periods: Turnstile Town, 1858-70; Youthful City, 1870-1904; The City Beautiful, 1904-23; Queen City, 1923 to World War II; and Vertical City, since World War II.

recorded interviews with prominent Denver area pioneers, Ann placed these fictional characters in these eras, where they migrated at first, then settled. For early eras, they must be where food is plentiful—first by the South Platte River, then along the foothills near present-day Golden. For later eras, they settled in Denver, and the changing garden reflected cultural processes at work over time. Where is this garden? She closed her eyes, circled her finger above a map of the Denver region. Her finger dropped on a plains subdivision developed in the 1880s. She selected as a model a particular brick and stone house on a busy street that once accommodated streetcars.

HABITATION ERA: PRE-1858 The banks of the stream protected the man's eyes from the sharp light (figure 4.6). A channel chiseled a new bank with vertical slopes. Saplings tumbled horizontally, their green leaves dipping like children's fingers in the flow. He could now see the opposite bank, hazy green with new grasses, where adolescent flapping cottonwoods sucked the nutrients from the scoured, renutrified sandbar. Wading across the four-inch-deep flow, he reached the other shore and planted seeds of his own gathering. Grasses with sweet seed heads and shiny awns grew well here and would be gathered again in a few months to supplement the berries, the beaver, the buffalo his tribe depended on. He clambered to the top of the bank and surveyed the plains

4.6
Plains streamside site prior to 1858.

stretching toward the western interruption of rock. Their temporary camp was established here in the patch of leafy shade left from a previous river meander, along the second terrace, more protected from flood than where he had just planted seed.

His stomach rumbled and he thought about food. Most food gained along this prairie sweep was on the run: rabbits, prairie dogs, buffalo. But the yucca found clinging to slopes provided starchy roots. Cacti could be stripped of spines and boiled, and their red fleshy fruits were a delicacy. The cherries that ripened along streambanks were relished. Sorrel leaves were chewed for sour pungency. Wild onions were gathered on the plains and added to spice the game. Grinding stones transferred hard seed into flour. Other than occasional grasses, few plants were tended here in the plains. But keen eyes aided the gathering of food from the plains. Trading for corn, pinyon nuts, and other food with distant men to the east and south helped supplement their repast. Their tribe would move on again, with the buffalo, in the fall. Plants would fruit, reseed, carry on the next cycle. Sometimes the tribe fed on them more than once, but not often. Occasionally trappers would come through this area, following the river and killing the beaver. They would bring unusual plants to eat and smoke. More of them were coming through more frequently. Change seemed imminent.

SURVIVAL ERA: 1858-1867 The Gales surveyed their property. Richard had moved west to Colorado with scores of other miners, seeking to stake or work claims and retire young and rich. Mining did not agree with him, however, and he decided more profit could be made supplying miners with food. No vegetables were available at all until a few settlers brought them into the town on wagons in 1859, and even then prices were high. Richard saw gold in the color of melons and squash. So he staked a claim by a creek near Golden City in 1859. No land office had opened yet; once Colorado lands had been surveyed, in 1862, he formalized his claim. He claimed 160 acres along the grassy foothills and creek bottom. His wife, Mary, moved out with him in 1861, and great strides had been made to change this grassy sweep into a home. Buildings were nestled on a terrace with a northwest bluff blocking westerly winter winds behind them. The house was oriented properly to the south, with the barn facing southeast. Gardens were also on the south side of the building, as were key use areas for repairing equipment. Storage areas were located to the north of the buildings. The stream wound away from the buildings, close enough to provide domestic water and shade from cottonwoods but far enough away to protect the homestead from flood.[14]

Cultivated fields hugged the area irrigated by the stream's diverted waters. Richard grew vegetables to sell to the miners in Golden City and occasionally settlers in Denver City, requiring hard work irrigating fields and then transporting vegetables in the wagon. On the whole, 1861 and 1862 were good years, but a drought in 1863 wiped out his crops, and the Gales used what water they had for Mary's kitchen garden.

Mary's garden was a sampler of necessary and favorite plants brought with her on the wagon west. She had dug and wrapped onion sets, garlic bulbs, and potato tubers—and at the last minute added purple iris rhizomes. She brought seeds for tomatoes, melons, and peppers, chosen carefully from seed catalogues before her departure—along with surreptitiously ordered zinnias and marigolds. Slips of raspberry bushes were rolled in newsprint with rose cuttings. She snipped Boston ivy vines and counted on their hardiness to survive the long journey west. She did not think she could bear living without the scent of spring lilacs, so saplings of these were added as well.

When Mary arrived, she caught her breath at her first sight of the rocky edge between mountains and plains. The house was well situated for her garden, and she helped excavate the fenced square of red, rocky soil that would help feed them (figure 4.7). The lithe woman pried loose the rounded rocks, quickly wearing out two shovels from the stones' grinding action, and pushed them to the edges to form a fence to keep cattle and horses out. She hauled soil from the stream edge and worked it into the gravely mix. The house's southern exposure proved unbearably hot in the summer, so she trimmed cuttings from the streamside cottonwoods and placed them on either side of the walkway, leaving room for them to grow. Winter winds still buffeted their home, so Richard brought home blue spruce seedlings from canyons west of their property to create a windscreen along the north side. The promise of leafy summer shade, win-

14. Homestead siting patterns in the Front Range region are described in Thorsheim n.d.

4.7 The Gale property near Golden in the 1860s.

ter light, and wind protection encouraged Mary as she hauled water from the stream in buckets to ensure the saplings' survival.

Soon her seeds, slips, bulbs, and tubers were planted. The lilacs were placed next to the front porch, on either side of the front step. They bloomed the next year, giving her deep satisfaction and a link with what she had left behind. Raspberries thrived against the wood fence. Roses enjoyed a place of honor in the front yard, where the full southern exposure would prompt them to bloom in the summer. The vegetables occupied the east side yard near the well. Melons and squash grew well in the mineral rich soil.

PROMOTION ERA: 1867-1904 The grasshoppers, fire, and floods of the 1860s created many challenges for Mary and Richard and gradually wore them down. Richard shifted his work toward buying and selling the produce of others, which required a move to town. They sold their homestead and bought a lot in a new suburb. Denver City proper had been a place they only infrequently visited, to deliver vegetables to the settlers—when prices were high enough, that is, to justify the expense. During her first visit in 1861, Mary had winced at the mud and dust, the brown slopes, the absence of trees, shrubs, or even the coagulating short grasses she had grown to admire on the ranch. Patches of cottonwood trees indicated where the banks of various intermittent streams were currently located. Individual trees were so rare and important they became known to the early settlers: a hackberry north of town marked the hill where a Sioux chief was buried in the early 1800s, according to local legend.[15] Because water was erratically supplied from artesian wells and occasionally flowing streams, any plant was appreciated in the eroded town. Mary had heard a story about one of the town's doctors who imported dandelions to hold the mud together.[16]

As the Gales moved to town in 1880, Mary surveyed the changes from the top of the wagon box. Windmills were enabling her neighbors to irrigate valuable acres for truck gardens. Some schools were surrounded by verdancy, thanks to the new technological twins of barbed-wire fencing, which kept out hungry animals, and windmills. But the biggest difference was seen inside the city's grid. Here, the first ditch, City Ditch, had been excavated to lend a sense of planted permanence to homesick settlers from the east. Rows of saplings lined the ditch and road edges, lawns held the mud together, and an explosion of imported plants had found their way through trial and error into city gardens, despite the increasing droughtiness of the High Plains in general.

Richard purchased a house lot, which would soon be served by streetcar, near 320 acres rumored to have been acquired by the city for a large park. The Gales would be outside the noise, smelter soot, stockyard stench, and crime of the inner city and would be able to enjoy the benefits of both country and city in their new location. The subdivision planned for spacious brick and stone houses with basements. Soil from the excavated basements had been piled in front of the house, toward the sidewalk, and behind the house, toward the back alley, forming a "Denver slope" that enabled positive drainage toward the street and clearly demarcated their property from the street. Along this street, silver maples and elm seedlings, supplied with water from lateral ditches, promised eventual shade.

Mary set to work on the plantings, unwrapping seedlings, bulbs, and cuttings moved once more from the east by way of their abandoned homestead

15. Ipsen 1995 and State Historical Society of Colorado, photograph F-7319

16. Leonard and Noel 1990, 27 nn.

4.8
The Gale's Denver house in the 1890s.

(figure 4.8). She eyed the neighbors' yards to update her sense of garden beauty and fashion. Over time, she and her neighbors covertly chose "The Unsinkable" Molly Brown's glorious garden surrounding the elaborate Queen Anne house as a model for their own gardens. Influenced by the latest style, Mary suddenly felt a piercing need for a Victorian rose garden, not just assorted shrubs to provide pleasurable scents and cut flowers. The roses should be to the east of the house. The top of the front slope area should sport symmetrical spot plantings—star-shaped would be most desirable. Her peonies were transplanted into the center of these beds and were surrounded by phlox and the lawn. A statue was located for the lawn—a cherub, of course. She hadn't the nerve or the money to install a marble nude statue, as the daring Mrs. Tabor had done on Sherman Street; besides, her interests were more dedicated to plants.[17] Weeping needle-leaved evergreens announced the path entryway and stairs. Vines growing up the house columns connected the house to the site. These would add beauty without hiding the new house's attractive stone foundation.

17. Noel and Norgren 1987, 8.

The yard was surrounded by wrought-iron fencing to keep out the occasional pig and to demarcate their suburban "estate." A backyard cutting garden, a birdbath with a concentric ring of flowers, and a peony bed provided, in Mary's mind, satisfying beauty. Vegetable and herb gardens were featured, which supplied most of their fresh vegetable needs. They could not completely leave their early success behind: they knew how to grow vegetables in this climate, and needed to, even as Richard's wholesale business flourished. A carriage house filled the corner of the property, approached from the back alley, where the incinerator was located.

ENHANCEMENT ERA: 1904-1944 The Barrs were lucky to buy into such a good neighborhood, Helen realized at first glance. John had done well, perusing the obituaries and then circling in on the Gale house just as the widowed Mrs. Gale was moving in with her daughter across town. Mary Gale had lived almost thirty years in the house and was well known and loved by her neighbors. She had been one of Denver's early Garden Club members, and her garden was renown in the vicinity. Most of her neighbors could thank Mary for their irises, raspberry slips, poppy seeds, and extra tomatoes for canning. Now the new owners had much work to do to stay in good stead with the neighbors while adapting the place to their own tastes.

The Barrs moved to Denver from Chicago, bringing with them first-hand experience with the City Beautiful movement, as demonstrated during the Columbian Exposition of 1893. They were attracted to Denver after reading issues of *Municipal Facts,* a publication by the City of Denver that sang the praises of the rapidly growing, self-promoting city. With its new auditorium, civic center, parks and parkways, large city lots, and street tree programs under way, Denver appealed to the Barrs as the place for William to recuperate from his plaguing asthma and continue his career as a developer.

Helen was attracted to the Gale property because the many mature plants reminded her of Chicago. She, too, loved to garden, but for many years she focused her updating efforts on the house. Indoor plumbing, electric lighting, and coal heating were installed. The carriage house was converted to a garage for their car, and the unused well was planted with flowers. When plants began

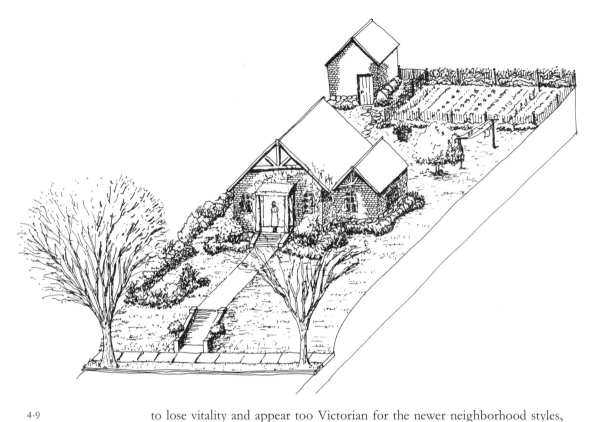

4.9
The Barr property in 1922.

18. Drawings from the McCrary Archives provide information about Denver landscape design in the 1920s.

to lose vitality and appear too Victorian for the newer neighborhood styles, Helen hired a locally admired landscape architect to help her upgrade her street appearance to match the newer, French-inspired homes springing up around her[18] (figure 4.9). First, the iron fence was removed from the front yard, as wayward farm animals and pets had ceased to trouble the increasingly elegant neighborhood and the street had long ago been paved and the lateral ditch concreted over. An openness between yards was currently the vogue, as if the lawn proceeded without end on at least one side of the property. Spirea shrubs on either side of the front walk marked the sidewalk entry to the property. Van Houtt spireas and Japanese barberries, the designer's signature combination, reliably denoted the front entrance. A planaria-shaped drift of shrubs and perennials fingered into the front lawn from the side yard, composed of French-hybrid lilacs, roses, staghorn sumac, European cranberry bush, iris, lemon daylilies, snowberries, phlox, peonies, and oriental poppies—all configured so that viewers from both street and window could see blooming flowers backed by a taller shrub background.

The back garden featured a single crabapple (several years later it would be debated whether this was the city's first crabapple, when the honor of having introduced the trees was granted to another landscape architect). In addition to the crabapple, the alley fence was screened by roses and a clothes line was accommodated; the fenced vegetable area remained. Helen's garden was practical to the rear of the house yet elegant in the front, with fingery flowerbeds and colorful, deciduous frailty set against the strong stone foundation. An early irrigation system was installed to minimize watering labor, and the garden thrived in this formerly arid landscape. American elm trees, personally handed out on Arbor Day by Mayor Robert Speer, reinforced the earlier trees planted after the City Ditch lateral reached the street in the 1870s. Overall, with the arching elms, shrub masses, and emerald lawn, Helen's garden looked daily more like the Chicago gardens she remembered fondly.

The Barrs prospered during their thirty years in Denver. John's asthma disappeared, his business boomed during the twenties, and his conservative investment practices left them well cushioned for the Depression. He did not live to see development grind to a halt as the United States entered the war in 1941. Their son and his family had inherited the house in 1940. John Jr., an engineer by training, returned to the property after the war, primed to make changes to bring the house into efficient, modern order.

DIFFUSION ERA: WORLD WAR II TO THE 1960S John Jr.'s wife, Nancy, worked at the Rocky Mountain Arsenal during the war, testing hand grenades. She was not afraid of hard work, but she did want their new house to be equipped with the latest labor-saving devices and focused her attention there first. These changes had implications for the garden as well. Their burgeoning family was outgrowing the elegant old home, and they added several rooms to the back of the house, toward the garden. Yet even then, the children's activities required more room. Thus, they looked to the garden to serve as additional outdoor living space. The clothesline had been replaced by an electric dryer, freeing up space on the south side of the house. They enclosed the back garden with

4.10
The Barr Jr. property in 1962.

19. U.S. Department of Agriculture and State Agricultural Colleges Cooperating Extension Service 1948, 12.

a redwood privacy fence and covered the garage with vines (figure 4.10). During the war, Nancy had pitched in to cultivate several of the more than forty thousand Victory Gardens in Denver. A thousand tons of tomatoes were produced in Denver's Victory Gardens in 1943, and Nancy swore she had canned most of them, profusely sweating over a city-loaned pressure cooker in mid-July. When the Liberty Garden movement was promoted door-to-door in 1951, she did not answer the door. And so, the vegetable garden lovingly nurtured by Mary Gale and Helen Barr was replaced with a swath of green Kentucky bluegrass. The Home Demonstration Club members had invited Nancy to join, but she by chance saw an article calling these clubs "a way to keep women busy and in a group that does no harm."[19] She felt that 4–H was bad enough, trapping her kids into raising chickens. Nancy wanted no part of these groups.

When her husband drove through a snowstorm in 1952 to attend a lawn meeting at the Garden Home Grange Hall, however, Nancy thought he was still suffering side effects of the war. Clearly, he had been infected with the Denver lawn craze and grew increasingly crazy over the years. It worsened in 1955, when the *Denver Post* and Western Federal Savings offered a prize to the most flawless lawn in the city's four quadrants. John accepted the challenge. First he had to rid the casually maintained lawn of that mortal enemy, crabgrass, a campaign he waged with Teutonic ferocity. He purchased arsenate of lead at the hardware store and spread the powder by hand. He calculated watering schedules, coverage, and pressure so that every blade was moist most of the time, as if they were in foggy London Town. These improvements gained him third prize in 1957. Three years later, chlordane's crabgrass-conquering power pushed him up to second prize. Industrial and commercial organizations then dropped out of the race, opening up more opportunities for the homeowners. John was the first to try out Dactual and Zytron, permanently removing crabgrass as even a visitor to his green quarter-acre. "Planting Bluegrass Lawns" pamphlets littered the living room after the local Lawn of the Month group met at their house.

Finally, in 1962, John won. His lawn was deemed utterly flawless. He was rewarded with lunch at the Denver Club, where the contest sponsors awarded him a majestic sterling silver trophy. Naturally, he built a special case in the living room and only half-jokingly called it his life's biggest accomplishment. Nancy feared this feat would define the rest of his life and that the minister would mention it in John's eventual eulogy, probably sped up somewhat by his having breathed the powders with which he laced the lawn.

Soon after John Jr.'s triumph, the Barrs began to long for a new house. There was always so much more work to do on an old house to keep it up-to-date. Following trends established in the new suburbs, Nancy had a nurseryman replace overgrown spireas and barberries with hardy junipers and then added more, to circle the house foundation like wagons. John's lawn passion ebbed and he tired of mowing the slope, so junipers were installed along the slope as well. Reducing maintenance time gave them more time to house hunt on the weekends, and soon they found a bigger, brand-new house southeast of town with a landscape already provided by the developer. They then joined their friends out in the new suburbs.

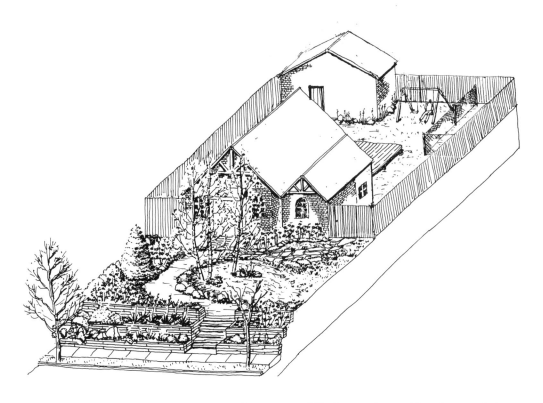

4.11
The Drury property in 1986.

CONFUSION ERA: 1960S-1990   The house changed hands several times during the 1960s and 1970s without too many changes made to house or garden. In 1976, it was sold to the Drurys, a young couple who were quite pleased with the brick and stone sturdiness of the house, especially in comparison with the pressboard and aluminum-sided houses they had been shown in outlying suburbs. The neighborhood was still attractive, although it was beginning to show its age. Many of the arching street trees had been removed because of the Dutch elm disease infestation, and the county extension agent was pleading with residents in older neighborhoods to replant. More than 60 percent of Denver's shade trees were American elms susceptible to the disease, and the gracious streets lost many of their shady denizens. Because the newly planted honey locust street trees were not yet tall enough to provide shade, the Drurys were troubled by the dry patches of bluegrass lawn and did not enjoy the overgrown prickly juniper leaves scratching their legs as they entered their front walk.

Judy and David Drury liked to garden, and they toured local nurseries and read magazines for ideas. They enjoyed the California look they saw in magazines more than the midwestern appeal of the neighborhood, so they began construction in the backyard, building a large redwood deck and extending the privacy walls to lasso more of the side yards (figure 4.11). They expanded the garage to accommodate a second car and added a manufactured swing set and a dog run. The droughts of 1976 and 1977 reduced the front lawn to brown patches, driving the Drurys to seek alternatives to the turf and junipers so prevalent in the region. Judy perused Denver's parkways and enjoyed hints of Denver's context: Colorado blue spruce and aspen evoked memories of mountains. After removing the junipered slope, much to the amazement of their neighbors, they purchased railroad ties from a nursery and hammered them into place to form a three-tiered terrace along the slope. Judy collected rocks from their travels into the mountains and walked to the nearby botanical garden for advice in planting a rock garden in the terraces. Over time, she focused on the rock garden, which boasted many specimens from around the world. As the shading honey locusts grew, her sun-loving plants were replaced with more shade-tolerant plants. The Drurys had relocated the steps up the slope, which connected with a curved walkway to the house, and on a berm in the front garden they placed an uneven number of aspen trees, more aesthetically pleasing, according to the experts whose gardening guides they had read, than an even numbers of trees.

By then, the term *Xeriscape* had been coined. Judy read about the practice in her Denver Botanic Gardens newsletter. It was a cumbersome term, she thought, but its water conservation gardening intent was good. With a few modifications, their garden qualified as a Xeriscape garden. She filled in planters with suggested plants such as potentillas, Oregon grape, and yuccas and then mulched with black plastic, rocks, and bark mulch. Their garden was photographed for the Denver Water Board Xeriscape calendar, which somewhat helped them defend it against attack from their lawn-attached neighbors. She found that the soils in the back corner of the property were unusually rich, but she continued to fret over the soils in the front yard, where perennials still would not grow. Eventually she created enough compost to replace these soils. Neighbors hinted at the use of herbicides by prior residents, so she dumped the previous soils in the landfill.

Judy and David hated to leave after doing all that work, especially because their water bills had only recently plummeted as the garden matured. Because they had created an unusual garden in the neighborhood, the appraiser had devalued the property below what it would have been had they left the turf and junipers. The next owners were luckier and moved in just as Xeriscape became more mainstream, and property values in general dramatically rose.

CONTEXT ERA: 1990S TO THE PRESENT The Barragans were lucky to buy the house before the 1994 Los Angeles earthquake struck, which sparked a surge in Denver's real estate market, according to one cynical newspaper report. Their own property in San Francisco had sold as soon as they placed it on the market, and they were able to pay cash for this character-filled house. They counted their blessings and tried to blend in.

They selected the property because it presented an alternative to the vacuity of developer-driven turf and tree landscapes and cookie-cutter houses. They liked the water-conserving garden. By now, however, soil pressure had pushed the railroad ties apart, weeds had overcome the black plastic and rocks, and the aspen were reaching the end of their short, citified life span. They joked about the hot tub and deck being their home away from home, although they had not had these luxuries in California. As the Barragans perused demonstration gardens and neighbors' gardens in the area, they found themselves drawn toward gardens that reflected a better sense of where they were, a sense of place. They wanted to be able to modify the property without wasting resources or money. How could they reduce heating and cooling bills through tree and shrub placement? How could they further reduce water use? Could birds make use of the yard as they migrated or sought food and shelter? Could they grow more of their own food and hobby plants? What building materials could they use that would say "Denver, Colorado"? They enjoyed the new infusion of dry-laid Lyons sandstone into highway interchanges and town welcome signs, but they preferred the use of recycled concrete sidewalk pieces, where the function of rock was present without the necessary scarring of another landscape and without the need for truck transport. They liked the use of aspen to connect city to mountains; yet these plants long for cool, moist pockets and higher elevations, not center stage in the plains with their roots covered with heat-absorbent black plastic. What appropriate plants and patterns of plants could provide that sense of connection to context?

The fingerprints of formative processes, of nature and culture, are evident in these stories. Through Ann's reading and interviewing, she saw times when climatic and biotic processes, such as drought and grasshoppers, drove people from their homes. But more often, such as during the crabgrass-versus-bluegrass battle, biotic processes such as competition are overwhelmed by people's need for order. At other times, like the era in which Ann was presently immersed, there is greater tolerance for the realities of the context: grasslands, wind, drought, and insects can be accommodated within the garden that is also culture. Like Mary Gale, Helen Barr, and the Barragans, she, too, was looking for local models to shape her garden. In the Context Era—an era best described by the Middle English and Latin roots of the word *context,* "to weave, to join together"—Ann turned to landscape models weaving together both nature and culture—plant patterns from her selected homeplace.

Juniper-dotted dry slopes in Jefferson County.

chapter five
patterns of place

ROOTS SUBSTITUTES   Ann's vehicle navigated the rural road's purposeful potholes, left intentionally to slow down tourist traffic. She pulled up at the state park gate and told the ranger the name of a particular family, and he allowed her free passage through the park to the inholdings where the daughters of the original homesteaders owned one of the most beautiful slices of Colorado imaginable. She felt privileged to know the ladies of this remote, wild, history-infused canyon. While working as a naturalist years earlier, Ann had lived in the canyon for three months in a 1930s stone cabin built by their brother. It seemed the sisters had a tale to tell about each stone in the canyon, some of which were incorporated into the cabin. They steeped her in stories.

Our family was the first white family to settle this area. That was 116 years ago. Our father and his brothers left the Isle of Man and came to New York City. There they were in a café, and they overheard men talking about the exciting land in the West. So they went West. They took a train to Golden in the 1870s and set up a freighting business for the mines there. Then they went to Leadville and set up a sawmill. Then they moved to Grand Lake and built cabins there. Eventually they found their way to this canyon to cut ties for a railroad, which had already been graded. The railroad went bust, but the brothers liked the area, set up a sawmill, and stayed. Our father considered several building sites for our home, but rejected the flattest, easiest ones due to proximity to the creek. "You build by a creek, you build a boat," he said. They built a boarding house, a two-story homestead, and eventually turned our home into a lodging ranch. You can still see our name painted onto rock way up where the old wagon road cut through the rock. Our mother was known for her chicken dinners, and folks still tell about the time someone gave our pet elk chewing gum. . . .

Father created a big vegetable garden by the creek, where he built a wood flume to irrigate it. He grew lettuce, beans, peas, and potatoes. We all helped create terraces around the house from stone they collected to help reduce flooding potential, erosion, and to provide garden terraces for our mother. She bought iris rhizomes and seeds from Long's Gardens in Boulder, started slips of lilacs, grew dahlias, gladiolus, and daffodils that they dug up every winter to protect the bulbs from freezing. See that big spruce tree over there? Mama planted it when it was a tiny seedling. Dug it up herself from South Draw.[1]

Ann basked in their rootedness, wearing it like a cloak, feeling the heavy significance of every view, every trail, every familiar plant. Rootedness was an unconscious part of their being, they breathed it with every breath. In her three short months and repeated visits later, she could only marvel at this sense of place she would never have but could only delightedly borrow for a few short hours at a time.

Ann considered what she did have, however, what she had acquired in her new homeplace within the short period of her recent residence. By attentively looking and learning, she had developed a capacity to predict: where debris

1. Recorded conversation with Helen Kneale, Eldorado Springs, Colo., 23 August 1996.

clogged curb gutters on her suburban cul-de-sac, she could expect certain plants to spring up as if born from divine intervention. She could drive Denver neighborhoods for the first time and, based upon which plants had been selected and the way they were arranged, pinpoint fairly accurately the original time of development, as well as when redevelopment had been deemed necessary by new owners. And, as she drove up from plains to foothills to mountains, she generally could predict her elevation by observing the aspect and species present. Conversely, if she knew her elevation and aspect, she could predict which plants generally would be present. She admitted that perhaps she was easily entertained, but she found these insights thrilling. For someone who had moved around so much in her search for a home, this predictive ability warmed her as much as her canyon friends' abilities to look at a large tree and remember when it was planted and in whose honor. The next best thing to being there, she supposed. Knowledge was her vehicle for becoming a "local."

DISTINGUISHING THE REGION'S PLANT PATTERNS Ann's collected information was bubbling up and spilling over, unsorted and still confusing to her. She wanted to use the information she had gained about processes to understand the repeated arrangements of plants spread out before her. These arrangements were her foothold on regional distinctiveness in the Denver area. She wanted to use the patterns in landscape design so that a fittedness emerged between place and new design. Ann hoped the information would help her gauge the extent to which new design either captured or detracted from the distinctiveness of the Denver region.

Rather than randomly collecting, and then using, repeated patterns, she wanted to sort what she had seen along her transect journey through the region. First, she extracted arrangements of plants that repeat three or more times (as well as a few anecdotal accidents that added spice to a region). Second, Ann selected those plant patterns that best reflect the waterstain—the evidence of water concentration as shouted out by the reactive presence of plants. She believed that the secret to seeing plant patterns in this region is to look for the waterstain. Water is a deciding criterion in semiarid regions because of its importance as both limiting factor and defining characteristic of the western landscape. Walter Prescott Webb suggests that shortage of water is the primary unity of the West. "Aridity, more than anything else, gives the western landscape its character," according to Wallace Stegner. A 1969 Denver Regional Council of Governments report states bluntly, "It is said that whenever you see a tree in Denver today it is there because somebody cared enough to water it." William Marsh asserts that running water heads the list of formative processes. "The work accomplished by runoff . . . exceeds that of all other formative processes by manifold, even in dry environments. Therefore we can safely conclude that the land forms we see in most landscapes are mainly water carved, water deposited, or influenced by water in some significant way." Plants, as well, are greatly influenced in their size, location, and distribution by moisture availability. Ann sought to capture the plant patterns that result from the way water naturally concentrates, without too much imported effort. The easier the relationship between plants and water, the better.[2]

Third, Ann wanted to acknowledge the influence of the geomorphic, climatic, biotic, and cultural processes upon the vegetation forming these predictable patterns. Some aspects of the processes appear more influential than others. For example, the petunia beds gracing so many suburban entrances in Denver are primarily caused by cultural processes—the need for order and attention—as opposed to the geologic uplift and subsequent erosion taking place millions of years ago. Although the latter clearly set the stage for this flat area now subdivided with homes, the cultural process of human affect plays the most apparent role. Thus, Ann grouped these manifestations of dominantly human processes together.

Ann scoured what she had seen and loosely grouped the plant patterns into different kinds of waterstains: those resulting from elevation, aspect, water concentration, soils, disturbance, production needs, protection needs, and pleasure needs. She hoped that grouping general vegetation responses to these outgrowths of the processes would encourage home owners and designers to seek out similar process-driven circumstances present on their own properties, choose plant patterns, and ultimately select plant species to suit the processes. The categorizing of waterstains helped her avoid seeing plant patterns as disembodied from the processes shaping them.

2. Webb 1931; Stegner 1992, 46; Denver Regional Council of Governments quote appears in Green Thumb Report 1971, 135; Marsh 1991, 40.

She again tripped over the importance of scale in presenting these patterns and remembered her flight over the area to gain a sense, first, of the largest scale. At this scale, the manifestation of processes most apparent in the Front Range is, of course, the great rising of the mountains from the plains (figure 5.1). Trees suddenly clad these slopes, slowly sprinkling occasional trees into the grassy plains. Water availability changes as more drought-prone soils feather down from the slopes and drought-tolerant plants flourish. As ecologist John Marr has written, "The conspicuous topographic break between the plains and the foothills of the Rocky Mountains is accompanied by an equally striking change in vegetation, from grassland to forest."[3] Similarly at the driving scale, underlying complex geology was revealed to Ann by distinct tree groupings and lines of shrubs where rocks surface (figure 5.2). And at the walking scale, she found blooming plants growing in fissures of rock where water had percolated and collected (figure 5.3). The same processes of moisture availability creating plant responses are evident at all three scales.

This repetition of patterns at varying scales has been well described by scientists and mathematicians. According to

5.1
Large-scale plant patterns are evident at the mountain-plains edge.

5.2
Medium-scale plant patterns are visible where trees rise from rocky soils.

5.3
Relationships between plants and water are evident at small scales.

---

3. Marr 1961, 21.

landscape ecologist Bruce Milne, "Natural landscapes possess remarkable regularity in the patterning, sizes, shapes, connectedness, and density of patches." He continues to describe "the pervasive fractal character of the landscape." Benoit Mandelbrot, a mathematician, discusses the remarkable repeated shapes of landscapes at a variety of scales. This regularity is described by fractals, which are mathematical representations of nature. One often-cited example of fractals in nature is the Maine coastline: At the largest scale, it is jagged, with numerous peninsulas. Each single penisula is also of a jagged form and is also composed of numerous penisulas; and so on down to minuscule scale. The shapes remain the same no matter what scale is used; the variable is the length of the measuring stick. Thus, the South Boulder open space, where these shifts between grasslands and forest are most evident, has a fractal consistency between flying and walking scales, and perhaps at much smaller scales as well.[4]

This similarity in scale relationships is important from several perspectives, Ann found. Dame Sylvia Crowe describes its importance from an aesthetic perspective, noting that humans deeply enjoy repetition of form at a variety of scales. "The landscapes most easily appreciated are those whose pattern is revealed on a large scale, as in the strong grouping of a mountain range, but the same composition can be discerned on a smaller scale in the grouping of rocks or the carving of a gnarled tree."[5] Ann remembered touring Machu Picchu in Peru years ago, where pulsing mists abscond with off-site steep mountain views on a regular basis. At one location along the edges of the ruins, a guide pointed out an upright six-foot-tall slab of rock carved into a seemingly random, undulating outline. At just that moment the mists cleared, and the slab's precise silhouette was visible in the ridges and peaks directly behind the slab in the distance. The clouds then closed over the off-site view again, leaving a perfect mirror image but at a much smaller scale. She had since forgotten the names of the many temples there, but this vivid image of the Incas' deliberate use of form repetition at smaller scales penetrated her memory of this trip.

Milne and others are currently studying implications of fractal relationships on ecological functioning. Studies have been conducted to ascertain whether landscapes with repeated fractal geometry at a variety of scales are effective in supporting various-scaled needs of animal and insect species. If so, then main-

4. Milne 1991, 81-82; Mandelbrot 1983.
5. Crowe and Mitchell 1988, 75.

taining a fractal geometry similar to that of the natural landscape would emerge as a landscape management goal. This has implications for designers as well as land managers. Milne concludes that more tools are needed to analyze landscape designs in terms of fractal geometry and that designs should strive to capture geometrical regularity similar to the regularity found in natural landscapes.

There are also pattern relationships in time, because processes can take place over long and short periods of time. As a rule, according to Milne, "short-lived processes (e.g., seedling establishment) occupy small areas, whereas persistent processes leave marks over hundreds of square kilometers. Thus, landscapes are affected by processes that vary across many temporal and spatial scales."[6]

Because "nomen est numen" (naming is knowing), Ann decided to name the patterns seen along her transect and group them according to relatively dominant processes. The following selected large-to-small-scaled, past-to-present patterns reflect remarkably complex relationships between interacting processes, relationships that evoke a sense of the region's response to the limiting and defining factors of water. They constitute a somewhat ordered smorgasbord of dynamic Denver.

Elevation. After familiarizing herself with descriptions of changes in the vegetation community along elevational gradients, Ann looked for evidence of these changes. She wanted to see clear shifts of vegetation, almost like milepost markers: "You have reached seventy-seven hundred feet. We are leaving ponderosa pine behind and arriving at Douglas fir forest." Although the vegetation shifts were not 100 percent predictable, since fire, logging, and insect outbreaks resulted in patchy plant checkerboards, the pattern expressions of elevational change from plains to mountaintop are dramatic at the flying and driving scales. Precipitation and evapotranspiration rates, sun and wind exposure, and gradients all increase as elevation increases, and they greatly influence plant responses. From a visual perspective, patterns include the stripes of plants along an elevational gradient, as shown in familiar section diagrams inspired by Marr's work (figure 5.4). This diagram reminded Ann of Ann Zwinger's eloquent description of driving along a mountain road: "The evergreen watermark now begins to stain lower on the slopes as the valley begins to rise."[7] It also

6. Milne 1991, 82.
7. Zwinger 1988, 6.

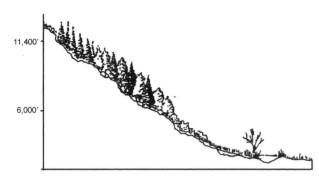

5.4
Vegetation stripes express the elevational gradient. *Based on data from Marr 1961*

hints at the hazards and stress of transplanting trees from montane meadows into suburban grassland settings, two thousand feet lower in elevation. They require cooler microclimates and protection from evaporative winds and sun to survive at lower elevations.

Ann recalled the luxury of following spring up the slopes of Mount Evans, the 14,264-foot peak west of Denver. She had found seasonal waves of plants blooming and bearing fruit earlier at lower elevations but shedding leaves earlier at upper elevations. The upper treeline was determined by harsh climatic conditions above 11,400 feet in elevation. Likewise, the lower treeline was determined by the presence of droughty, fine-grained soils and competition by grasses. In between, a distinct band of trees between 6,000 and 11,400 feet was still visible from the plains. The lower treeline was obscured, however, by the steady westward march of urban forests. Ann would have liked to see designers and developers acknowledge this signature of place and preserve it instead of masking it further.

Aspect. *Aspect* is defined as "a position facing or commanding a given direction; exposure." And so, as Ann learned, north was quite legible within the Denver Front Range area, particularly within the foothills and High Plains to the southeast. *Aspect* also means "a particular facial expression; mien, air." And aspect in the Denver Front Range is, Ann mused, a reliable "facial expression" of the region: like a rough five o'clock shadow, trees and shrubs precisely trace the line of a north-facing slope in the foothills, and shrubs do the same along gentler slopes on the High Plains (figure 5.5).

Branson and Shown, in their study of north- and south-facing slopes in the Denver area, comment that the "marked contrasts in vegetation types on hillsides with varying slopes and different exposures are a familiar feature of most landscapes with moderate to large topographic relief."[8] Ann had observed this pattern while hiking, noting that ponderosa pines seem to invade foothills

8. Branson and Shown 1989, 1.

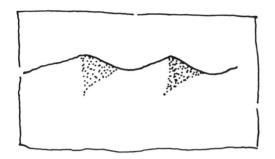 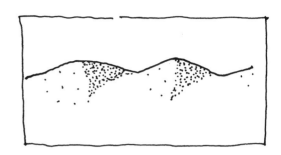

grasslands on north-facing slopes at a greater rate than on south-facing slopes. This phenomenon is confirmed by geographer Joy Mast, whose research tracks pine invasion over time through historical aerial photos and geographic information systems models.[9] The familiarity of the densely clad northern exposures and sparsely sprinkled, sun-saturated southern exposures is easily read by those who look (figure 5.6). Again, fire, insect outbreak, logging, and landscaping can interrupt the clarity of these contrasts; nevertheless, like a familiar smile or a warm glance, aspect patterns express that north is different than south, and their order and beauty are remarkable. Contrasts are notable at smaller scales as well, often wherever there is a vertical surface. Along a row of honey locust trees planted, under landscape architect DeBoer's direction, near Berkeley Park, Ann found lichens growing on the north side of street trees, attesting to the manifestation of aspect influences on vegetation (figure 5.7).

Water concentration. "Where water concentrates, plants respond." This phrase had become Ann's mantra for the Front Range. She recognized that plants respond to

5.5
Trees and shrubs render north-facing slopes visible.

5.6
Isolated larger plants create a patina of dots on south-facing slopes.

5.7
Lichens indicate the north face of an eighty-year-old honey locust tree.

9. Mast, Veblen, and Hodgson 1997.

PATTERNS OF PLACE 115

varying moisture levels within all the patterns she described—the factors leading to water concentrating in different areas are closely related to slope and the underlying soil's ability to hold water—but she thought of water concentration patterns as those inscribed by plants' responses to water in the form of streams, reservoirs, leaks, puddles, and so on. She consulted older aerial photos and those she had taken when flying over the region; these photos provided a horizontal view of plant responses to water concentration. Her fingers immediately traced the tree-demarcated stream courses veining through the study area. Former river meanders were evidenced by ghostly crescents of aged cottonwoods, revealing the river's past courses (figure 5.8). She found tree-ringed reservoirs and ponds where water levels remain stable (figure 5.9). Where water levels change dramatically, as a result of water storage or energy generation practices, bodies of water were edged by stony, steep, uneven terraces and weedy annual plants (figure 5.10). Throughout the region, ditches knit the land together with scraggly cottonwood stitches. Where ditches were stabilized with concrete, remnant or newly planted trees were evident. Where ditches were not lined with con-

opposite, from top
5.8
Crescents of cottonwoods trace former river meanders.

5.9
Plants ring reservoirs where water levels are relatively stable.

5.10
Weed-ringed reservoirs are notable where water levels frequently change.

this page, top
5.11
Plants stain the toes of slopes.

bottom
5.12
Plants radiating outward in wetlands are influenced by water availability.

crete, Ann noticed, the shrub layer often reappeared. Gullies, where surface water flows intermittently, were lined with stripes of plants—sedges, rushes, golden banner, and other herbaceous species in the gully bottoms and along the margins—and hawthorns and chokecherries formed a tangled overstory. She found that where impermeable soils coincide with the base of slopes, predictable changes in plant species, densities, and colors occur (figure 5.11). Wetland patches glistened green, distinct from the arid matrix. Ann felt that she was examining colorized black-and-white photographs, with green staining these key points and lines.

When she examined a number of these wetlands, she found that certain plants seem to occupy predictable niches, depending on water depths (figure

PATTERNS OF PLACE 117

5.12). She confirmed this by reading reports on wetland restoration within the region and learning more about these patterns and associated plants.[10] She frequently saw rings of plants radiating outward from deeper water to upland locations, with plants such as pondweed floating in the middle of a pond. Moving toward shallower water, several species were often present "with their feet in the water," such as shield-shaped arrowhead and water plantain. Bulrushes and cattails often occur in large stands in wetlands with reliable water sources, although they also withstand seasonal drought. These plants are considered "obligate" wetland species, Ann read, those plants which most reliably occur in wetlands.

Moving upland, "facultative wetland" plants, those which are usually found in wetlands, occur, such as sedges, rushes, foxtail barley, and redtop. "Facultative" species such as wild licorice can be found one-third to two-thirds of the time in wetlands, and "facultative upland" species such as timothy are more indicative of nonwetland areas, although there is a 1–33 percent chance of their being located in wetlands' outer rings. Plant sorting is quite dynamic, however, as wetlands develop and change over time. Because water levels in many wetlands drop during the summer due to evaporation, plant composition can change seasonally, with weedy species such as bindweed and cocklebur invading areas where former anaerobic soils and inundated conditions previously favored only certain species. Over longer periods, longer-lived species such as sedges and prairie cordgrass can replace short-lived perennials and become dominant. During exceptionally dry years, aggressive species tend to proliferate and are most abundant in the aquatic zones. Eventually, successional processes result in ponds filling with sediments, with upland species likely to be present. Ann noted other wetland patterns along her transect as well, such as cordgrass meadows responding to a water seep and blanketing dry grassland areas in green (figure 5.13).

At the smallest scale, she often found hardy plants responding to puddles, broken irrigation heads, leaky pipes, and clogged gutters and heads. She admired these determined pioneers.

---

10. Cooper 1987, 1990.

Soil moisture availability. Abrupt transitions between different plant communities often indicate changes in soil texture and moisture availability. In fact, although county soil surveys are determined through soils tests and geologic evidence, much of soil mapping is also determined by studying aerial photos, identifying plants, and classifying soils based on the relatively predictable relationship between soil and plants. Soils greatly affect moisture availability for plants, and distinct vegetation changes often indicate underlying contact between soil types. With the help of plants, Ann noted soil type variability throughout the study area. Within the grasslands, occasional ponderosa pine (also called rock pine by turn-of-the-century botanist Francis Ramaley) and shrub islands indicate isolated sites of rocky soil conditions. Rocky reservoirs were formed here, collecting water for probing root systems (figure 5.14). John Marr writes of the plant patterns in the foothills, "Within this area, regional climate is suitable for both grasses and trees; differences in soil or topography, or both, determine which of the two vegetation types will occupy a given locality. Fine, deep soil supports grassland; coarse rocky soil and even fractured rock outcrops support pine."[11] Recalling an earlier hike in the open space near Boulder, Ann remembered being drawn across the grassy plains toward a seemingly regular square shrub footprint (figure 5.15). Puzzled, she soon discovered that the square was a rock pile formed by long-gone ranchers, most likely used to enclose or exclude cattle from the area. Entwined skunkbrush and snowberry shrubs had colonized the

5.13
Cordgrass meadow blanket is a response to a water seep.

5.14
Rocky reservoirs support pines within grasslands.

11. Marr 1961, 22.

5.15
An orderly shrubbed square delineates a former cattle enclosure.

area where the rocks interrupted the fine-grained soils of the surrounding sod, calling attention to the past with orderly shrubbed lines.

Although trees and shrubs tend to catch our eye in the grasslands, grasses should be admired for their superior ability to sequester water for their own use, the ecologist and long-time Front Range resident David Buckner gently reminded Ann as she quizzed him about this region. He painted a picture of vast areas of homogeneous, fine-grained plains soils fully occupied by grasses, those superior moisture extractors capable of excluding all trees and shrubs, unless disadvantaged by overgrazing or construction. His vivid appreciation for plains grasslands made her suspect that many of the shrubby patches she noted were like scabs, covering cuts and slices into the otherwise resilient grassland skin.[12]

Buckner noted another pattern prevalent in urban environments, one that Ann had witnessed in a friend's garden. The friend, wanting to do the right thing in conserving water, had planted a blue grama and buffalo grass lawn. However, adjacent yards were composed of irrigated grasses. Irrigation water soaked into the soil and flowed toward the friend's yard, allowing more aggres-

12. David Buckner, letter to author, 1 December 1997, and telephone conversation with author, 10 December 1997.

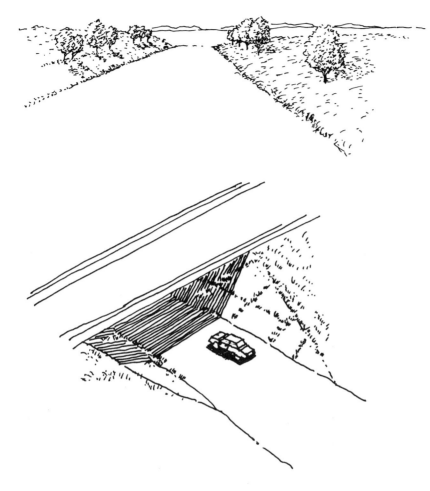

5.16 Cottonwood lines designate changes in soil permeability.

5.17 Plants colonize concrete joints.

sive weeds and imported grasses to outcompete the dryland grass mix. Buckner commented that in urban settings, the ecological base conditions have been shifted a few notches toward the moister extreme by the cumulative effects of irrigation and the growth of trees and structures. These limit the bite of winds that define many of the environmental limits for plant growth in the Front Range. As a result, despite our best intentions, soil moisture availability is limiting our ability to replenish native species in urban settings, sometimes resulting in patchy, weedy, unsuccessful attempts.

Changes between permeable and impermeable materials are frequently announced by plants, Ann found. She noticed this phenomenon as she drove through road cuts striped with a line of cottonwoods growing at the contact between a rock cap and a shale footing (figure 5.16). The same forces shape numerous other patterns in the region. Edges of impermeable asphalt or concrete roads and paths are typically lined with a distinct row of plants taking advantage of additional runoff that collects at these edges. Cracks and joints in these impermeable surfaces are invariably colonized by aggressive opportunists, causing maintenance headaches for those surprised to see the plants in their newly designed concrete embankments. She had grown accustomed to seeing plants, usually Eurasian steppe annuals, thriving along sloped overpass embankments; her favorite crack plants, growing along one slope near an overpass, almost spelled out the word "Hi" (figure 5.17). She personally felt an affinity for these crack plants, perhaps because, as Robert Frost observed, "People are inexterminable—like flies and bed bugs. There will always be some that survive in cracks and crevices—that's us."[13]

Soil elements. Plants respond to concentrations of various elements in Front Range soils. Salt concentrations in soil and water, for example, evoke predictable responses in plants. Many plants are highly intolerant of salts, and certain other species, such as salt grass, alkaligrass, alkaline sacaton, and tamarisk, thrive in highly alkaline or salty soils and are often found where salt naturally concentrates, such as in alkali wetlands and reservoir edges. Because Denver still used salt mixed with sand to clear winter roads, concentrations of salt also occurred along roadsides and sidewalks. Ann noted the salt grass sprouting from cracks along Denver's downtown sidewalks, forming a formidable sod along sidewalk edges. Colorado State University has developed a commercially available alkaligrass seed for roadside edges that takes advantage of the waterstain where saline-loaded snow water is piled and absorbed.

The presence of other plants in the Front Range also indicates elements in the soil. Prince's plume, a spiky, showy plant of mesas, shales, and plains, is a good indicator of the poisonous element selenium. Many species of the genus *Astragalus* also absorb selenium and cause cattle ailments known as "the blind staggers" or "alkali disease," according to botanist William Weber.[14] A good

13. Quoted in Rodis and Odell 1992, 131.
14. Weber 1976, 222.

thing to know, she thought, when siting playgrounds, a well, or a pasture. At smaller scales, Ann enjoyed the predictable association between fruiting shrubs and their inevitable location at the base of a bird-perch fence post—a seeding concentration of sorts (figure 5.18).

Presence or lack of disturbance. "For every truth, the opposite is also true." With this Zenlike phrase echoing in her ears, Ann went for a hike. She climbed to the top of a slope and enjoyed the sudden sky views afforded by burned and broken tree limbs. She hiked through dense ponderosa pine forest until she came to the patch of burned trees, the result of a fire in the Boulder open space a number of years ago, which had been quickly extinguished. Blackened trunks sported machine-gunned sapsucker feeding holes and punched-out woodpecker nesting holes. A riot of sun-loving herbaceous plants rampaged where flames had once licked, and new even-aged pine seedlings reached upward to shade the forest floor once again. She was seeing a typical disturbance patch—a hole carved out of the forest—and at the same time she was seeing evidence of lack of disturbance (figure 5.19). Because lightning and aboriginal fires no longer burn the piedmont every twenty-five to forty years—they were now firmly suppressed by local firefighters—this forest had built up a high fuel load and burned fiercely. Had it not been suppressed it could have been part of an enormous conflagration. Thus, this pattern of patchy burns is evidence of both disturbance, from fire, and lack of disturbance, from fire suppression.

Through the naked trunks Ann could see the mountain slopes to the west. Green ponderosa and Douglas fir trees were evenly mixed with grey, foliage-stripped trees along

5.18
Fence post plants are evidence of bird perches.

5.19
Fire disturbance patch is carved from a ponderosa pine forest.

the slopes. Again, both disturbance and lack of disturbance were visible in the tweedy forest. Logging, fires, and grazing massively altered forests of the Front Range from 50 to 130 years ago. Trees have regenerated under fire-suppression policies, with the result being long-term change in forest character from open woodlands to dense forests. Trees growing closer together have been weakened and are susceptible to the insect outbreaks that sweep these forests, leaving the corpses interspersed among those still alive and well.

Ann found several studies indicating that grazing creates many vegetation patterns. Botanist S. V. Clark and others studying the effects of grazing at Rocky Flats conclude that there are obvious plant patterns resulting from grazing, not just from water availability. On alluvium, for example, broad-leaved herbaceous pasture plants such as Klamath weed and nailwort replace Junegrass- and wheatgrass-dominated prairie when grazing pressure is high. If grazing increases further, ragweed, Klamath weed, and barren areas replace the pasture, giving the grasslands a patchy, weedy appearance. Native bunchgrasses such as needle-and-thread grass and western wheatgrass disappear when overgrazed.[15] Patches of plants such as prickly pear and Spanish bayonet are considered "unpalatable remains" because cows do not fancy them; they tend to dot an overgrazed landscape. According to William McGinnies' analysis of High Plains photos taken at repeated intervals from 1904 to 1986, small differences in soil texture can have dramatic effects on native species composition. For example, in High Plains areas studied, vegetation changed from short-grass prairie to wire-grass stands as a result of continuous heavy grazing. The author concludes that cows' teeth cause less damage to plants than do their feet: soil texture and permeability changes occur as a result of repeated trampling over long periods of time, allowing plants with a greater tolerance for soil compaction to thrive[16] (figure 5.20).

Other grazing disturbance patterns on the High Plains, according to McGinnies, include the disappearance of bunchgrasses, particularly little bluestem, and the increase of sand sagebrush where tall-grass species once thrived. Drought is a likely accomplice. McGinnies concludes that in the foothills areas, within the complex zone between mountain and plains vegetation, reduced grazing pressure following previous heavy grazing can lead to increas-

15. Clark et al. 1980, 49.
16. McGinnies 1991, 157.

5.20 Compaction causes vegetation changes.

ing invasion of ponderosa pine. So, Ann thought, fire suppression and reduced grazing pressure together are among the causes of the changing look of the South Boulder open space.

Gullies northwest of Colorado Springs were also investigated for vegetation changes from 1905 to 1986. Investigators found that blue grama "heals" disturbed sites and that tree and shrub species proliferate in ungrazed gullies. Blue grama is seen as a resilient plant able to recover from extreme overgrazing, plowing, and drought. Little bluestem is less able to bounce back and has been replaced by other species.

Bulldozers and bulls can cause similar plant responses. Ann could recognize the bulldozer's increasing impact as, over time, grazing pressure had decreased and urbanization pressure had increased. She found many locations where opportunistic plants thrived, especially where construction had been begun but was never completed and where once-cared-for vegetation had been abandoned. These locations struck her as being in the city's peripheral vision, much like homeless people. Plants like horseweed, cheeseweed, bindweed, and many others are adaptable to the harsh conditions of abandoned areas. Their numerous seeds disperse well, plant parts regenerate new growth, basal leaf arrangements withstand trampling, they grow and set seed rapidly, and they form deep tap roots, as any gardener knows. Some are indicator species that tell a story. Prickly lettuce is nicknamed "compass plant" because its leaves grow in a north-south direction when in full sun. Plantain has been called "white man's footsteps" because it appeared and spread simultaneously with the first human settlement in the region. And an abundance of native pineapple weed tells much

5.21
"Golems" and "wraiths" pile up against fences.

about dog use of the property and informs on the owners who did not "scoop the poop." As compensation, Ann mused, the foliage has a mitigating pineapple aroma when crushed.

Dame Sylvia Crowe has described patterns that have a powerful effect on people, including the pattern of prevailing against adverse conditions, such as an oasis in the desert, wind-clipped alpine plants, and a hedgerow surviving long after the protected farms are gone. Weeds in vacant lots capture this spirit in a more subtle way (figure 5.21). Bill Mollison, of "permaculture" fame, ascribes unfamiliar names to weeds, which Ann instantly appreciated: Tumbleweed-like plants, or those substantial rolling balls like ironweed, which disperse spiny seeds, are known as "golems." "Wraiths" are dry, light, airy panicles, such as mustards and amaranths. According to Ann's dictionary, a *golem*, from Jewish folklore, is "an artificially created human being endowed with life by supernatural means." A wraith is "the ghost of a dead person." Every weed-wrestling gardener in windy areas can be convinced quite easily that some plants are supernaturally persistent, she was certain. Ann was not suggesting that we include golem and wraith patterns in our gardens, but because they grow with inadvertent water, she considered them interesting, challenging, and certainly worth observing.[17]

Urbanization within the region occurred over a period of 150 years, but native plants were not completely removed. As habitat decreased, plants migrated into infrequently disturbed, remnant areas and persisted. Photographer Robert Adams has commented on urban disturbance patterns seen repeatedly throughout the Denver area: "In Denver's vacant lots one can still find, no matter how numerous the food wrappers and pieces of styrofoam, an old tough green—Spanish bayonet, cactus, and sage."[18] Ann often glimpsed fugitive native grasses along railroad rights-of-way, road edges, river corridors, and other unmanicured areas (figure 5.22). As Denver's interest in greenway design grew, however, many natives were displaced by turf and trees, victims of vegetation gentrification.

5.22
Native plants often repopulate unmanicured areas such as pipeline corridors.
Photo by Nat Kuykendall

Production needs. Productive vegetation patterns are those in which plants are managed for economic production, usually for food, such as crops or grasses intended for grazing. Aerial views of the study area reveal quilts of various themes: squares aligned with the American Survey, 133-acre pivot-irrigated circles, grids of orchards, and plants growing along fences and canals. Wherever water was applied, plants responded, forming regular patterns related to the efficiency of irrigation technology. The efficiency of haying operations is also evident from aerial photos. It took Ann quite a while to determine that the long white stripes and gravestone-like spotting of fields on aerial photos were rows of cut hay awaiting baling and the bales themselves. Many times the hay stripes circled an unmown area that apparently was too steep or wet to run machinery over; a bagel effect was formed in these cases. Hay lines also veered around lone cottonwood trees, usually centered in a field (figure 5.23). She saw this vestige repeatedly in the region, attesting to water's underground presence. The ghosts of waterstains often showed through a disked field; when flying over the eastern

17. Vessel and Wong 1987; Crowe and Mitchell 1988; Mollison 1990, 396.
18. Adams 1977, 7.

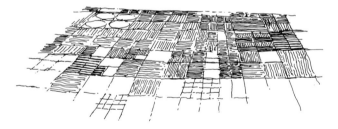

5.23
A lone cottonwood is centered in a field.

5.24
Waterstains appear through a disked field.

5.25
Checkerboarded productive patterns grow more pronounced over time.

portion of the study area, she could see scattered pockmarks of former wetlands still legible in the uniformly plowed fields (figure 5.24). Back on the ground, Ann looked again at old aerial photos; the pattern of fields informed her about when an area had been settled or subdivided. Fence lines separated section-sized homesteads of the late 1800s, with fields alternating their stripe directions. As these sections were further subdivided in the 1920s and 1930s, the stripes became more and more checkerboarded (figure 5.25).

While driving, she traveled along quilt pieces of rich corn green. The borders of these fields are frequently manipulated to make sure waterlines are in good repair. This soil disturbance creates perfect opportunity for summer annuals such as sunflowers to germinate (figure 5.26), forming a vivid pattern of green squares within a golden frame. Driving through Denver neighborhoods, Ann saw evidence of community garden patches, one of which had been in the same location since the Victory Garden days. Corn tassels, usually the tallest features of the gardens, announced these happy patches.

Productive patterns are also the result of landscapes primarily shaped for economic production or transportation.

These include undesigned arrangements of plants surrounding factories and those lining railroad corridors and highways. At one point many of these sites have been disturbed, sometimes repeatedly. However, many others have been allowed to stabilize and have often been reclaimed by native species. Mae Watts writes about railroad corridors as the last refugia of native tall-grass prairie species in Illinois.[19] Indeed, needle-and-thread grass, rabbitbrush, and other extremely hardy native plants crowd the edges of Denver area rail corridors and roadsides.

At the smaller scales, productive patterns show up in backyards, usually in rectangles and squares devoted to vegetables. Ann's favorites were the vegetables growing in unexpected places, like corn thriving in a sliver of soil along the Cherry Creek railing in the former warehouse district, the vegetables and sunflowers at the Denver Art Museum entrance, the three corn plants sprouting voluntarily along a neighbor's front walk, and the Colorado Rockies–sized zucchini baseball bats growing innocently from a self-sprouted plant on a compost heap (figure 5.27). It would be difficult to predict the exact location of some of these unplanned patterns. But, she learned from seeing these incongruities repeated throughout the region, they will occur. And she liked them best.

Protection needs. For a variety of reasons, many of the patterns related to human need for comfort and protection are disappearing quickly, so Ann paid close attention to those repeated along her transect. It struck her that the best

5.26
Sunflowers frame agricultural fields.
Illustration by Devon Kohen

5.27
An agricultural sliver along downtown Denver's Cherry Creek.

19. Watts 1975.

PATTERNS OF PLACE   129

demonstration of this need for protection is in areas planted prior to widespread availability of electricity and air conditioning. They are easy to spot, especially in the plains: just look up and out. The farmhouses are now crowded by the dense blue spruces or Douglas firs on the north and west edges and cottonwoods on the south and east sides (figure 5.28). Somewhere in there there's a farmhouse, Ann thought. These trees are useful for microclimate control but also for orientation: one farmer, describing the dense plantings he irrigated by hand, confessed that he had planted them so that he could always find his way safely back to the homestead if he got disoriented out in the fields.

Often, full-grown trees are removed because the overdensity of plants obscures the sunlight from windows and provokes residents' claustrophobia, but most often these patterns are disap-

5.28
Microclimate protection patterns are notable at older homesteads.

5.29
Homestead trees shade southeast building corners.

pearing as a result of development. Back in the Boulder open space, where the previously described shrubbed rock fence breaks through the grassland sod, Ann discovered a single cottonwood trunk lying on the ground, riddled with oval-shaped woodpecker holes. The ragged-edged trunk told a story of drought and high winds, which eventually brought the tree down. A familiar shrub grew nearby: a lone lilac surviving without any irrigation. She had never noticed a house foundation; but now, knowing where to look in the tall grasses, she found one to the northeast of where she stood. The umbrageous cottonwood had protected the southwest corner of the house, reduced glare, and provided comfort for these unknown early residents. The "homestead tree" was a pattern she frequently found in the region (figure 5.29).

Ann could still see remnants of hedgerow and windbreak patterns. Early settlers lined fields with trees to block winds and reduce soil erosion. The lines ranged in width from a single tree to a dense aggregate of conifers and deciduous trees, many imported from similar arid steppelike environments. Aerial photos of the Rocky Mountain Arsenal near Commerce City show windbreaks run amok; early ranchers most likely planted the New Mexico locust around their homes and outbuildings to block harsh, snow-laden winds (figure 5.30). Over the fifty years following the Army's condemnation of the ranches as part of the development of the arsenal, the locusts have expanded to form dense thickets and now provide excellent cover for wildlife species.

Snow fences are another form of windbreak that protect highways and interchanges throughout the region, as well as driveways and rural roads. Sometimes these are planted with evergreens and other wind-blocking plants. Snow is caught by the fence and plants, resulting in higher water availability and dense plant growth (figure 5.31). Ann noted that such fences usually parallel the highway, but she did enjoy one series of fences that were angled to capture snow drifts in such a way that they resembled old Burma Shave signs.

Irrigation ditches skirting fields support cottonwood hedgerows that serve dual functions of habitat and windbreaks. As water supply for the region

5.30
New Mexican locust thickets provided windbreaks for early Denver residents (aerial view).

5.31
Snow fences concentrate water and irrigate planted shrubs.

PATTERNS OF PLACE 131

5.32
Mayor Speer distributed saplings for street tree plantings (1909), creating "urban reprieves."
Photo from the Denver Public Library, Western History Department

20. U.S. Department of Agriculture and State Agricultural Colleges Cooperating Extension Service 1965.
21. U.S. Department of Agriculture and State Agricultural Colleges Cooperating Extension Service 1948.

becomes an increasing concern, interest in covering the irrigation ditches to reduce evaporation is growing. Ann saw the familiar cottonwood field edges as disappearing relicts. Interest in planting hedgerows seems to reemerge at intervals: The Junior Forester Program began in 1949, with young men planting dense layers of trees and shrubs at field edges. According to Extension Service records, ten thousand trees were planted, starting in 1965, on farms of at least two-and-one-half acres, for shelter belts and wildife protection.[20] These are most noticeable in the plains portions of the study area, and many are being reinforced by new property owners for additional purposes of privacy. In urban settings, the need for climate control and order is derived from dense street tree plantings and cooling urban parks and parkways, originally envisioned in 1858 and eventually threading throughout the Denver urban core as "urban reprieves."

American elms and "soft maples" were the most common species given to home owners, who had first to prove they could take care of the trees, during the 1909 free tree giveaways (figure 5.32). Ann wondered what residents had to do to prove they were worthy of the seedlings—show up with a bucket of water? In 1948, Dutch elm disease made its first appearance in Denver, attacking the elms that made up 60 percent of Denver's shade trees.[21] More recent protection patterns are visible in the region; more than one suburban resident has strategically placed cactus species beneath windows, to dissuade potential intruders.

Pleasure needs. Plant patterns resulting from our need for pleasure abound. Again, Ann interpreted "pleasure" as encompassing those things that separate garden from wildland: selected colors, textures, forms, scents, scale, lines; meaningful groupings of plants expressing an idea or symbol; ordered arrangements that help us derive a sense of human intention. Three themes emerge repeatedly in the pleasurable use of plants in Denver: a sense of oasis, property definition, and welcome. Ann found these themes evident throughout the region's matrix, concentrated in well-defined corridors and in notable patch patterns.

At the largest scale, Denver's transformation from High Plains grassland to a second- and third-generation urban forest matrix indicates the importance of a sense of oasis, a response to both protective and pleasure needs. In the late 1800s, small patches of green were placed where there was the most need for shade and food and in places frequently viewed by the residents and visitors. Vegetation responses to human needs for pleasure are most distinctly seen during times when water is scarce: priorities become very clear when seedlings are watered by hand. Early settlers interrupted the vast plains with green imports, ringing the houses so that from a distance they could easily find their way home. Towns such as Lafayette and Brighton could be seen from a distance on the plains, their vertical vegetated stature discernible from great distances. As Kenneth Helphand writes, "On the plains, trees are not a symbol of nature but of civilization. They are the sign of human presence."[22] Towns became reprieves from the dusty plains, and tree-lined streets hearkened back to eastern city order. Parks were developed to provide a sense of urban oasis as well, based upon those in temperate climates, as the green lungs of the city.

As early as the 1860s, landscape architect Frederick Law Olmsted, the codesigner of the quintessential temperate-climate urban park, New York's Central Park, urged that design criteria specifically developed for semiarid landscapes be used to limit irrigated areas and restrict views of dry middleground landscape. He found to his dismay that his clients preferred his pastoral park

22. Helphand and Manchester 1991, 171.

designs for temperate climates and, against his advice, transposed them to semiarid locations. Olmsted's parks in Chicago and New York appealed more to Denver's city fathers and served as "passive beauty spots" in the hard urban environment. Thus the sense of oasis was enlarged.[23]

As water became more available through ditches and dams, the desire for green also grew. Helphand comments sympathetically on this repeated phenomenon: "Our plant choices reflect a cultural heritage, perhaps a species heritage, in the preference for green itself and for the expanse of a lawn. Preferences are also born of familiarity, the comfort of the known. . . . The front lawn is the American garden, the base on which we build our home, the true frame of our dwellings. Representing domesticity, it is an atavistic attachment to the land and reminder of a rural past."[24] Such American gardens dominate much of Denver's landscape, from residential lawns to mown roadsides to sports patches of soccer and baseball fields and golf courses. From the air, these sports patches are striking in their regularity of rule and challenge. Baseball diamonds appear as if giant pendulums have worn off the lawn through regular rubbing. Measurements stand out in regulation-sized football and soccer fields. Golf courses appear to be stroked from giant fingers, smearing smooth green paths among the textured trees and traps. The oasis theme is like a reversed negative in Denver and many arid and semiarid cities, where an overwhelmingly brown matrix with a few green patches, the natural configuration, has become a green matrix with a few brown patches. Ann remembered a cartoon, entitled "Oasis," that showed a verdant suburban landscape with a single house's fenced backyard planted with desert species.[25] Now the oasis patches in Denver are the native grasslands.

Beginning in 1864, cottonwood branches were trimmed and placed along Denver's streets to provide eventual shade corridors and a sense of aligned order. Tree plantings were later supported by and proliferated along the Denver irrigation ditch network, reinforcing their orderly lines. As houses were built, plants also defined property boundaries and cinched the houses themselves, as evidenced by innumerable "juniper belts" at the foundation edges and along fence lines (figure 5.33). In aerial photos Ann repeatedly saw suburban checkerboards, with larger plants designating the property lines on the boards. Many

23. Beveridge 1995, 252.
24. Helphand and Manchester 1991, 171.
25. Billout 1997, 103.

corridors of plants were created. She was convinced people responded to lines with plants: Rather than deliberately shaping spaces, people tend to look at their property and wherever they see an edge—of the house, the walk, or a property line—they place lines of plants, sometimes curvy to give a "natural" appearance, sometimes straight. Lining entrance drives with plants, particularly blue spruce, is a repeated pattern within the region (figure 5.34).

Notable patches include the blazing flowerbed "beauty spots" welcoming people to city parks and civic features. Saco DeBoer, writing about the flower beds he designed for Denver parks and parkways, has noted that "flowers give people a friendly feeling toward a city. . . . There is no better memorial than a flower garden. . . . Once the city takes the lead, the citizens will follow and plant gardens on their own."²⁶ As a result, intricate weaves of radiant annuals and perennials spot the edges of parks and parkways to draw attention and provide DeBoer's friendly feeling (figure 5.35). As Lady Bird Johnson once commented, "Flowers in a city are like lipstick on a woman—it just makes you look better to have a little color."²⁷ However, Ann had heard others refer to these parks, with their floriferous flauntings, as being "all tarted up." These beauty spots are now repeated at larger scales at entrances to cities within the region, as well as at smaller scales in

5.33
Shrubs reinforce property boundaries in many Denver neighborhoods. *Photo by Kiku Kurahashi*

5.34
Blue spruce frequently line driveways.

---

26. DeBoer 1972, 204, 206.
27. Quoted in Rodis and Odell 1992, 222.

PATTERNS OF PLACE 135

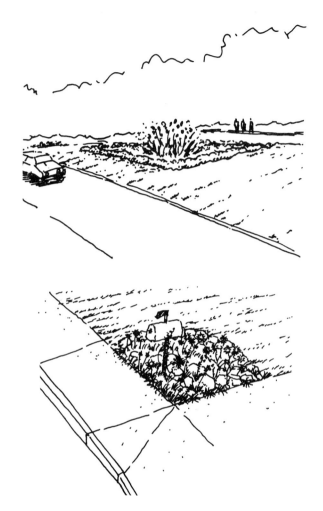

5.35
"Beauty spots" call attention to Denver's numerous parks and parkways.

5.36
Mailboxes typically are set in floriferous patches.

commercial and residential development entryways, providing a sense of welcome. At the smallest scale, mailboxes and paths connecting driveways to front doors receive special attention in introducing the property owner's sense of order and beauty. Usually, bright perennials or annuals announce these entrance points (figure 5.36). "Mail dominance," Ann thought as she photographed yet one more mailbox surrounded by an explosion of flowers in an otherwise unremarkable front yard. In more recently designed gardens, she found drought-tolerant plants gracing these key welcome spots.

Although Ann enjoyed many aspects of the region's green matrix—the notable corridors and the colorful patches defined by property and irrigation lines—she had to acknowledge that these patterns were unsustainable as currently expressed within the region. Their survival depended on a life-support system of imported water, fertilizer, and maintenance. Throughout the settled history of Denver, the gestures of oasis, property definition, and welcome have been universally employed, as they may be for all settled populations. Ann returned to one of the questions with which she had begun her study: How can we acknowledge these human impulses through planting design in a way that does not violate our desire to create sustainable landscapes?

Ignoring these fundamental drives because they do not conform to resource conservation goals will only further delay the capturing and honoring of the

5.37
The mowed strip along the open-space edge is a "cue to care."

inherent patterns disappearing so quickly in the region. People may continue to reject the guilt sparked by conservation: "I know I should conserve water, but I don't want to live without roses." They may not know the joy of acknowledging their own drives along with other processes at play: "I can have roses in the waterstained area of my property." In her article, "Messy Ecosystems, Orderly Frames," landscape architect Joan Nassauer writes that ecological design will not increase in acceptability until we recognize that people need to express "cues to care."[28] These can include a mowed strip at the edge of wildflower plantings or a neat fence along the edge of a restored grassland (figure 5.37). Ann believed that the beauty spots at walkway entrances and mailboxes were examples of such cues to care. Designing them to meet people's needs and at the same time conserve resources is the challenge of pattern-based design. As we traverse the ground from unsustainable landscape design toward design that survives on its own and supports other species, Ann thought, we must include signals to remind ourselves that what initially seems to lack order is actually intentionally cared for.

Despite a design's best intentions, she concluded, some plant patterns hound us like an uninvited Field of Dreams: build it and they will come. What we now build will become the stage upon which future formative processes act. If we build a sloped concrete embankment, we invite seed dispersal in the fertile but

28. Nassauer 1995, 167.

PATTERNS OF PLACE 137

cramped concrete-joint seedbed. If we house people in even the most famous or rustic national park area, we should expect them to express themselves with favorite plants in key locations. For example, at Yellowstone National Park, Ann once saw petunias framing an employee's window view of bubbling geysers. Even though they often had to haul water with a bucket, her octogenarian friends in the canyon irrigated the small patch of frail grass underneath the towering ponderosa pines, just as their parents had after importing the seed from an eastern nursery one hundred years ago. Plant patterns are derived from natural and cultural drives, and in designing we must acknowledge these forces, because many of the patterns will be expressed whether we want them or not. Sometimes we can learn to want the inevitable patterns—maybe choose the embankment crack plants instead of being assigned weedy-looking Eurasian species. Sometimes we can ease inevitable ones into more appropriate expressions—native perennials requiring no additional water instead of those Yellowstone petunias.

Ann felt that the beauty of seeing and understanding these patterns was the sense of being attached to something larger than, say, the currently marketed landscape style. She would never have the firm rootedness of her friends in the canyon to give her a similar sense of attachment. But every once in a while, when she saw evidence of larger forces at work and their resultant sensible patterns, she felt a stirring connection. What was it, exactly? She decided Elaine Penwardin had expressed it better than she ever would:

> While pursuing the humblest occupations—such as planting or cutting flowers, I had perceived, as a chink of light through a door opened quickly, a greater plan of things than our programme for the year, a larger world than that surrounding us, and one universal pattern of things, in which all existence has its place. . . . I have felt peace descend on me while I have handled plants, so that a rhythm and harmony of being has been brought about. That harmony is the beginning of health. . . . There is a universal pattern, a pattern that flows like a stream, like the moving pattern of a dance. It is possible even through such contact with the earth as I have had, to be drawn into that pattern and move with it.[29]

29. Quoted in Lewis 1996, iii.

Joseph Campbell once commented on the difference between living as if we were in the center of a wheel or on its spoke: When we are in the center, life revolves, and we move in a smooth, steady progression. When we operate on the spoke, much more effort must be exerted to withstand the constant rising and falling.[30] Ann suspected that designing with these patterns could flow as easily as Penwardin's stream or dance or Campbell's center of the wheel. She looked forward to finding out.

30. Campbell 1988.

Small residential pond captures roof runoff and sump pump water.

chapter six
the stumbling-forward ache

DESIGN TIME Ann's love for the house was cinched by a note on the appraiser's form commenting, "Lack of lawn devalues the property"—just her kind of place. Ann and her husband were helpless against the pull of purchasing the tiny property adjacent to the South Boulder open space (figure 6.1). Her attachment to this place had consistently grown as she learned about processes and how to recognize their manifestation in patterns. She could see many of them from the kitchen window, feel the wind against the house in winter, see deer masticating neighbors' roses but leaving her devalued grasses alone. Yet she also felt the pull of her own processes: the need for production, protection, and pleasure. She needed a garden. She successfully avoided the cafeteria of brilliant annuals at various home improvement centers, realizing they were a temporary plant fix and she had greater needs than that. She knew she would change this property in some way to reflect their immediate need for privacy and shelter from snow and wind. She wanted her garden to be more edible for them than

6.1
South Boulder neighborhood and the open-space edge (aerial view).

for the deer. She also had to have soil under her fingers and an outlet for the gardening urge. She had Steinbeck's "stumbling-forward ache," the universal human need to improve one's surroundings according to his or her needs.

Her neighbors invited her to see their yards and subtly suggested she improve the weedy look of her property. Their houses had been built almost two decades ago, and many still sported the encircling junipers, as well as lawns with token trees in the front. The next-door neighbor had hired a landscape architect to implement a Xeriscape design. Colorful flowers dotted the silvery perennial border, set off by a small patch of green grass in back. The forms were sweeping and curved and responded to the property boundaries and structures. To copy either of these models would have been simple, but Ann was motivated by a desire to create landscape connections, to find good work and joy, not by the need to keep up with the Joneses. Her studies of the region prodded her to create a different approach.

SETTING GOALS AND OBJECTIVES   What did she want most from this place? Ann looked at her neighborhood's splashy summer colors, the English countryside borders, the turf and trees as foreground to the looming mountains and their savanna skirts. She did not want to erase legibility as she imposed her own needs. She wanted to set the stage for the interaction of formative processes, her own included. She wanted the landscape to continue to function well—to acknowledge and accommodate flows of wind, water, nutrients, energy, people, and other species—so that she was not fighting fundamental forces such as gravity or the need for other species to survive. She wanted to work with these processes she struggled to understand.

Ann also wanted to design for what she had come to think of as positive human response. She wanted to be comfortable in her garden, sheltered and shielded from the climate's extremes as well as from a sense of being overly exposed to neighbors or potential criminals. She delighted in sensual stimuli and knew her garden could provide scents, tastes, textures, and sounds. She wanted change to be a built-in component, allowing her critical eye to learn lessons from everyday changes and her understanding of patterns to grow as she watched them unfold before her. She also wanted a place in which to reflect upon her own unfolding changes. Gardens she admired in magazines included pieces of people's lives featured in them—mirrors, plates, photos, memorable relics from travels. She liked the balance between these personal pieces and the sense of larger responsibility that design for positive function provides.

Another bridge between positive function and positive human response, which she shared with all her neighbors, was the desire for gardens to be affordable over time. Her neighbor's juniper belt garden was inexpensive to install: sod, three trees, fifteen junipers. But, as the design aged, the lawn still needed water, mowing, weeding. The junipers had to be beaten back from the windows at regular intervals. Maintenance was becoming more expensive because of the rise in water and energy prices since the garden had been installed. Similarly, the neighboring Xeriscape garden featured many colorful plants, but they had short life spans and required frequent replacement. Trimming was required to keep the distinction between perennial border and lawn intact. The Xeriscape garden conserved water and supported a diversity of species, but it did not present the strong sense of region that she desired. Ann sought to build an affordable garden that would change and grow and maintain its acceptability to her. This would require designing with as little intervention in the formative processes as possible.

Her thoughts invariably sorted themselves into phraseology familiar from her training. She realized she had just set the goals for her design work: to create both positive site function and positive human response. She then tested her goals. Perhaps the goal of positive site function was too narrowly defined? Recently, planting designers have begun to describe their work in terms of meeting functional, ecological, and aesthetic purposes.[1] Functional goals are met when the site meets human needs, such as the need for movement, for safety, for climatic protection. Ecological purposes are met when important plant communities are maintained and habitat is provided for other species. Aesthetic purposes are met if a sense of beauty accompanies the design. Ann felt all three purposes could be wrapped into the dual goals of positive site function and human response. When site functions, or flows, are deliberately attended to, designers account for energy flow, nutrient cycling, plant and wildlife habitat needs, water flow, people's access requirements, and so on. Positive site function folds together the first two purposes other designers describe. Ann was satisfied by this because she saw no line between ecological and other types of design, a hotly debated subject within her profession. A place that functions well meets the basic physical needs of humans and other species. Period. She felt designers should aim for no less.

The test continued: If her goal was positive human response, did that mean artistic expression that deliberately provokes fear or disgust is bad design? She considered this, thinking of a design competition that entailed designing a warning system to ward off future generations from trespassing onto nuclear waste sites.[2] What universal symbols could be created to communicate the message, "Keep Out"? The winning entry surrounded the nuclear waste site with towering black metal thorns. Her immediate reaction to the photographs was to catch her breath—the designer indeed had captured a universal repellent, drawn from both the botanical world and the fanged animal world. Yes, the

1. Robinson 1992, 3-8.
2. *Los Angeles Times* 1992, B6.

design was ugly and evoked negative responses—but with an eye to the positive aim of protecting the safety of future inhabitants.

She contrasted this intentionally bleak design with a plaza she had once visited near the Denver Tech Center after reading its numerous kudos.[3] This corporate plaza was located between two buildings encased in reflective glass and provided workers with needed outdoor space for relaxing, lunching, and now, smoking. The site, with stunning views of the Front Range, invited lingering and the clearing of one's head of workday details and concerns. Ann had needed such relief after driving along her transect across the region, and she stopped around lunchtime in mid-July to eat a sandwich. One lone smoker huddled against a wall; otherwise, the plaza was deserted. Few plants tarnished this slick statement. Metallic statues representing fantasy figures, mirror-glass-enclosed chillers, and vents from the underground parking lot cast the few shadows present. Because none of the surrounding walls was appropriately sized for seating, she stood and unwrapped her sandwich. Hot afternoon winds dried the bread. Her eyes squinted from the glaring sun reflecting off the white squares and mirrors; her feet were heated by the absorbent black squares. Ann struggled to find the praise-givers' voices, but she was too hot and uncomfortable to appreciate the boldness and innovation. In this case, she felt that the design should have gone further to mitigate the unnecessary negative response she experienced. Providing shaded places to sit would have been a good start. Others agreed, apparently, and during her last visit, she was amazed to find the plaza under significant reconstruction. Aspen trees were being planted in the numerous planters to provide needed shade. Looking to the reflective glass and sunny exposure, she hoped they would not one day be known as sacrificial aspen trees.

Once her design goals of achieving positive site function and human response had been set, more specific objectives flowed from them. Such objectives are the conscience of any design project, whether a Xeriscape or a traditional planting design, and are usually developed with widespread participation by people involved in the design. For their homeplace design project, her husband and son had designated her as their proxy. She held up to the scrutiny of

3. Goldstein 1983; Johnson 1983; Brown 1991; Olin 1995.

imagined critics her list of objectives that anyone designing within this and other regions could use.

Create positive function by acknowledging and designing for flows:
— decrease off-site water importation and flow
— decrease cooling and heating requirements
— minimize use of direct and indirect energy
— retain on-site nutrients as much as possible
— provide for species' habitat and movement needs

Create positive human response by respecting psychological, cultural, physical, social, and economic needs:
— allow for individual site interpretation and meaning
— acknowledge historical and cultural affiliations
— provide comfort, visual and sensual pleasure, and safety
— create places for privacy and social interaction
— create designs that are affordable over time

Ann's marching orders were developing, and she knew these objectives would be refined with each project she undertook. She felt that by following these objectives, she and others who might use this approach in the future would be closer to creating appropriate design responses for the region. The objectives were intended to acknowledge, consider, and "do the right thing" with the elements that make a region unique: its water, soil, climate, species, history, culture, money, people.

Goals and objectives, as snapshots of current values, tend to change depending on the needs of society and the designer, as she had learned earlier by tracing the landscape fate of particular Denver region landscapes. Ann's three decades of environmental and cultural awareness had infiltrated her humble planting design project for her own garden. She realized that these objectives, too, would develop further and change over the course of her lifetime. In fact, it was daunting to consider that society's future values might render these conscientiously crafted goals and objectives dated or passé. As the urban planner

Jane Jacobs has recently said, "You can be sure of one thing: The architecture and site planning that is being created now will be despised at some point. In fact the process may have already begun. . . . [People] should not put so much faith in the belief that the tastes of this particular decade are the right ones."[4]

Yet Ann felt her objectives were sufficiently general, appropriate, and flexible. The objectives pointed toward survival and enjoyment of both present and future generations. Incorporating these design goals and objectives into people's inherent drive to change their surroundings certainly would create more durable, responsible, beloved places than much of what she saw proliferating in Denver's current boom economy. Her imagined critics poked and prodded, raised one eyebrow, then the other, and sniffed at the list. Finally, they promised they would be back to add and subtract at the first whiff of values changes.

She pushed her luck by looking through the many patterns she had drawn and described throughout her search. Are all patterns created equal? Are all available for use in design as long as they are locally derived? Then she scanned her objectives list. Some of the patterns repeated throughout the region did not meet these objectives. Juniper belts around houses are not affordable over time, do not provide safety as the plants grow above window ledges, do not provide diversity for species habitat. Bluegrass expanses are terribly common but require imported water, fossil fuel, and labor to maintain them. Air quality is reduced by the blowing and mowing required by these expanses. Herbicides, pesticides, and mowing pretty well scare off any beasts from making bluegrass their home, so diversity of both plants and animals suffers. Out, out, out. Her goals were in business already.

LEARNING ABOUT THE SITE   Ann continued assembling her thoughts in terms of design process. So far, she had derived a "feel" for the region by looking and reading at a variety of scales. Repeated phenomena or patterns registered in her gray matter. As she systematically studied formative processes of this region, her collection of regional plant patterns enlarged and jelled. Spring fever and her recent purchase of a new house fomented her urge to merge hands and soil and roots. She must have a garden. She developed her conscience and aims through goals and objectives. Now she needed to know her property bet-

4. Proffitt 1997, M3.

facing page
6.2
A step-by-step approach to determining shadow lengths.

ter to conduct what sounded so clinical: site inventory and analysis. Where's my white lab coat?, she thought, slamming the door on her way out to her garden-to-be.

She took her appraiser's map with her, acquired at the closing. Had it been misplaced, she knew a plot plan could be acquired through various means, either from the original developer or architect or through the county or city. In the worst-case scenario, if no plot plan existed, she could make one. A site survey plotted the location of house foundations, trees, walks and drives, and elevations and contours. In Ann's case, the previous owner had passed along the developer's original drawings. The backyard landscape on the plan, almost two decades old, was labeled to be seeded with a foothills tall-grass mix, including many nonnative grasses. Adjacent open-space lands were also seeded with this mix, accounting for her property's high degree of plant and visual continuity, barely interrupted by the split-rail fence. In the tiny front yard contractors had piled rocks excavated from the foundation. Ann pictured herself in a chain gang, atoning for some forgotten crime, removing those rocks to rediscover soil. Previous owners had clearly not been interested in gardens, except for literal rock gardens.

By talking with rangers and planners at local city offices, drawing from her earlier reading about landscape processes, and observing, Ann learned much about critical factors determining plant success: soil (and, in her case, rocks), water availability, sun exposure, existing on-site and nearby plants and seed sources, and local disturbance factors such as deer, insects, and other marauders such as kids' feet and dogs' and cats' digging paws. The order of investigating these factors roughly paralleled the order of her previous look at regional processes and patterns.

The soil on the Crane's property was derived from the eroding mountains that eventually tumbled down to this mesa, where plenty of reminders of origins remained. Her shovel penetrated about six inches of grass root–bound, deep-brown soil before bouncing off a rock. An old saying came back to her: You don't dig the soil here, you pry it. At the low point in her backyard, however, the shovel struck pay dirt: saturated deep black soils, perhaps Valmont clay loam present in adjacent open-space wetlands. It was a waterstain indicated by

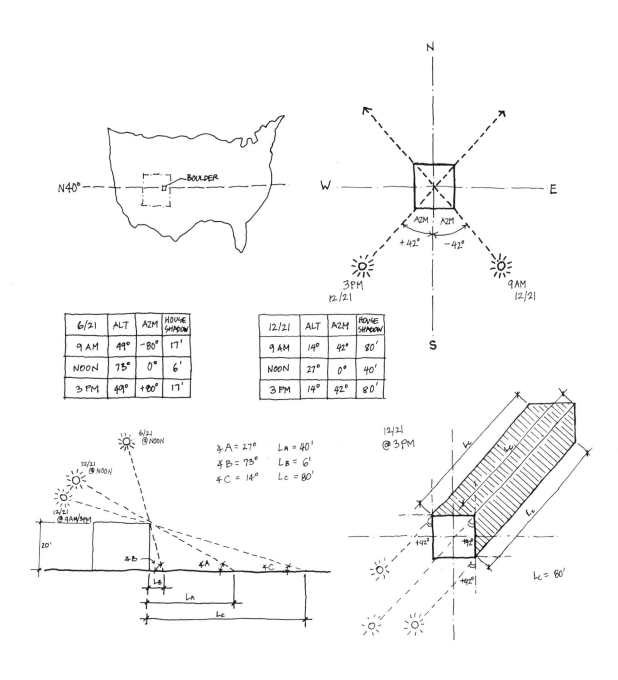

THE STUMBLING-FORWARD ACHE 149

greener grasses, mostly invading Kentucky bluegrass but also some Canada bluegrass, Junegrass, and a big dose of Canada thistle. Water availability was high here where drainage collected. Water availability was lowest next to her house on the south-facing side. Roof runoff was announced by greener plants at the pan drainage point.

Solar radiation was intense in this region, as she had learned earlier. She needed to know exactly where and when sun and shade would affect her site, because plants have adapted specific solar tolerances. She drew shadow diagrams to show the angle and length of shadow during key times: summer and winter solstice and at the typical garden-use times of 9:00 A.M., noon, and 3:00 P.M. These were deceptively simple to draw; yet she knew from her experience as a student that precise shadow diagrams were a valuable design tool. Several ingredients were needed for this solar diagram recipe: location and height of nearby vertical structures measurable on site, key times of day and year, latitude of the site as found on a globe or in an atlas, and altitude and azimuth angles, which could be found in a typical graphic standards book available at any library's reference desk. Using the process she had sketched out, Ann could derive sun and shadow patterns on her site for any time of year (figure 6.2).

Identifying plants on-site was pretty easy, once she discovered that tall foothills seed mix had been used. She went to a local seed store and asked what the typical ingredients of such a mix were, and sure enough, these were all present. Some, like annual ryegrass in the wetter site locations and crested wheatgrass in the drier locations, dominated others. The rock pile sported a native leadplant and milkweed, among other plants. Ann examined the base of the fence posts with great anticipation. Sure enough, a skunkbrush shrub guarded one and a Boulder raspberry another. Bird droppings graced the top of the post as well, making her feel a bit cocky in her predictive abilities. She confirmed the plants' identities by taking samples to a particularly helpful and knowledgeable ranger at the City of Boulder Mountain Parks station in Chatauqua Park, who readily identified them for her without making her feel like a dolt. As Ann surveyed her yard's grasses and rocks, she knew from observing surrounding disturbed areas that if she jostled the soils she would open the site up to local invaders such as thistle, burdock, and perhaps spotted knapweed from adjacent

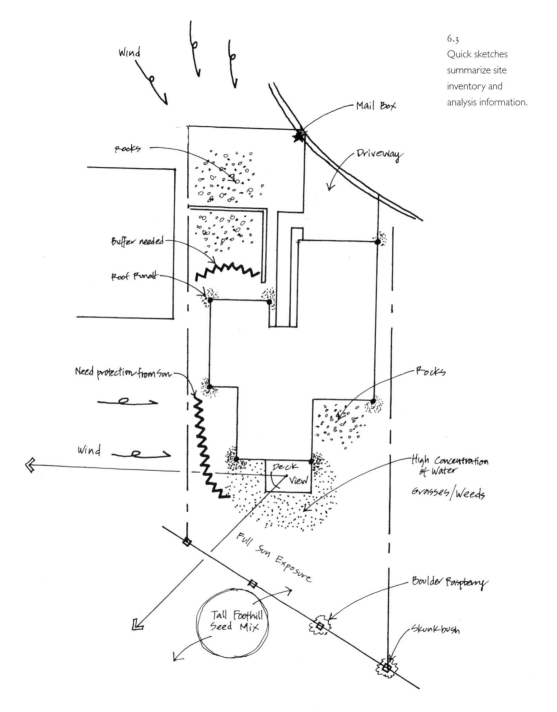

6.3 Quick sketches summarize site inventory and analysis information.

trails. No false promises for a maintenance-free garden called to her like the Lorelei. She knew she was in for some vigilant work. She recorded her findings in a plan view diagram of their property (figure 6.3).

The processes shaping Ann's site were becoming clear to her: geomorphic processes had shaped the landforms, leaving a rock mulch that deterred her shovel's progress. An impermeable soil lens underlaid the low point, supporting her very own waterstain. Climatic processes created the semiaridity, the hot exposures, the buffeted northwestern exposures. Biotic and climatic processes brought thistles to newly disturbed areas. Birds were agents of the fruit-bearing shrubs' relocation. Cultural processes of production, protection, and pleasure were largely absent in the plants themselves—thus the hard sell from her new neighbors to tidy up the place a bit, maybe plant something by that mailbox. Her discussions with planners at City Hall further informed her about the human need for order in the guise of relevant ordinances and codes she must obey, such as not allowing runoff to trespass onto her neighbor's property and maintaining certain setbacks.

Had she not already examined the area for dominant processes and repeated plant patterns, she would have done so now. With any luck, she thought, there may someday be a guidebook that allows others to conduct an investigation of processes and patterns, too.

Finally, Ann focused on other challengers to her garden's success. Digging up and importing soil would attract cats. Creating a bird habitat garden would as well. Dogs were kept at bay by the fence. Deer—well, her approach was to plant one plant for her and one for the deer. But she did pore over the city's list of plants that are unpalatable to deer and found her variety was still satisfyingly wide.

CHOOSING THE SITE'S PROGRAM Ann now had a site inventory drawing, complete with comments regarding her garden's pros and cons. She knew what she wanted to accomplish. Now she needed to determine her desired program: the nouns of her site. She rubbed her hands together like Simon LeGree. She wanted great mountain views and comfortable, protected seating—prospect and refuge. These are classic human needs, according to Jay

Appleton's theory of human survival needs. She wanted a waterstained area for bird habitat, a perennial garden, protection from winter winds and summer's scalding sun, private areas, and a place to honor the importance of mail. She also wanted her painstakingly collected rocks, china sherds, and durable mementos placed throughout the garden to tell her family's history. Her husband wanted a place for an inverted V ham radio antenna and softening of the harsh reflective driveway where he would work on cars. What a guy program, she thought. Their children—a second was on the way— could use the garden to develop fine motor skills and inquisitive minds. Large motor skills could be exercised on nearby hiking trails and playgrounds. Their tiny plot did not have to provide all things for everyone at all times. Her neighbors needed to be included in programming as well, they reminded her. The design could not block their views or result in water flowing onto their property.

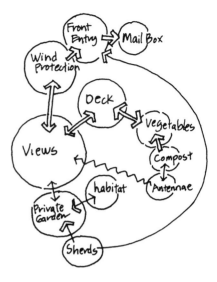

6.4
Program relationships are shown through "bubble diagrams."

She considered relationships between these program elements by drawing circles of different sizes, to represent the relative importance of each one, and arrows of different sizes between the circles, to indicate the strength of relationships and proximity (figure 6.4). "Mountain views" had the largest circle and were closely tied to "deck," "compost pile" was related to "vegetables," and so on. Ann remembered that she had often skipped this step as a student designer; but over time she found that the diagrams reminded her of her relative priorities and where program elements would best be located in relation to each other.

DEVELOPING PATTERN-BASED GUIDELINES Before applying the program to her site, Ann developed guidelines from her goals, objectives, patterns, and processes. One of her favorite design authors, Clare Cooper Marcus, had written an intriguing pamphlet in 1985 entitled *Design Guidelines: A Bridge between Research and Decision Making*. Marcus notes that designers working in highly productive and high-pressure design offices often require specialized information about settings or users, but time is rarely available for in-depth investigation. Design researchers can assist by translating research into a useful form, such as design guidelines. Marcus describes three types of guidelines: behavioral guidelines, in which a statement of research observations is made without instructing the designer as to what the design response should be; performance standards, in which suggestions are made to open up design possibilities; and prescriptive guidelines, in which design actions are detailed, with few variations left open to the designer. Ann wondered which type of guidelines would be most useful in communicating her pattern-based design method. The patterns she had described could be classified as behavioral guidelines: for example, plants tend to grow at greater sizes and densities where there is more water. Prescriptive guidelines would tell designers the precise spacing and species necessary for achieving this pattern. She opted for the middle approach, creating performance standards, to suggest how to place plants in accordance with larger geomorphic, climatic, biotic, and cultural processes as expressed through the Denver region's plant patterns. Ann organized these guidelines, applicable at a variety of scales, and arranged them in roughly the same order as her patterns. Although, admittedly, guidelines run the risk of oversimplifying complex relationships, she would use them as suggestions when designing her garden.

Aspect. Celebrate differences in moisture availability between northern and southern exposures at similar elevations by placing larger plants, planting at greater densities, or selecting more mesic species for northern exposures. This can happen where grade changes are notable, such as along the sides of large rocks, houses, and walls and on foothills slopes.

Water concentration. Announce water concentration at slope breaks or concavities by using larger plants here than on the slopes. When unirrigated slopes of similar soil composition and texture are uniformly terraced, upper and lower slopes typically provide greater moisture availability. Upper slopes capture more frequent rainfalls that are not intense enough to cause flows and soil erosion to lower terraces. The top terraces capture water from a larger watershed, slow water's erosive force, and allow water to infiltrate. The lower terraces sustain more moisture-loving plants, as all unabsorbed water and soil from larger storms concentrates here.

Create "shrub skirts" around the base of trees, using drought-tolerant shrubs, to increase plant and wildlife diversity and allow shrubs to take advantage of the cooler microclimate.

Plan for and incorporate plants that respond to breaks in impermeable surfaces. Find acceptable early successional species that can outcompete the "weeds." Many showy species, such as several aster species and penstemons, compete well with roadside weeds. From an aesthetic standpoint, some weedy species, such as crane's bill and daisy fleabane, may be more acceptable than others. Species that spread into wetlands or other critical habitat, such as purple loosestrife, must be avoided.

Waterstains where snow concentrates, saturating soils for long periods, can be reinforced with larger plants or denser plantings than those in the surrounding matrix. This helps reinforce the snow-blocking abilities of snow fences and links plants to water availability.

Soil. Reflect soil shifts from fine- to coarse-grained materials with plants of graduating sizes. Associate shrubs and trees with rock outcrops in fine-grained plains soils.

Where fine-grained soils coincide with a water source, creating an impermeable layer, allow plants to reflect variable water levels, with submerged aquatics at deepest locations. Expect seasonal changes in species distribution as the wetland dries and fills with sediments. Good sources for wetland species are now becoming commercially available within the region.

Plan for and incorporate wildlife-dispersed plants at edges of fence posts, telephone poles, and other vertical surfaces where nutrient-rich and seed-bearing soils accumulate. Fruit-bearing shrubs such as skunkbrush, Boulder raspberry, snowberry, Oregon grape, and currants are frequently seeded candidates for this strategic location.

Protection. Utilize homestead trees on southwest corners of buildings to recall earlier planting patterns and provide microclimate comfort for the building interiors. Cottonwood is the historical species, but it has invasive roots and weak branches. Western hackberry, green ash, Kentucky coffee tree, and bur oak are drought-tolerant alternatives.

Associate spiny barrier plants under windows vulnerable to break-ins. Prickly pear, yucca, and barberry are good candidates for providing vegetation barriers.

Pleasure. Utilize notable plants in key locations to provide "polite introductions" or "beauty spots." This trend of announcing entries, intersections, and key locations has permeated every design era in the Denver area and may be a universal ordering signal.

Combinations. Create microclimate oases where people or other species require respite from harsh climatic conditions and where water concentrates with a minimum of importation. Where trees are needed for shade on southern exposures, create indentations in flat grades to collect and hold water to provide supplemental moisture availability. Utilize swales and terraces to allow percolation of summer storm water and irrigation for needed shade trees. Shade from trees also reduces evaporation from swales.

Create beauty spots where there is human need for order as well as a water concentration. Where entries are marked by notable plants, reinforce their presence by shaping landforms to collect additional water to support plants with higher water needs. For example, use roof runoff to water an entry sign planting. The water can freeze and thaw in winter as well as provide additional summer water for plants if the erosive force is reduced. Allées of trees should be reinforced by swales to provide water infiltration.

Allow historical plantings that do not respond to geomorphic, climatic, or biotic processes to shine as green gems in the semiarid west. Selected historical properties designed when water limitations were unacknowledged are worthy of preservation and of the extra water needed to support them. Newly designed areas must reflect current awareness of water conservation, however, and wean themselves from the matrix pattern of the green oasis.

Combine productive patterns, many of which have been developed for irrigation effectiveness, with water concentration patterns. Plant more mesic productive species at bases of slopes and along irrigation canals. Use more mesic productive species within pivot-irrigated circles, and cultivate remaining wedges with productive nonirrigated plants, such as sunflowers.

CREATING BENEFICIAL CHANGE THROUGH DESIGN
Ann imagined herself under a deadline and prepared to draw up a plan for her residential garden. Guidelines gave her a variety of design inspirations and shortened her research time. Now she turned her attention to design (figures 6.5 and 6.6). She allowed the numerous facts and suggestions to sift together; she doodled, pulling ideas from personal preferences, memories, and relative forces on the property to create the overall frame of forms. For example, the house was rectangular and the corners, walls, and its entrances had certain lines of force, often called force lines, that extended beyond the

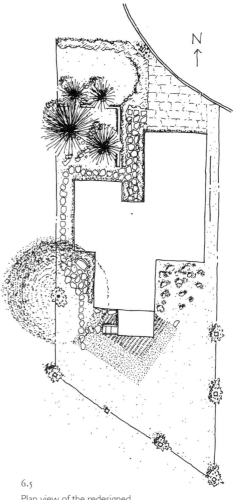

6.5
Plan view of the redesigned garden reflects use of the region's waterstain patterns.

6.6
Sketch of redesigned garden shows wetland ring, homestead tree, bird-perch shrubs, and other water concentration patterns.

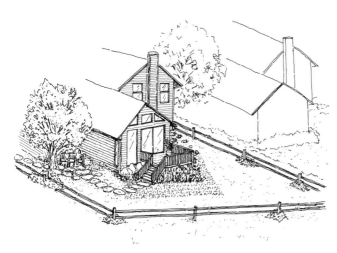

house itself. Ann projected them further, into the garden. They clashed with both the directions her eyes move, toward the mountains and toward the fence line. She liked the regularity of the rectangular forms of the house but felt a strong pull to the mountain view. By shifting the forms toward the mountains, Ann was able to bring the view, the fence line, and the house forms into alignment. The front and side yards were very small and dominated by the streets and property boundaries. She honored these boundaries and maintained their ordered forms.

After refining the framework, she considered dominant processes. Closest to the back deck was the most waterstained portion of the lot. She used wetland ring patterns here to announce this location, seeking local wetland plants that tolerated inundation and some drought. One was a species of rush, another was sun sedge. She expanded from this waterstained core with increasingly drought-tolerant grasslike plants to blend grasses into the existing matrix. She acknowledged biotic processes by adding a few more fruiting shrubs to the fence posts, leaving one unplanted. A homestead tree would grace the southwest corner. She opted for the historical cottonwood as it was so symbolic of her own aging progress: first a coarse-leaved gawky youth shooting up in all directions, then a svelte young adult with lithe limbs, later a broad-beamed adult with arms reaching out to protect and shelter, and finally a dome-headed matriarch, riddled and pocked with woodpecker holes, deeply furrowed and a bit brittle as her balance shifted from nurturing others to requiring more and more care to stay healthy. Yep, cottonwood it would be for that southwest corner, with a shrub skirt of skunkbrush beneath it. They would normally have a similar life span, she and the tree, but because she was planting this garden while in her late thirties, she selected a fairly large tree. For shade, she told her husband, keeping the analogy to herself.

Under the cottonwood's canopy she located a small private garden featuring a garden seat, broken concrete pavers with chamomile planted in the cracks, and a backdrop of lamb's ears, creeping grape holly, and coral bells near the house wall, supplementally watered by roof runoff. She added her son's favorite collected rocks at key locations through this garden and the side yards, along with pieces of mirror and pottery, mementos in an expandable life collection.

Grasses extended along the sunny side yards, underneath her husband's radio antenna, interplanted with bright perennials such as asters and penstemons. The southeast side of her house would be graced by aromatic, drought-tolerant shrubs—silver sage and skunkbrush—like those seen in the open space. Rocks piled here would serve as catchment areas for shrub roots; where the rocks emerged from the grass sod, shrubs would be planted.

The north side of the house was acknowledged with two ponderosa pines taking advantage of the cooler microclimate and providing a wind buffer. Because soils in this region are not expansive clays, Ann could plant trees closer to the house than would be prudent in many other Denver area yards. She removed the asphalt driveway and walkway and replaced both with recycled broken concrete pavers. She would sweep early successional plant seeds into the cracks, hoping for asters, daisy fleabanes, and crane's bill to drive out undesired weed species and soften the hard work and walk surfaces. In acknowledgment of the neighborhood full of dogs, she concentrated pineapple weed along the street edge. She also transplanted one weedy compass plant on the north side of the mailbox as a joke, though the subtlety was mostly for her own enjoyment. Colorful, durable perennials joined the compass plant at the mailbox post, and she created a low spot here and along the path edges for these taller plants. Her neighbor's malfunctioning irrigation system provided plenty of summer water to keep these pleasurably healthy. Her productive plant needs were met by tubs of heritage plants placed in a neat grid pattern on her south-facing deck. Roof runoff was collected in a temporary holding tank to water the tubs, and her sump pump water was funneled to the wetland ring.

EVALUATING THE DESIGN Ann's neighbors had never seen a design quite like this, but they found it appealing, and it met their needs for basic orderliness and the protection of views and property values. The deer recognized the lack of junk food plants and passed the place by as if it were in its previous state. She indulged in her vegetable gardening urge, providing herself with prospect and refuge, production and protection, process and pattern. She felt a symbolic link to the plants growing where her husband worked on cars, to the cottonwood, to her garden travelogue. In about six months, she would save some money by cut-

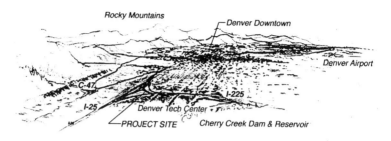

6.7
Location of Interstates 25 and 225 interchange.

6.8
View of existing embankments.

ting off the irrigation, after her plants became established. The garden could grow and change without her begrudgingly maintaining it, although she felt a commitment to look after the cottonwood limbs. She anticipated the bird-planted shrub at the fence post, and perhaps late successional species like ponderosa pine, would colonize the rock piles and upper wetland rings, if fire did not clear the seedlings out.

The place was an ecosystem, linked to its setting by thousands of strands—a system of the *oikos*, the home.

BRANCHING OUT After working at a residential scale, Ann grew increasingly interested in trying out pattern-based methods in other settings. A friend caught the fever from her and joined her. They experimented with the pattern-based design method at a tempting site, the Interstate 25 and Interstate 225 interchange in southeast Denver (figure 6.7).

Sprinkler arcs again swished and rotated over the south-facing turf slopes at midday as Ann and her friend Kiku sped by the interchange near the Denver Tech Center. The steepest slopes along the underpasses were graced by pon-

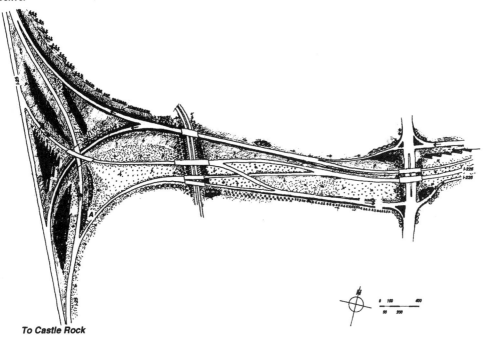

6.9
Plan view of redesigned interchange shows water-stain patterns.

derosa pine and juniper. Recently, crews had given up on mowing the cattails at the toes of the steep embankment slopes. Otherwise, the intersection reflected the neat patterns of mowers and spray heads and might as easily have been located in Tulsa, New York, or Los Angeles (figure 6.8). This highly visible, nondescript site was one of her friend's pet peeves. Because the I-225 corridor was mentioned in the Denver Regional Council of Governments' *2015: Interim Regional Transportation Plan* as a candidate for a rapid transit corridor, Ann felt that the intersection would one day be redesigned.[5] What would a pattern-based approach look like on this site? They returned to the studio in Ann's home, rolled up their sleeves, and began chiseling away at the challenging site design.

Ann and Kiku first set down their objectives for the intersection design: to provide erosion control, acknowledge water concentrations, and enhance the driver's experience and safety. The site was complex and analysis a bit tedious: slope maps of the interchange resembled a *Gray's Anatomy* drawing of arm muscles, with many slope areas steeper than 20 percent. Aspect maps with north, northeast, east, southeast, south, southwest, west, and northwest slopes shaded

5. Denver Regional Council of Governments 1995.

THE STUMBLING-FORWARD ACHE 161

in various colors looked like a fractured stained-glass window. Tracing the intersection's open views with dashes and enclosed views with dots created an intriguing visual Morse code. Only the map showing existing vegetation was simple: a few circles for the trees and shrubs floating in a green turf. Over the next few weeks, Kiku reread seminal books regarding driver experience and road design and dug into various highway and bioengineering reports.[6] From her analysis and references, they created a system of alternatives emphasizing highway safety, driver experience, and natural processes. These were then combined into one design, which drew from the region's dominant plant patterns (figure 6.9).

For reasons of safety, all intersections and on-ramps were kept open for clear traffic views and safety in merging. Snow fencing was used to block drifting snow from merging lanes. The driver's experience was thus enhanced without detracting from safety and smooth highway flows. This was accomplished by acknowledging transitions, such as the approach of a major overpass where views of the mountains and surrounding city are captivating. Anticipation of the views was built by reinforcing approaches with rows of trees, the strongest vertical elements in the plan. These were kept far enough from the roadway to avoid icing problems. Kiku used the same technique to reinforce upcoming street overpasses as well. Important nodes, where traffic exiting from the formal Denver Tech Center and the adjacent commercial developments entered the community, were marked with detailed human-scale plants to link the interchange with its local context and to tie it into an "urban reprieve" pattern.

On a gradient from wet to dry, they placed the deepest waterstains at toes of slopes with tall grasses and perennials. Wetland plants grew there at present, but primarily because of runoff from irrigation systems. Irrigation was intended only to establish plants and would be eliminated following establishment. North-facing slopes supported midgrass prairie, with the tallest grasses again appearing at the toes of slopes. Shrub stripes traced the snow fencing alignment, taking advantage of stored moisture (figure 6.10). Swales at low points at the base of slopes held water to support the deciduous trees in the overpass and community transition areas. Road runoff was also directed toward these plants. Ponderosa pines were planted among boulders at the low point of a slope, uti-

6. See Appleyard, Lynch, and Myer 1964; Lynch 1960.

lizing a "rocky reservoir" pattern. Shrubs were planted under the pines to take advantage of the trees' microclimate. The driest slopes supported short-grass prairie species, such as blue grama, buffalo grass, and needle-and-thread grass, which might grow more luxuriously along the impermeable edges of roads. These slopes were dotted with a scattered pattern of yuccas at the slope edges and opuntia mixed in with the grasses to give the dotted-swiss pattern prevalent on south-facing mesa slopes nearby. The nearly vertical underpass slopes were now lined with concrete; plants seen as weeds were invading the cracks. These would be replaced with a deliberate concrete pattern reinforced by more desirable "crack" plants, such as asters and fleabane (figure 6.11). Why not? It would happen anyway, whether they designed for it or not. Plants selected were native and adapted nonnative species that could tolerate the various water conditions, excluding those, like Russian olives, that were invaders.

6.10
Use of snow fences, runoff water, and toe of slope patterns.

6.11
South-facing slope, rocky reservoir, crack plants, beauty spot, runoff, and toe of slope patterns.

The key to the success of projects like this is the care exhibited toward soil preparation during construction and maintenance following construction. Adequate topsoil must be preserved and replaced, and if soils are mechanically compacted a wide variety of plants will not survive. Weed control is always a serious concern during the period of plant establishment, and the waterstained areas are likely to require more weeding than the drier areas. Maintenance is critical until plants are established. This fact needs to be more widely accepted, Ann grumbled. She had been told of another recent large-scale highway job for which much money had been spent on the design but decisions made in the field during construction usually favored the ease of the contractor rather than the success of seeds and seedlings. Many inspired and well-intended design ideas failed as a result.

Kiku helpfully passed along to Ann the layers of interim drawings necessary to create this plan. The stack of forty-five thin tracing sheets was an inch thick. This was a complex site, one that could be designed to inform visitors and residents about the forces and considerations at play in this active region. As a result of this redesign, maintenance dollars could be slashed, water usage minimized, and the region's character maximized as the plants changed and grew in a self-maintaining manner.

PROGRESS REPORT Ann reread an early draft of her progress report to the foundation that had funded part of her study. She had written the grant proposal long ago, requesting funds to develop a method of planting design that captured a region's unique character. To win the grant, she had to specify her method; in effect, she had had to do the study before she could request funds to do the study. She must have bluffed convincingly, because the funds did come her way. In retrospect, she saw that only recently had her Polaroid photo developed fully; now she could write the report more accurately.

In her report, Ann advised those interested in using this planting design approach in other regions to start at the regional scale. Examine the formative processes. Look for their evidence in repeated plant arrangements. Understand that these patterns are responses to formative processes, not clip art to be inserted by computer operators into designs (she made a mental note to go back and tone down her rhetoric). Develop design goals along the lines of creating beneficial site function and human response. Tailor more specific objectives from this broad umbrella, drawing on widespread practices of user participation.

At the site scale, refine objectives further. Use site, behavioral, and program analysis tools to understand the site context and desires for the design. Pay close attention to the formative processes in place on and near the site. Develop design concepts and alternatives in as many modes as possible—plan, section, elevation, perspective, 3-D computer models, clay, mashed potatoes, if necessary—using every ounce of creativity that can be mustered. Utilize applicable guidelines in applying patterns to the site's new or existing processes. First select plant criteria, and then select plants. Mix and stir, taste and correct seasoning.

Ann sighed and looked out the window, her computer screen trance broken. She did not mean to sound flippant; the foundation reviewers must know by her previous reports that she had trouble keeping food analogies out of her writing. The design process did require mixing and stirring; it was not a linear trajectory. It required much tasting and correcting to evaluate whether resulting plant locations were appropriate. But listing steps did not target what she liked best about the method: she liked that it awakened her to see her surroundings with a type of clarity she had not experienced in any of her other homes; she liked that the method acknowledges the "inherentisms" of people and place, without reinforcing the supposed dialectic between designing for humans or nature; she liked that the patterns are like prairie grasses: you see them above ground, but most of the plant—its roots—is underground; when you see a pattern you are mostly seeing formative processes. She liked the fact that she could use the patterns and guidelines as inspiration, not as dictation. And she liked the honesty she saw in the resultant designs. "A tree is there" not only "because someone cared enough to water it," as the saying about Denver proclaimed, but because someone cared enough to put it in the waterstain, where it had a better chance of surviving on its own. The "least effort principle" again. Making smart and lazy decisions, not dumb, hardworking ones.

Ann felt her ache to change a place, to rearrange the furniture so that it was more comfortable and fit better, was beginning to be assuaged by these design experiments. Watching the plants in her garden take root and leaf out after their first long winter provided a sense that she could settle down and yet move at the same time, albeit vicariously, through her changing, growing garden. Steinbeck describes the "aching to create beyond the single need," and Ann knew she would begin to ply her pattern-based trade whenever a design opportunity arose.[7] She also knew she would be drawn to view other projects in the region built with similar goals and objectives, to see that the design approach did not address just her single, personal need. Then, perhaps, she would be able to finish this report.

7. Steinbeck 1939, 164.

Walkway at Jefferson County Government Center.
Photo by Civitas, Inc.

chapter seven
planting evidence

DESIGNS UNDER WAY "I don't get it," said the bearded man, looking out the shuttle window, to his travel companion. "Why are these silver whirligigs attached to the tunnel?" "They're for, you know, aesthetics." "Oh. I thought they helped the train go faster."

Ann, too, had been looking out the train window, greatly admiring the innumerable silver Mylar fans firmly attached to the tunnel walls, whipping about from the strong tunnel winds the train generated. The display was a celebration of process and flows — winds blow here! — whether the fans helped the train go faster or not. She was glad this art piece appeared here, at the Denver International Airport. Located on the edge of the High Plains, the airport was buffeted by great Chinooks, and the fans made her anticipate the winds that would give her a horizontal hairdo once she emerged from the terminal.

Ann had just flown back from Atlanta, Georgia. From her window seat, she admired the grids of pines planted at the entrances to the airport, welcoming

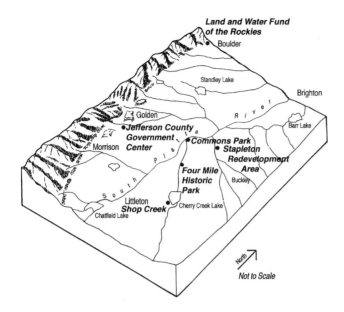

7.1
Location of six designs reflecting regional patterns and processes.

people to an orderly setting but also triggering images of the extensive, efficiently planted southern pine forests covering the southeast landscape beyond the city. Ann sensed that the recognition of processes and regional context was growing quickly in the field of design, even though the connection was not fully recognized by all those who benefited from it, such as the man on the train. She resolved to investigate built and unbuilt landscapes, closer to her Denver home, that reflect the legibility of the region's waterstains and thus anchor the designs to their regional context. She was especially interested in the ways in which planting designs are conceived, as evidence of the region's processes and patterns.

After talking with many designers in the region and touring recently built projects, Ann selected six works that stood out from the rest as best revealing the connection between process and place (figure 7.1). These diverse projects were representative of both public and private interests, varied in scale, and included "clean slate" as well as retrofitted design sites. They were evenly dispersed throughout her study area, she found, and would serve as good models for much of the region. She toured them again and spoke with their designers and clients.

SHOP CREEK Ann's first site was Shop Creek, in the southeastern portion of her study area in Cherry Creek State Park. Shop Creek, once a highly eroded high-prairie stream connecting to the Cherry Creek reservoir, had grown in volume and velocity as a result of increased runoff from gutters, driveways, and cul-de-sacs of the adjacent new suburbs. Because its flow collected silts and chemical pollutants from construction sites, the suburbs, and the park itself, the creek was also a significant source of phosphorous pollution to the nearby reservoir. A multidisciplinary team of engineers and landscape architects was hired by the city of Aurora's Urban Drainage and Flood Control District and the Cherry Creek Basin Authority to stabilize the stream, revegetate it for increased wildlife habitat, and reduce phosphorous pollution by 50 percent. Rather than construct typical "dragon's teeth" concrete stream structures to slow the velocity and erosive impact of the water, the team developed an innovative, context-fitted approach to achieve their goals (figure 7.2).

The system begins with water flowing from the adjacent tidy suburb into Shop Creek and into the park. A retention pond first collects the water, allowing

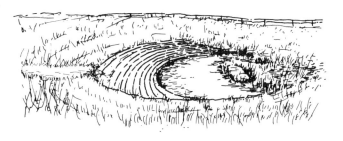

silts and sediments to settle. The stream proceeds through five crescent-shaped drop structures or dams. Each dam, formed of a mix of native soil and portland cement, stops the water, which then flows through a culvert to a lower pool on the other side of the structure. The pipes carry everyday water into the eyelike ponds, with storm flows cascading over the top of the soil-cement dams. As water leaves each pond, it flows into shallow, primordial soup-like wetlands, where cattail and bulrush root systems remove phosphorous and other chemicals from the water (figure 7.3). Eventually, the stream meets the Cherry Creek reservoir, with phosphorous levels reduced by 50 percent.

7.2
Aerial view of Shop Creek drop structures near Cherry Creek State Park.
Photo by Wenk Associates

7.3
Crescent-shaped Shop Creek drop structures.

The landscape architect William Wenk, of Wenk Associates, a Denver-based design firm, related to Ann his sources of design inspiration: in studying erosion in western settings, he had been struck by the eventually stabilized slope forms of western mesas and southeastern Utah stream courses. The slopes of both are nearly vertical yet very stable. The rock formations exposed by eroding streams are "very hydraulically efficient," Wenk told her, meaning they contain and convey large amounts of water.[1] Wenk captured this mesa-streambank form in the creation of the semicircular concrete retention basins that hold water, reduce its force, and provide irrigation for lush wetland growth and habitat. Site soil and portland cement were mixed together to form the vertical slope over which stream water pours. This concrete mix was compacted everywhere but at the edges, so that the edges erode more quickly and change shape according to weathering. The resulting jagged-edged surface is quite reminiscent of mesas and exposed rock stream courses.

Water can have recognizable positive and negative effects in this plains environment. Where water concentrates, plants respond, and the resulting wetlands help designers achieve their goals of reducing pollution, erosion, and increasing habitat. Where too much water concentrates, however, such as in the cut channels formed by speedy suburban runoff, plants cannot colonize successfully and maintain their hold on quickly disappearing substrates; the stream eats up more and more upland vegetation. This is water without the stain. Wenk and company restored a functioning stream system in a way that allows dynamic processes of colonization, deposition, and erosion to continue.

But as Ann investigated these forms in the state park grasslands one summer afternoon, she was not reminded of mesas or Utah streambeds; these landforms were too distant from where she stood. Mesas play no direct role in the processes of this plains site and so provided little sense of context for her. However, she applauded the designers' perhaps inadvertent recollection of a nearby form, one that troubled her every time she heard a reservoir deemed a "lake," such as the Cherry Creek "Lake" she had seen moments earlier. Lake edges meet the water surface. And because water is concentrated at this location, in a natural lake system vegetation appears to rise straight out from the water. The banks of reservoirs, however, are marked by jagged edges like those notable in Wenk's soil cement forms. Reservoir levels fluctuate, drowning or desiccating whatever vegetation happens to colonize the reservoir edge. This inhospitable, sterile edge is further endangered by maintenance forces actively removing vegetation from reservoir edges during high water periods. "Why?" Ann asked one reser-

1. William Wenk, telephone conversation, 12 December 1997.

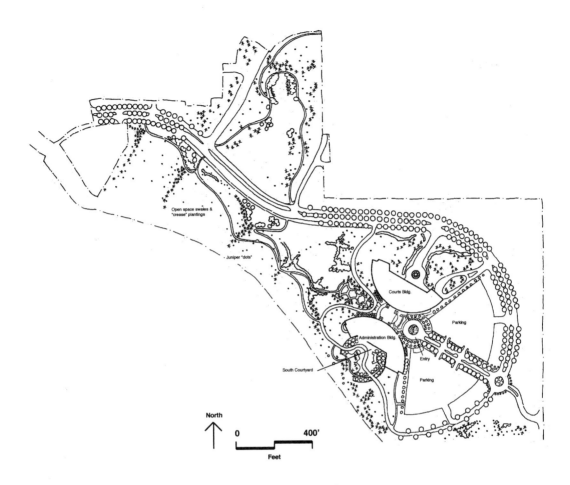

7.4
Plan view of Jefferson County Government Center complex.

voir manager. She was told that managers feared that under various environmental regulations they would be responsible for protecting any wetland species that became established along this edge during high-water seasons. If that were the case they could no longer raise and lower the reservoir levels without being under intense scrutiny.

Wenk's forms perfectly captured that barren, ragged, manipulated reservoir edge but created an antidote to its sterility by using native soil and encouraging the presence of abundant, flourishing wetland plants and birds. The crescent shapes recall the legible cottonwood meanders seen along streams in aerial photos. In plan view, the soil-edged drop structures fleetingly reminded Ann of the scattered pockmarks seen particularly well in aerial photographs of this short-grass prairie: prairie dog burrows and towns. She knew in her bones that a good design evokes many interpretations, and this one had a particularly strong attachment to processes and place.

JEFFERSON COUNTY GOVERNMENT CENTER Ann next visited the west-central portion of her study area, where a recently built project graciously captures the waterstain of nearby foothills and mountain landscapes. The Jefferson County Government Center, east of Golden, is an enormous complex of elegant courtrooms and offices, with a four-story, neoclassical atrium (figure 7.4). Landscaped areas include an entry parkway and turnaround, the south memorial courtyard, or "Courage Garden," which commemorates those who risked their lives in service to the county, the west courtyard with its series of turf terraces, and surrounding open-space slopes. Since construction began in 1990, Ann had frequently stopped at this site to watch it grow.

The landscape architectural firm Civitas was hired by the county to provide a landscape design. "The main purpose," according to principal landscape architect Todd Johnson, now with the firm Design Workshop, "was to delight the visitor and engage her or him with nature." To accomplish this simply stated purpose, Johnson concentrated on creating a pleasing aesthetic for the semiarid climate of the region, using design principles of form, line, color, and texture. This meant consciously abandoning the approach often taught in design schools—to imagine carving spaces from an existing forest area—which Johnson felt was inappropriate for the dry, open plains. The second purpose was to respond to the landform of the foothills and plains. "We shouldn't be afraid to manipulate the landforms, especially as a way of making people aware of this place. They are in a special place, poised between the Great Plains and the Front Range. Here people can be aware both of what landscape architects do and how we contribute to people's experience of place." The third aim was to create formal areas, where the landscape responds to the buildings, and informal areas, where the landscape responds to adjacent open-space views. Juxtaposing formal and informal areas is a critical design challenge and is "where the expression of both is most vivid," Johnson noted.[2]

2. Todd Johnson, telephone conversations, 11 November 1996, 14 November 1997.

The informal areas, with their graded open-space slopes, greatly appealed to Ann (figure 7.5). These slopes provide middleground views to building users gazing toward the nearby mountains. Ann admired the designer's careful grading and, most of all, the association of trees with the graded swales cutting through the slopes. These tree-planted creases immediately strike the waterstain chord. She had seen the same processes of gravity and climate producing similar plant/slope relationships a few minutes west of the site in Clear Creek Canyon. Ann enjoyed the contrast between the densely planted swales and the drier site areas, where oneseed junipers dot outer slopes in a pattern of distribution. These woody evergreens evenly space themselves, as if by contract, to share the scarce rain and snow (figure 7.6).

Todd Johnson spoke convincingly of the swales' purpose in fulfilling the creation of a semiarid landscape aesthetic. He acknowledged soil as the landscape's basic building block, in the same way that, according to Louis Kahn, the brick is architecture's fundamental unit. Johnson's description reminded Ann of the ranger's hands modeling the rise and fall of the Rockies when she was first learning about geomorphic processes.

7.5 Plantings in the slope crease respond to regional context.

7.6 Junipers spot dry slopes at Jefferson County Government Center complex.

> Soil starts from parent material, is weathered, then moves into low places where moisture gathers. This soil becomes rich with weathering and decay and soon a whole environment evolves from these conditions. And

PLANTING EVIDENCE 173

so the basis of this design type is to ask how the soil arrived, its moisture content, and what special environments ensue. Then you ascribe various values to the land: the lower the depression where water gathers, the greater comfort and richness it offers. . . . It is related to the fundamentals of how we perceive the environment as systems of contrast, offering choices of places for us to visit. It is no longer so important to completely abstract the landscape, to completely falsify it.

However, Johnson remarked, we should not be afraid to manipulate it to intensify the sense of where we are. Through a simple yet profound gesture of plants, water, and grades working together, his work in the outer portions of the site collars and intensifies the sense of the great semiarid edge between mountains and plains. Capturing these signatures of place offers much beauty and information, Ann concluded.

The project teases, though, she thought; the design knowingly and deliberately reflects its context in the place closest to its source of inspiration. The lawn terraces, or "plates," drip with water close to the building and then thrust into grasslands that grow drier with distance from the building. The proportion of formal, building-inspired space was too great for Ann's liking, but perhaps that was her jewel box bias rearing its head again. She liked the sturdy honesty of the open-space slopes as a container for the water-rich gardens but would have liked to see more modest gems in both gardens and building. She could see that in making their decisions the designer's were quite cognizant of the tension between the Front Range's diverse context: the entry drive turnaround features a yin-yang circle design with slabby, jutting stones rising from spotted shrublands, counterbalanced by an equal proportion of mowed urban lawn (figure 7.7). Ann imagined flattening

7.7
Jefferson County Government Center complex entry drive turnaround.

174 WATERSTAINED LANDSCAPES

and tilting the circle so that the irrigation water concentrated on the lawn portion, firmly anchoring the waterstain.

As she walked along the path that intersected one of the swales, Ann reflected on the project's significance. It was one of the first in the region to acknowledge the beauty of regional processes and patterns and to inject them into a highly visible, traditionally staid governmental environment. She felt this project was the bellwether of many good designs to come.

LAND AND WATER FUND OF THE ROCKIES COMMERCIAL RETROFIT

The Land and Water Fund of the Rockies (the LAW Fund) is a nonprofit organization that provides legal assistance to individuals and communities engaged in environmental protection. The headquarters are located at the busy intersection of Broadway and Baseline in Boulder, in a recently retrofitted building originally constructed in the 1960s. The founder and past president, Frances (Kelley) Green, desired an educational, water-conserving landscape design to complement the building, which had been redesigned to incorporate a number of energy-efficient features.

Prior to the start of construction, Ann visited the site and spoke with Green about the project.[3] Green was determined to house the LAW Fund in a setting appropriate to its environmental purposes—scenery to match its society, Ann thought, in apology to Wallace Stegner. The landscape architects William Wenk and Joan Woodward worked with Green to expand the goals from water conservation to encompass additional objectives. These objectives included reducing nonpoint urban runoff by holding water on site as much as possible, creating a larger diversity of plants for increased habitat, providing microclimate comfort, reducing maintenance needs and energy inputs from power tools, honoring the pedestrian and bicyclist and reducing the impact of autos, providing educational opportunities, and celebrating the site context. These were part of the overall goals of creating positive site function and human response. They also wanted water, where it did occur, to be legible.

Ann toured the half-acre site prior to its construction. Cars dominated sight and sound. The site was breathtakingly noisy from forty-mile-an-hour traffic and braking squeals as cars approached the busy intersection. A parking area,

3. Frances Green, personal communication, Boulder, Colo., 11 September 1996, 10 October 1997.

7.8
Plan view of the Land and Water Fund of the Rockies redesign.

7.9
Land and Water Fund of the Rockies entrance sign demonstrates relationships between plants and water.
Redrawn after illustration by Wenk Associates

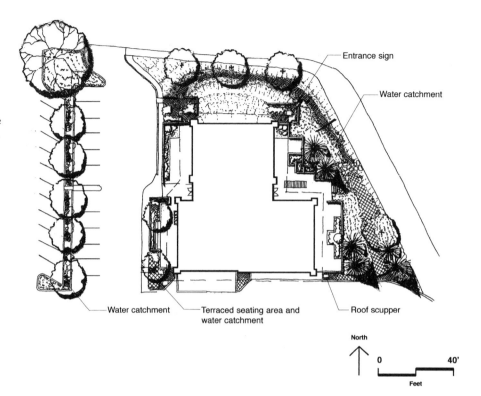

176 WATERSTAINED LANDSCAPES

accommodating thirty-two cars, provided the foreground to mountain views from west-facing office windows. Building entrances catered to motorists and largely ignored pedestrians and bicyclists. The property seemed tired to her. Originally, its perimeter and inner courtyards were designed to recall a Japanese garden, using native plants instead of traditional Asian species. But in thirty years, junipers, blue spruce, skunkbrush, Oregon grape, and other plants had imbibed available nutrients and irrigation water, and now their branches blocked walkways, windows, and light. She saw a maintenance worker shearing back the biomass and dumping trimmings in the trash. Water flowed from the irrigated lawn to catch basins and out eventually to Skunk Creek, a tributary of Boulder Creek.

As Ann looked on, Green spread out the landscape designs on a conference table, discussing first the plan's highlights and then its significance (figure 7.8). Green animatedly described how water was celebrated on-site wherever it flowed or stalled. Parking lot, roof, and slope runoff was directed to an encircling swale. Where the water paused, the highest water-use plants such as Nebraska sedge, Bebb's sedge, spike rush, and three square muscled for position. Seating terraces on the west side were designed with plants that tolerate both drought and inundation, including red day lilies. Existing spruce and pines were maintained, their shady microclimates used to support layers of plants for wildlife habitat. Rocks formed reservoirs underneath trees for the dwarf mahonia groundcover layer.

The LAW Fund sign was relocated beneath a drain spout where roof runoff would irrigate larger, more colorful plants in the planter below, such as rushes, sedges in the wetter areas, and day lilies and sage in the drier areas (figure 7.9). In winter, runoff would freeze and thaw, creating a dynamic introduction to the attention to process inherent in the design. Pedestrians and bicyclists could appreciate this detail, which might be missed by drivers; the intent of the design was to favor those on foot or bicycle tires whenever possible.

The parking area had been reduced in size and creased so that runoff was collected and filtered by a central rock and vegetation median strip. Parking spaces were planted with drought-tolerant hackberries to reduce glare and urban heat-island effect while allowing mountain views from second-story windows, since hackberries tend to grow slowly when unirrigated. Ann learned that the client desired all parking spaces to be reduced in size, assuming, because the building occupants were environmentalists, that compact spaces would be the norm; ironically, she saw that almost all of these outdoors buffs drove oversized sports utility vehicles. However, half of the stalls were designed for compact spaces, and employees were encouraged to use alternative modes of transportation to reduce stress on the remaining parking spaces. This seemed reasonable since the site was adjacent to a wide-ranging bicycle trail network and the LAW Fund subsidized the cost of employees' bus passes.

In a future design phase, productive planting areas would be created around employee kitchen and lunch areas, with herbs and grapes and other edible foods nearby. Courtyard gardens included shade- and drought-tolerant plants, featuring aromatic and colorful plants, such as dwarf mahonia, coral bells, bluebells, and sweet woodruff.

The scale of the project was small, but, as Green pointed out, the scale of significance was much larger. For example, the design was one of twenty projects receiving a national endorsement from the National Forum on Nonpoint Source Pollution as a model for retrofitting commercial areas for runoff reduction. Most cities in the semiarid West allow storm water to drain directly into storm sewers and then into watercourses. This explained those conspicuous stencils of bony fish Ann saw painted next to storm sewer inlets to remind people not to dump toxins into streams through the storm sewers. When Boulder resource managers installed monitoring devices in Boulder Creek to trace pollutant sources, they found that 70 percent of pollutants, including sediments, nitrates, phosphates, pesticides, heavy metals, oils, and gas, were derived from storm runoff. Oil and gas pollutants are particularly concentrated in arid cities where rainfall is infrequent. When large storms occur, toxic levels of these pollutants end up in streams, affecting aquatic ecosystems.

The LAW Fund project was designed to retain a five-year-flood event and allow runoff to percolate before entering Skunk Creek. A five-year-flood event did not sound significant to Ann until she realized that it produced half the water volume of a one-hundred-year-flood event. If all new commercial and residential developments were designed to retain water for such flood events, flooding and pollution would be substantially reduced within the city, requiring less culvert enlargement in the city and reservoir enlargement outside the city. Because plants utilized respond to quantities of water naturally falling on-site or concentrating in certain locations, no additional "drain" on city water supplies would be incurred.

The design was revolutionary when Ann considered its application beyond the half-acre scale. Creating an education center on-site could spread this gospel further; she hoped the "contagion effect," where one pioneering neighbor creates an innovative style that spreads to neighboring sites, would take effect here as well.

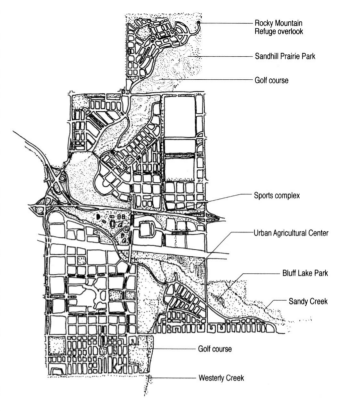

7.10
Stapleton Development Plan highlights creek corridors and parkways connecting through neighborhoods.
Based on data from Stapleton Redevelopment Foundation et al. 1995

STAPLETON DEVELOPMENT PLAN

Ann paged through the attractive Stapleton Development Plan book as she awaited her appointment with core planning team member Mark Johnson of Civitas. The 1995 plan reflects the history and results of a lengthy planning process to determine the fate of the forty-seven-hundred-acre former airport and its connections to the urban and natural fabric (figure 7.10). The intent of the planning team of landscape architects, architects, and engineers was to create a series of multiuse communities based upon patterns inherent in Denver's neighborhoods. These would be interconnected on- and off-site by parkways that also served as storm water, recreation, and habitat corridors. Ann was meeting with Johnson to discuss the design process he had used to reveal the site's potential.

Ann was ushered into an office. She had been forewarned of Mark's rapid-fire conversational style, and she was armed with three pens, an oversized note-

PLANTING EVIDENCE 179

book, and a tape recorder to capture his perspective on the Stapleton project. On the surface he appeared lanky and relaxed, yet his responses to her questions arrived as if on a tightly coiled spring. She worked to keep up.[4]

What was the overall concept? The concept involved trying to uncover the natural foundations of the site and the forces at work on it, both historically and today. The intent was to take advantage of these forces to reveal patterns that may have been there or could be there to create functional open space for those who live and work at Stapleton. This system would connect Stapleton to a regional open-space system, to the Rocky Mountain Arsenal National Wildlife Refuge, to the Lowry Air Force Base site, and to the surrounding neighborhoods.

The process I used was to excavate historical photographs and maps dating back to the 1860s. We could see patterns of agriculture, settlement, mining, and railroads. I inferred from these patterns the forces shaping them. For example, there once was a little town called Independent that was connected to coal mines to the east of the Stapleton site by a railroad. The railroad line had a kink in it. By studying 1938 stereo photos, we found that the railroad line curled around a sand dune with a wetland in the middle of it.

We also found that agriculture and airport development had greatly altered surface water flow. For example, Sand Creek had been relocated to the north through filling and bank stabilization. Although soil structure could not be replaced at the previous stream site since it had been filled, perhaps water could be reintroduced in these locations. So we looked for natural patterns that could be utilized along with community development patterns. When we overlaid both of these, we found that the Denver tradition of parks and parkways could be the stitches to knit the community and natural landscapes together. The Stapleton Plan outlines the development of the Sand Creek system, the Westerly Creek system, and the northeast prairie system and connects these into the surrounding neighborhoods and new villages through the use of parkways. The parkways reflect the historical vision Kessler had for Denver. But they are

4. Mark Johnson, personal communication, Denver, Colo., 20 August 1994, 25 February 1997, 14 November 1997.

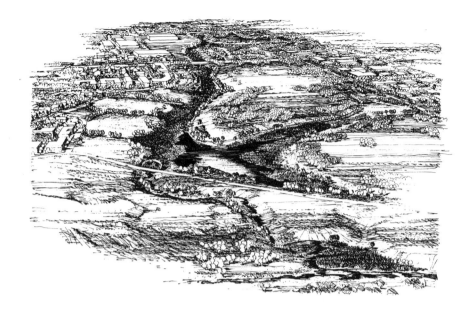

7.11
Westerly Creek corridor.
Illustration by Wenk Associates, in Stapleton Redevelopment Foundation et al. 1995

wider and serve more than recreational and aesthetic functions. They are intended to provide native habitat, storm water management, and treatment.

Other landscape architecture firms were among the eighteen subcontractors contributing to the plan. The Philadelphia-based design firm Andropogon was involved in analyzing natural systems of the site and detailing restoration strategies. Wenk Associates was instrumental in developing the design for an open-space system and creating compelling illustrations of its functioning (figure 7.11). Open space on the northern half of the site was designed to retain the hundred-year-flood event on-site, saving an estimated twenty million dollars in construction costs for storm-sewer outfalls. For example, Westerly Creek would be carved out of runway concrete to again escort storm flows. The stream system would function as a community gill, filtering pollutants and breathing organic life into the urban configuration. Drainage fingers flowed from adjacent developments into Westerly Creek, gloved with cottonwoods and willows and beckoning pedestrians to partake of the regional walkway net-

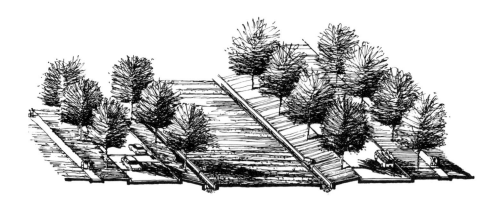

7.12
Integrated surface storm-water system from Stapleton Development Plan. *Illustration by Wenk Associates, in Stapleton Redevelopment Foundation et al. 1995*

work. These walks and stream flows led to detention ponds and wetlands, where nutrients and pollutants filtered out. Wetlands throughout the system allowed infiltration of water to replenish groundwater supplies. Drop structures stabilized the streambed, slowing the erosive force of runoff. Upstream water-treatment practices included treatment of parking lot oils and pollutants before they entered the streams. Runoff would be used to irrigate shade trees and groundcovers.

In examining the plans for Stapleton, Ann traced functioning processes at both large and small scales. Her eye was drawn to the entire project's ear-shaped runoff system, rendered varying shades of green and gold, depending on water concentrations. Swales, channels, runnels, streams all obviated the need for expensive subsurface storm water systems. They accommodated recreational desires such as golf, walking, and biking. They allowed stressed species to survive. They accepted pollutant-laden water from adjacent developments such as the Montebello Industrial Park, cleansed it, then returned it to the Rocky Mountain Arsenal refuge for wildlife habitat. At smaller scales, her fingers raked through parking lots, following the straight rows of channels that collected runoff and sustained landscape plantings (figure 7.12). The parkways served multiple purposes of recreation, water conveyance and detention, and habitat. Johnson suspected that the edges of parkways would still retain a traditional formal edge, harkening back to the City Beautiful parks and parkways.

Ann noted the plan's waterstain patterns, reminiscent of the larger Denver region. They included streams with accompanying cottonwood and willow meanders. Rolling sand hills with tall grasses pocked the lower, moister areas, and short grasses carpeted drier slopes. Tree-lined parkways linked old and new development. Grass-lined swales captured runoff on these parkways instead of flushing water to the storm drainage system. Larger grasses would one day sort themselves to mark the moister areas. Detention basins, disguised as playas, would sustain plants that withstand drought and inundation. Where groundwater contact was maintained, wetlands of spike rushes and other species would proliferate. Sports patterns of ball fields and golf courses were present, with the latter featuring habitat development and sand hill prairie integration. Wetland patches sparkled in wooded, layered drainage corridors, increasing habitat for many species. Agricultural quilt patterns were reflected in the new community farm. Beauty spots recalling Denver's parkway heritage demarcated important intersections, utilizing more perennials and drought-tolerant plants than in DeBoer's day. Although planting design scale had not been detailed as of her interview with Johnson, the intent was to restore four native prairie habitats over 150 acres and to include plants within the more traditional parkways that were beautiful and had value for insects and wildlife.

It was clear to Ann that the Stapleton Development Plan, combined with plans for the adjacent Rocky Mountain Arsenal and Lowry Air Force Base, were imprinting regional patterns into new public and private development on a scale not seen before in Denver's development history. According to the plaque she studied on the office wall, the project had won the 1996 Colorado Chapter of the American Society of Landscape Architects' President's Award and would surely capture the attention of planners and designers across the country.

Before she left, Ann asked Johnson about his perspective on patterns in the Denver region. He thought they were obvious and essential building blocks in design. She was relieved by his response because another seasoned Denver designer she had interviewed insisted that Denver was too confusing to have discernible patterns. What were Johnson's favorite patterns? He said that there were many, but currently he most enjoyed the sand hill prairie cut by washes. Ann was surprised by his response, thinking that few people are really aware of these areas far from the region's population center. But then Johnson relayed

7.13
Four-Mile Historic Park plan, 1981. (Four-mile house located in park, center.)
Redrawn after illustration by Jerry Shapins and Ann Moss

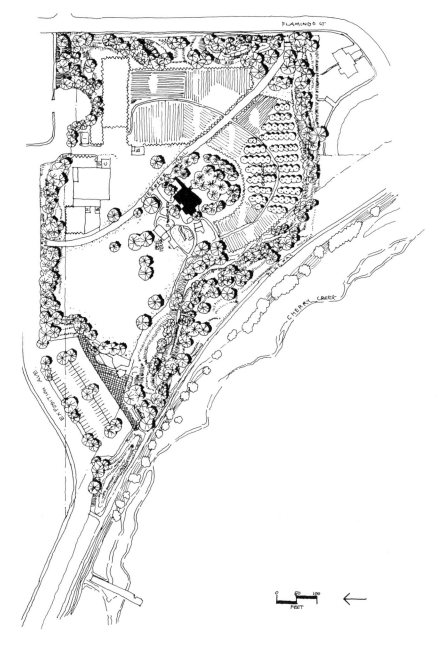

184 WATERSTAINED LANDSCAPES

that he was a pilot, as she should have guessed, and was quite familiar with the region's signatures from the air. Ann wondered how flying lessons could be made a part of every designer's basic training.

FOUR-MILE HISTORIC PARK   Ann first discovered the Four-Mile Historic Park, a rustic anomaly in a glossy commercial Denver neighborhood, while driving the route of her transect across Denver. Having recently journeyed to the region herself, she was curious to tour this once-vibrant rest stop that had greeted westering travelers before they reached Denver. Four-Mile House, built in 1858, was the last stagecoach station on the Cherokee Trail east of Denver. Here, travelers could buy vegetables grown on the property, camp in the shade from creekside cottonwoods and other planted trees, drink and dance in the saloon, and dine with other travelers. The owners of Four-Mile House profited from flourishing business between 1858 and 1872. With the arrival of trains to the Denver region, however, stagecoach business declined, and the enterprise failed. The park was purchased in 1975 by the city and county of Denver, and designers and historians were consulted to learn how best to rehabilitate and interpret the 14 acres remaining from the original 640-acre plot. In the early 1980s, designers Ann Moss and Jerry Shapins were asked to create a master plan for the property so that it could be developed into a historical interpretive park (figure 7.13). Ann met for dinner one evening with Moss and Shapins, who generously reconstructed their memories of the project, resurrected slides, and told anecdotes. They were a perfect complement to one another, taking turns in being alternately laid-back and intense. Moss would describe the intensity of the design process, and Shapins would talk about how much fun it had been. Shapins would then describe some of the frustrations, and Moss would inject comments about how positive the experience had been.[5]

In their investigation, Moss and Shapins found scant information about the Four-Mile House landscape itself. They did learn that the settlement, located near an oxbow of Cherry Creek, was in an advantageous location, with rich soils from frequent flooding. At first, settlers had grown crops without irrigation, but these failed during dry years. A knoll protected the house from flooding, and eventually water was channeled through this knoll to reach crops. A garden

5. Ann Moss and Jerry Shapins, personal communication, Boulder, Colo., 28 August 1994, 2 September 1996, 17 November 1997.

just beyond the kitchen door was watered with a bucket from a well. Irrigation ditches were excavated in 1868, providing additional irrigated acreage. Originally park supporters wanted to capture a snapshot of life in 1859, the stage's busiest year. However, the setting would have been so barren at that early point that designers stretched the interpretive period to include the Victorian era that reached Denver in the 1880s.

Moss and Shapins approached the design by visiting the region's remaining ranches and homesteads, reading period newspaper articles and books, and excavating the site's Homestead Act papers from 1866. They analyzed typical uses of Front Range homestead properties, building orientation, microclimate responses, and garden and crop siting. They then grouped repeated configurations into patterns. This study of patterns gave them likely locations for many of the disappeared uses at Four-Mile House. Shapins described their system: using a method of stating questions, facts, and deductions and exploring design implications, they were able to reason where elements such as corrals, sheds, pastures, and windbreaks would have been found. For example, where were the Four-Mile House barn structures located in 1864? In fact, no one knew. The design team deduced that the barns would have been adjacent to the creek or the well, for water, and also downwind of the house. These deductions were derived from patterns of most ranches in the region and guided the property's reconstruction.

Under the designers' guidance, the historical resource maintained a landscape emphasis. A swale was dug to replicate Cherry Creek's 1872 alignment. Because of sandy soils, however, the diverted water percolated through the soil, leaving a dry surface. This proved to be excellent cottonwood habitat, and seeds soon blew in to colonize the swale. Crops were planted, their location determined by water availability; those planted closer to Cherry Creek, such as corn and potatoes, required more water than the wheat and oats planted upslope. Plants popular in the early settlement and Victorian eras were brought in, such as lilacs, roses, kitchen plants, herbs, and fruit trees. Some of the largest trees surrounding the house remained from the earliest days, reflecting the microclimate comfort patterns typical of these eras, when water was hauled in buckets from a well. When she visited the park, Ann peered into the no-longer-functioning well on the property and noted thriving raspberry shoots highlighting this former water source. Another shrub flourished next to a rain-gutter outlet.

The two designers stressed that although this was not an authentic restoration of a particular preirrigation and prerailroad landscape, the design reflected the region at a similar time period and was designed with as many clues about the region at that time as could be found. The property reflected principles such as water conservation (prior to ditch construction in 1868), productivity, and meaning. It was a waterstain from a time when the property was on the edge of civilization and the clarity of people's intentions was evident in the land. Community, profit, survival, and beauty were all legible in the landscape.

A new planning effort was under way for Four-Mile House, according to Executive Director Jim Hartman, that would revisit the park's interpretive emphases and programs.[6] The dilemma of accommodating groups with certain comfort and safety requirements in a historical environment precipitated the need for the plan update. Irrigation ditches conflicted with schoolchildren's feet. Tender plants needed regular irrigation to withstand trampling—should a new irrigation system be installed? Ann hoped that planners would maintain the legibility of the historical waterstain patterns. She felt that there were many lessons to be learned at Four-Mile House that could be applied to residences throughout the region. Moss and Shapins agreed; as the three of them finished their dinner, they clinked their glasses together and made a toast to the health of residences and commercial enterprises with dooryard gardens, shaded porches, and raspberries growing in the waterstain. These were the types of places that would welcome you—no matter how long your particular journey had been.

COMMONS PARK   Honest, Ann thought, she did not intend to promote particular design firms as she explored work under way in the Denver region. When she first started her study, there were not many projects to highlight as particularly regionally distinctive. By the time she was finishing her survey, however, several inspiring projects had been initiated. Ann felt she would be remiss if she did not include the Commons Park Master Plan, which was hot off the presses in 1998, when she was drawing her work to a close.

The Denver Department of Parks and Recreation hired Civitas and Jones and

6. Jim Hartman, personal communication, Denver, Colo., 8 October 1997, 28 August 1998.

Jones, a Seattle landscape architecture firm, to spearhead the design of the twenty-six-acre critical park area along the South Platte River. Commons Park is part of the Riverfront Park system of parks within downtown Denver.[7] The vision for this system was to provide along the river both natural habitat and diversity of river-based places for people to enjoy. Commons Park, one of the largest parcels in the park system, connects to downtown at the confluence of Sixteenth Street, the Highland neighborhood, and the South Platte bikeway. Intended uses include passive and active park activities such as walking, jogging, education, informal sports, bicycling, and picnicking.

The design team's goal was to create a regionally rooted and culturally inclusive place. The park was intended to be a respite and retreat for urban dwellers, with an emphasis on youths and the benefits they might derive from such a place. The context of place was woven into all design decisions, beginning with Denver Parks and Recreation's interest in designating the site as a natural area. This designation would signal that management of the park was different from that of other urban park areas and cue users not to expect the usual turf and tree configuration. Design participants included landscape architects, architects, ecologists, engineers, and an educational futurist, all offering their perspectives on what elements and processes define the region.

Ann felt a twinge of sadness mixed with delight in perusing the seven work-session books produced by the team. The design process looked like it had been energized with the power of revealing the region. Mark Johnson commented that throughout the process, intellectual sparks had flown. These sparks are recorded in the process books, along with jokes and spirited discussion. She felt sad that she had not been a fly on the wall yet delighted that the time had come for such regional revelation and reveling.

The Commons Park Master Plan and Guidelines summed up the design, planned for construction beginning in 1998. Ann could detect the pulse of processes as she studied the plans, starting with the South Platte's dynamic role in the park (figure 7.14). The design pulled at the river's fringes, creating five striated swales that cut into the park site. During major storms, the swales allow the river to lap up against protective stone-outcrop weirs. Resilient wetland plantings of cordgrass, sedges, and rushes mark the wettest locations, those

7. Mark Naylor, Civitas project manager, telephone conversation, 11 November 1997.

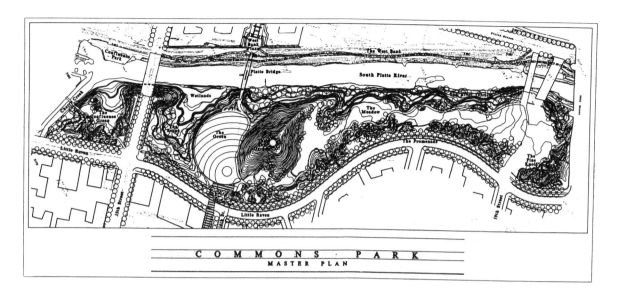

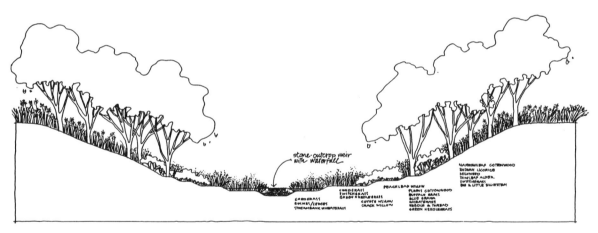

7.14
Commons Park plan.
Illustration by Civitas, Inc.

7.15
Swale section showing plant stripes responding to water availability.
Illustration by Civitas, Inc./Jones and Jones

7.16
Trees are planted in the waterstain.
Illustration by Civitas, Inc./Jeffrey Joyce

most vulnerable to flooding, in the swale bottoms (figure 7.15). The edges of the swales step upward toward the park, with each higher terrace reflecting less water availability. Wheatgrass, switchgrass, and green needlegrass mark the next drier terrace, then peach-leaved willow and short grasses, then forests of narrowleaf cottonwood, thin-leaf alder, bluestems, and switchgrass. All layers provide greatly needed habitat along the South Platte River, a migratory lifeline for birds. According to project manager Mark Naylor, the South Platte River's hundred-year-flood stage could be accommodated easily within the banks and provide water storage space for more constricted areas downstream as well.

Ann then considered the flow of water from the city toward the river. The sixty-foot-wide swales control and direct the flows of urban runoff volumes toward the river. During low river flows, runoff from the adjacent Little Raven Promenade and developments supply the required water IV to support swale plants during droughtier summer months, when rainfall is a daily, intense afternoon occurrence. Runoff is filtered through "stormceptors" that remove the first flush of oil, debris, and sediment prior to flowing in the swale systems during one-to-two-year-storm events. Larger storms bypass the swale system and flow directly to the river.

Waterstains are distinguished throughout the design as urban runoff is captured, filtered, and manipulated on its way to the South Platte River (figure 7.16). Nonpotable ditch water and runoff appear in key "seep" locations, demarcated with plum, chokecherry, and hawthorn thickets or cottonwoods. Rocks, because of their water-shedding properties, are incorporated into these areas to form reservoirs for plant roots. Irrigated open lawn areas allow views into the park and support Frisbee and other unstructured play activities but are more limited in size than in most traditional urban parks. Bur oaks and other shade trees zigzag along the promenade, a more water-conserving alternative to the elms and maples of DeBoer's and Kessler's days. Grassy prairie knolls, planted with mixed grasses, mark the driest locations. Ann expected that a green crease would one day mark the knoll edge.

Park highlights include the "Sky Garden," an encircled area emphasizing upward views of Denver's cerulean sky. Dolmen-like stone markers are located along the park edge and incorporated into the picnic structures. Ann noted that the quick character sketches of picnic shelters include skylights to allow sky glimpses while providing weather protection for users. Stone benches are curved to afford better socialization and comfort and also to recall the flowing river, not far from users' feet. Fountains were designed for a series of small garden rooms along the Little Raven Promenade, and according to early sketches, they appear to interpret water's every effect in Denver: a grid of channels recalls agricultural fields, water cracks through concrete, riparian ribbons intersect neat tree grids, splash pools recall mountain springs—all possible forms seem represented, to bring home the importance of water in a semiarid environment.

Mark Naylor spoke with Ann about the "vital tension" of adjacency in the Commons Park plan: "The tree-planted Promenade is where city and park meet with great rigor. It is a new take on Denver's park tradition. Instead of a park's lawn coming to the city's arboreal edge, inviting pedestrians to enter, the natural landscape's influence is at the edge of Commons Park, highly visible and really a part of the promenade."[8]

After speaking with project managers who had worked extensively with community groups to ensure the social as well as ecological fit of this project, Ann came away with the feeling that Denver was at last being pinned to place by projects such as these. Geomorphic processes of flooding and erosion are addressed by accommodating hundred-year floods, protecting soils from erosive forces, and planting riparian wetlands like those that once fringed the South Platte River. Climatic processes are celebrated through sky-featuring devices at large and small scales. Biotic process are honored by increasing riparian habitat within the urban environment through the five swales. Cultural processes are fulfilled by inviting people into the park and offering them protection through use of landforms, water, and accompanying plants and through specially crafted features such as lights, shelters, benches, and toilet facilities. Pleasure is also provided: settings for play, views, learning, and meaning. The place, poised on the edge of a great river system and city, manages to acknowledge both in an interpretive rather than didactic way. Patterns Ann discovered through her study are prevalent: wetland rings transformed into swale stripes, rocky reservoirs for larger trees, the green crease, affiliations of varying plants with varying water concentrations.

Ann trusted she was not being premature in her enthusiasm for the potential place. She did wonder, however, how habitat values could be preserved when so many people could potentially access the swales and disturb nesting species. Education might be effective in deterring people's use of these areas, but it was difficult to estimate the extent of conflict at this early stage. It struck her that an excellent design or ecology graduate thesis topic had emerged: to monitor and assess Commons Park's habitat functioning and human use over time.

She also realized that many waterstains would not be legible because automated irrigation systems obscure the contrast between wet and dry areas. Although turf areas are reduced in size in comparison with most urban parks, decision makers had not heeded Stegner's advice to "get over the color green" in appreciating the inherent, changing colors of the semiarid West. Ann also ques-

8. Mark Naylor, telephone conversation, 26 January 1998.

tioned whether the design included perhaps too many folly-like fountains celebrating water in this semiarid environment. This was admittedly her bias, though, and she hoped fountains would have multipurpose functions rather than existing as landscape one-liners. Overall, she appreciated the plan's fundamental accord between processes and place and hoped it would be appropriately maintained and spark equally inspired design within other portions of the Riverfront Park system.

All six projects she described are evidence of a changing sensibility toward design in the Denver region. No *Municipal Facts* publications touts them as being as grand as Paris or New York City, as was done in Mayor Speer's day around the turn of the century. Many were rather humble works that sought to integrate ecological functioning with human well-being. If she imagined she could reach into a map of the region and pull from the map any one of these designs, like a slice of cheesy pizza, she pictured the innumerable strings and connections stretching to hold these designs to their locations. Water, species, nutrients, soil, pedestrians, memories, recollections formed the connections: these designs could not be easily relocated elsewhere with the same fit.

Ann hoped the same was true for her.

Colorado, Here We Go. . . .
Illustration by Cindy Enright/ Denver Post

chapter eight
there's no home like place

MOVING AGAIN Packing the office for the upcoming move was the hardest part. All that paper hovering in piles now needed to fit into the already full file cabinet. Ann checked her watch and listened to the noisy activity in the next room, where the kids were separating the toys needed for the move's duration from those they possibly could live without for the next few weeks. The dreaded file cabinet needed weeding and she knew it. She had a few minutes to get started. She bravely opened the drawer labeled "projects." Toss, toss, toss, away went the relicts from her years in the Denver region. Inevitably, her efficient intentions stalled cold when she found the map of the Denver Front Range urban corridor with the bold X drawn across it. Smudges, a boot print, and a coffee cup ring attested to the map's past value to her. This map, with its tic marks along the transects, had motivated her to get out of her car every three miles along one arm, and every five miles along the other, to look, draw, write, and look again, carefully, to understand the patterns and processes of her new home. A torrent of images washed across her view. She could envision many of the stops she made along the transect arms as she had first investigated her new homeplace years ago: the perfect lawns in residential areas, the plastic palm trees outside a glitzy retail shopping center, the abandoned stockyards and weedy remnant expanses in industrial areas, the views of the mountains from ranch lands at what were at the time the edges of town.

Ann and her family were moving again. This map reminded her of their earlier intentions to stay here in this selected homeplace and send down permanent roots. She, who had moved sixteen times during the fifteen years following her graduation from college, was going to move just one more time. Then she would join the "Don't Move" movement, so to speak, a vocal group from the 1990s who felt that staying put and attending to the daily threats to local well-being would benefit the planet. With the high influx of people into the Denver area at the time of her arrival, it seemed that she was indeed a part of a major migration into more amiable places than the huge urban cores of cities like Los Angeles. But the Denver Front Range corridor had consequently swelled and rippled, splashing over the mountain lip and washing eastward over the plains. The corridor, with a few notable exceptions in Boulder and other counties where substantial open-space buffers had been preserved, had indeed expanded to connect Pueblo to Cheyenne and beyond with relentless commercial enterprises, residences, entertainment facilities, and roads.

She had done her part, both good and bad. True, she and her family added to the numbers causing the population crush. Yet, when Ann had finished her pattern-based design study and applied what she had learned to the freelance design jobs she landed, she worked hard to learn from and spare distinctive features of the region. As a result, Ann had greatly enjoyed the work environment here. She found, however, that her other two motivations, joy and connection to landscape, had been joined by another: the timeless concern for her children and a nagging desire to raise them in a smaller community. She thought back to the fractal geometry of landscapes and wondered if she had some kind of inborn need for fractal structure, where the edge of development could not exceed a certain perimeter and the patches of undeveloped land must be of a certain minimal proportion of the whole.

She reread her demographers, eventually, and discovered that their Denver move had been a part of an interim move; the next migration, complete with its attendant computer-facilitated place independence, was moving toward the tiny communities and unsettled counties across the country. Here land had been abandoned in earlier busts or had not been developed for community life beyond a small town because the area served as ranch, farm, or forest land. These small communities were coming to life as exiles from big cities purchased property, started business enterprises, and located employees here. And so again Ann and her husband systematically scoured small communities in the semiarid West, because she could not part with her waterstain lenses on the world, and decided to move north to a new community.

Two peering faces from the room next door brought her back to her task at hand. But instead of pitching or filing the map, she tucked it in her pocket and decided to retrace her transect once more before leaving the region.

X REDUX Ann stood on the hogback overlook once again, this time with informed eyes, not the fresh eyes of a relative newcomer and student straight out of school. She was still armed with a sense of caring, however; she truly wanted to see what differences the passage of time had made in the Denver area landscape. The urban forest had grown taller, and the successional edge was still visible because new rings of houses had been added to the marching force toward the west. Two-toned planting schemes were visible even from these heights—bright deciduous trees to the south and east, dark evergreens on the north, to block winds. The pattern was repeated and reinforced by the old Rooney homestead, well preserved in its original 1880 condition. Many of the real estate signs had been replaced by open-space signs at the foot of the red rocks. Trails had grown in size and popularity and definition, yet they still blazed through mountain mahogany slopes on the north and grass- and juniper-dotted slopes on the south. Traces of a fire now showed at the tree trunks, a picnicker's illegal barbecue gone astray, but former ranch meadows were luxuriant with revived grasses. North was quite evident, she was pleased to note. Orientation to processes and place was well anchored here.

Other stops along her X were revealing. Many positive steps had been taken to weave resource conservation together with the preservation of regional character. Streams previously culverted had been opened to the light of day and celebrated through public arts programs. Residential and commercial areas now often contained waterstain patterns previously seen only in wild and remnant areas. Former emerald-green lawn expanses of the suburbs were now grey green with more drought-tolerant grasses and pocked with greener bowl formations to serve as temporary water catchment areas. Gutter water, no longer considered "nuisance water," was captured to water key locations of blazing perennials and edible plants around mailboxes and building entrances. According to the regional plan approved many years previously, the region would develop into centers connected by transportation routes, still allowing occasional undeveloped roadside or railside areas to remain.[1] Along roadsides she noted aesthetic arrangements of snow fences and large shrub stripes behind them. Low points supported wetland vegetation, ephemeral with the summer's progressing heat.

Her tour took her by the preserved City Beautiful–era parks and parkways, still glowing with verdant green lawns, flower beds, and shade trees, the exceptional expenditure of water deemed worthwhile by this community adamant about preserving its past. In former ranchlands, many communities germinated with neat rows of gridded streets and alleys, community features strategically located at ends of axial streets, and people enjoying front porches. The street trees were more drought tolerant and were reinforced in their rows by low points where runoff collected. Salt was no longer used on city streets to melt snow—other temperature-increasing compounds had been applied—and water that previously rushed to storm sewers was now percolated through medians and roadside plantings as much as possible. Other communities in former agricultural landscapes had been designed with the pivot irrigation patterns inspiring their forms. The pivot areas were still croplands, though they now used recycled grey water instead of ancient groundwater, and the leftover areas from the circle within a grid were colonized by dense community housing in some areas and by connected wild patches in others.

Ann was relieved in part by much of what she saw in this last look at the region; she experienced a sense of fittedness and felt attuned to the climate, landforms, and people of this place. But a sense of loss also pervaded her opti-

1. Denver Regional Council of Governments 1992.

mism; so much of the former ranchland had been developed that many of the old pattern-ridden homesteads, the telltale slopes and green slope toes, and the orienting windrows were gone. She remembered pulling off the road at the first sight of the then-new developments near Golden, speechless, because these brand-new houses had been thrust into hillsides with wide roads carving the slopes, instant shamrock-green lawns, and puddles of token pine trees and drought-tolerant plants flowing down the slope to the entrance signs. Soon she could not even look at these developments, they were so unacceptable to her sense of what the region could express. These development types—rapid, profitable, market-dictating, with an estimated life cycle of thirty years, precisely tuned to the average mortgage—were still spreading (Wallace Stegner calls them "Denver's ringworm suburbs on the apron of the Front Range"). In an article entitled "New West, True West," Donald Worster writes, "This region offers for study all the greed, violence, beauty, ambition, and variety anyone could use." Yes, Ann saw that in these new developments. Yet she also noted positive change spreading slowly but determinedly in ever-connecting constellations along her transect: as Worster continues, "Given enough time and effort, it may someday also offer a story of careful, lasting adaptation of people to the land."[2]

Alternatives to these worn-out development models had been produced by the efforts of an increasing number of talented designers to capture the essence of the region's inspiring context. She hoped her work was a part of Worster's "time and effort" and had contributed a sensible, responsive method to shape planting designs in ways that did not glorify the good old days but extracted from the past and present essential considerations to promote the survival and legibility of future garden designs in this region. She agreed with landscape architect Laurie Olin's statement that rational, nonnostalgic methods that could help designers create designs scaled to the project and true to the region had not yet been developed.[3] Ann felt satisfied, though, that the pattern-based method was a valid approach toward addressing that project scale in a holistic, accountable, regional manner. The method did not promote pristine reproductions of earlier eras or vapid, "politically correct," self-righteous gardens. As she perused designs utilizing this method, she saw gardens that could change com-

2. Stegner 1992, 104; Worster 1987, 156.
3. Olin 1995, 249.

fortably over time. They showed the value of water and accommodated other species. The gardens reflected an appreciation of people's basic needs to garden, to have beauty spots of color and fragrance and occasional extravagance, and they connected with, and sometimes drew from, the fascinating stories and experiences native to this soil.

ON IMPURE LANDSCAPE As Ann contemplated her own pattern-based garden, with its role for chewing animals, branch-breaking wind, both sluggish and rapid water flow, compost accumulation, curious and property value–minded neighbors, and collected stones, feathers, grass seeds, and memories, she recalled an unusual prose piece, "On Impure Poetry," by poet Pablo Neruda:

> It is very appropriate, at certain times of the day or night, to look deeply into objects at rest: wheels which have traversed vast dusty spaces, bearing great cargos of vegetables or minerals, sacks from the coal yards, barrels, baskets, the handles and grips of the carpenter's tools. They exude the touch of man and the earth as a lesson to the tormented poet. Worn surfaces, the mark hands have left on things, the aura, sometimes tragic and always wistful, of these objects lend to reality a fascination not to be taken lightly.
>
> The flawed confusion of human beings shows in them, the proliferation, materials used and discarded, the prints of feet and fingers, the permanent mark of humanity on the inside and outside of all objects.
>
> That is the kind of poetry we should be after, poetry worn away as if by acid by the labor of hands, impregnated with sweat and smoke, smelling of lilies and of urine, splashed by the variety of what we do, legally or illegally.
>
> A poetry as impure as old clothes, as a body, with its foodstains and its shame, with wrinkles, observations, dreams, wakefulness, prophecies, declarations of love and hate, stupidities, shocks, idylls, political beliefs, negations, doubts, affirmations, taxes.[4]

4. This translation is from Reid 1996, 64. See also Neruda 1983.

This is the kind of landscape we should be after, too. A landscape known for forces that shape it, with green at the base of its chin, with wrinkles pronounced by shaggy shrubs, with darkened triangles where extra humidity gathers, with death and excrement giving birth and nutrients to the next generation, with salt and salt grass crusting alkaline edges where water once stood. The fascination offered by seeing and understanding the patina of process cannot be overestimated. The permanent mark of humanity is on the inside and the outside of landscapes, too—yes—this we see and expect when we look at our groomed, plumbed, trimmed homes. Yet the permanent mark of this landscape on humanity is becoming evident in key locations as regional materials infiltrate airports and highway exchanges, as water is held and valued, as renewable energy sources outpace fossil fuels in doing our work for us, as people read and appreciate the waterstain in this dry, golden, breathing hinge of mountains and plains. The self-conscious movement toward acknowledging the patterns and processes of this valued region has buffered its inhabitants from becoming crushed by deadening national conformity, to paraphrase geographer Josiah Royce. This is not simply nostalgia (although *nostalgia* is defined as "homesickness" in her dictionary, a more-than-appropriate reaction to the rapid change around us); this is honor, appreciation, pluck, doggedness.

A WESTERN SENSE OF PLACE The train moved the Cranes toward their new destination. From the window Ann saw tall trees clustered around the north edge of buildings. These trees pointed them to their next homeplace, where they would once again begin the act of seeing, learning, and discerning that "sense of place." Ann wrestled one more time with her invisible critic. Was she selling out by moving again? Was all this investigation into seeing and shaping the region's distinctiveness a fraud? She had caught herself over the years trying to borrow her friends' deep rootedness through osmosis but realized that this was where the fraud was. With her split-household upbringing, moving was a part of her. And, not surprisingly, she found herself drawn to the West, about which Stegner has remarked, "Whatever it might want to be, the West is still primarily a series of brief visitations or a trail to somewhere else."[5] Like so many others involved in recent migrations, Ann could not borrow rootedness; she

5. Stegner 1992, 72.

had to look at what she individually offered to cultivate her own sense of place. So she provided a means by which to see, understand, and appropriately shape places, whether she stayed or left. And to do this she needed to care while she was there. These twin offerings of caring and knowing what to do about it, in a design sense, were her substitutes for long-term attachment, because she, and many like her, could not settle down in one place after all, especially in the West.

She also came to realize that the waterstains in the semiarid West were more than a way of seeing. They were a way of being. She became suspicious when she was repeatedly drawn to edgy places and anomalous examples of gardens thriving against the odds, like the lilac shrub so far from a garden in the Boulder open space. Kenneth Helphand writes, "When we see a garden eecked out of difficult or forbidding terrain, or in uncommon associations—a garden out of place—along a railroad track, or a home garden in an industrial area or a parking lot, it captures our attention, even admiration. . . . In all these situations there is not only a shock of recognition of the garden's form and elements, but also a renewed appreciation of the garden's transformative power to beautify, comfort, and convey meaning."[6]

Ann appreciated the waterstains and "uncommon associations" within the Denver region because, for whatever reason, she related so much to being on the outside looking in. She preferred the blemished, tarnished quality of the stepsister-like word, *waterstain,* to the dignified, well-bred *watermark.* She admired brown with a speck of green rather than green with some or no brown. Being in a droughty environment made the rare gems of water more valued. Her sturdy jewel box concept from graduate school was back to haunt her again, she was amused to discover. Maybe a waterstain is like love, she considered. Maybe love is hard to come by in a split and frequently uprooted family. Maybe inundation, whether it be love or water, is too much to handle. Maybe, Ann thought, the beauty of the semiarid West is its ability to face drought and not take water for granted, to greatly appreciate it where it occurred, just as she did with love. The concept of the waterstain is growing in its applicability, she found. Apparently the waterstain, like a garden, has that "transformative power to . . . convey meaning."

6. Helphand 1997, 105.

Her mind snagged upon a treasure geographer Yi-Fu Tuan once planted in *Space and Place,* an idea as wonderful as all the collected objects she had ever put in her pockets combined: a sense of place, he writes, may be a "quality of awareness poised between being rooted in place, which is unconscious, and being alienated, which goes with exacerbated consciousness."[7] Alienation, then, is a necessary part of that sense of place, especially in the West—a comforting thought, Ann mused, as she could almost hear the train stretching and snapping her years of ties, attachments, and bonds to the Denver region. There's no home like place, she thought, secretly clicking her heels around the luggage at her feet.

7. Tuan 1977, 202.

appendix

PLANT NAMES

(Unless otherwise noted in the text, plant nomenclature is from Weber 1990 and *Sunset Western Garden Book* 1988.)

Common Name	Botanical Name
Alder	*Alnus incana* subsp. *tenuifolia*
Alkaligrass	*Puccinellia distans* 'Fults'
Alkaline sacaton	*Sporobolus airoides*
American elm	*Ulmus americana*
Arnica	*Arnica cordifolia*
Arnica	*Arnica fulgens*
Arrowhead	*Sagittaria cuneata*
Aster	*Aster spp.*
Bastard-toadflax	*Comandra umbellata*
Beggar's tick	*Lappula marginata*
Big bluestem	*Andropogon gerardii*
Bindweed	*Convolvulus arvensis*
Bitterbrush	*Purshia tridentata*
Black-eyed Susan	*Rudbeckia laciniata*
Blue grama	*Chondrosum gracile*
Blue sage	*Salvia azurea*
Bluebells	*Mertensia ciliata*
Boston ivy	*Parthenocissus tricuspidata*
Boulder raspberry	*Oreobatus deliciosus*
Box elder	*Negundo aceroides* subsp. *interius*
Broadleaf cattail	*Typha latifolia*

Buffalo grass	*Buchloë dactyloides*
Bulrush	*Scirpus spp.*
Bur oak	*Quercus macrocarpa*
Burdock	*Arctium minus*
Canada thistle	*Cirsium arvense*
Canada bluegrass	*Poa compressa*
Canada wild rye	*Elymus canadensis*
Chamomile	*Chamaemelum nobile*
Cheatgrass	*Anisantha tectorum*
Cheeseweed	*Malva neglecta*
Chokecherry	*Padus virginiana subsp. melanocarpa*
Cocklebur	*Xanthium strumarium*
Colorado blue spruce	*Picea pungens*
Columbine	*Aquilegia coerulea*
Common juniper	*Juniperus communis*
Coral bells	*Heuchera sanguinea*
Cottonwood	*Populus x acuminata*
Cottonwood	*Populus deltoides subspecies monilifera*
Crab apple	*Malus spp.*
Crack willow	*Salix fragilis*
Crane's bill	*Erodium ciculata*
Creeping mahonia	*Mahonia repens*
Crested wheatgrass	*Agropyron cristatum*
Douglas fir	*Pseudotsuga menziesii*
Duckweed	*Lemna turionifera*
European cranberry bush	*Viburnum opulus*
Fleabane	*Erigeron divergens*
Forget-me-not	*Myosotis scorpioides*
Foxtail barley	*Hordeum vulgare*
Geranium	*Geranium richardsonii*
Golden banner	*Thermopsis divaricarpa*
Green ash	*Fraxinus pensylvanica var. lanceolata*
Green needlegrass	*Stipa viridula*

Gumweed	*Grindelia squarrosa*
Hardy pink ice plant	*Delospermum cooperi*
Hawthorn	*Crataegus macrantha var. occidentalis*
Honey locust	*Gleditsia triacanthos inermis*
Horseweed	*Conyza canadensis*
Indiangrass	*Sorghastrum avenaceum*
Iris	*Iris pallida dalmatica*
Ironweed	*Bassia sieversiana*
Japanese barberry	*Berberis thunbergii*
Junegrass	*Koeleria macrantha*
Kentucky coffee tree	*Gymnocladus dioica*
Kentucky bluegrass	*Poa pratensis*
Kinnikinnick	*Arctostaphylos uva-ursi*
Klamath weed	*Hypericum perforatum*
Lamb's ears	*Stachys lanata*
Leadplant	*Amorpha nana*
Lemon daylily	*Hemerocallis lilioasphodelus*
Lilac	*Syringa vulgaris var. M. Le Gray*
Little bluestem	*Schizachyrium scoparium*
Marigold	*Tagetes erecta*
Milk vetch	*Astragalus spp.*
Milkweed	*Asclepias speciosa*
Monkshood	*Aconitum columbianum*
Mountain mahogany	*Cercocarpus montanus*
Nailwort	*Paronychia jamesii*
Narrowleaf cottonwood	*Populus angustifolia*
Needle-and-thread	*Stipa comata*
New Mexico locust	*Robinia neomexicana*
Ninebark	*Physocarpus monogynus*
Oneseed juniper	*Sabina monospermum*
Oregon grape	*Mahonia aquifolium*
Oriental poppy	*Papaver orientale*
Paperbark birch	*Betula papyrifera*

Peach-leaved willow	*Salix amygdaloides*
Penstemon	*Penstemon spp.*
Peony	*Paeonia spp.*
Pfitzer juniper	*Juniperus chinensis pfitzeriana*
Phlox	*Phlox paniculata*
Pineapple weed	*Lepidotheca suaveolens*
Pinon pine	*Pinus edulis*
Plantain	*Plantago major*
Ponderosa pine	*Pinus ponderosa*
Pondweed	*Potamogeton pectinatus*
Prairie cordgrass	*Spartina pectinata*
Prickly poppy	*Argemone polythemos*
Prickly pear	*Opuntia macrorhizae*
Prickly pear	*Opuntia polyacantha*
Prickly lettuce	*Lactuca serriola*
Prince's plume	*Stanleya pinnata*
Quaking aspen	*Populus tremuloides*
Rabbitbrush	*Chrysothamnus nauseosus*
Ragweed	*Ambrosia trifida*
Raspberry	*Rubus spp.*
Red osier	*Swida sericea*
Redtop	*Agrostis gigantea*
River birch	*Betula fontinalis*
Rocky Mountain beeplant	*Cleome serrulata*
Rush	*Juncus spp.*
Rush	*Juncus arcticus*
Russian olive	*Elaeagnus angustifolia*
Russian thistle	*Salsola australis*
Sage	*Salvia spp.*
Salt grass	*Distichlis spicata subsp. stricta*
Sand sagebrush	*Oligosporus filifolius*
Sandbar willow	*Salix exigua*

Scrub oak	*Quercus gambelii*
Sedge	*Carex spp.*
Shrubby cinquefoil	*Pentaphylloides floribunda*
Siberian elm	*Ulmus pumila*
Silver sage	*Artemisia frigida*
Silver maple	*Acer saccharinum*
Skunkbrush	*Rhus aromatica subsp. trilobata*
Smooth monkeyflower	*Mimulus glabratus*
Snowberry	*Symphoricarpos albus*
Spanish bayonet, yucca	*Yucca glauca*
Spirea	*Spiraea thunbergii*
Spleenwort	*Asplenium andrewsii*
Spotted knapweed	*Acosta maculosa*
Staghorn sumac	*Rhus typhina*
Sun sedge	*Carex pensylvanica subsp. heliophila*
Sunflower	*Helianthus annuus*
Sweet woodruff	*Galium odoratum*
Switchgrass	*Panicum virgatum*
Tamarisk	*Tamarix ramosissima*
Three square	*Scirpus americanus*
Timothy	*Phleum pratense*
Van Houtt spirea	*Spiraea vanhouttei*
Virgin's bower	*Clematis ligusticifolia*
Water plantain	*Alisma triviale*
Wax currant	*Ribes cereum*
Waxflower	*Jamesia americana*
Weeping juniper	*Juniperus scopulorum 'Tolleson's Weeping'*
Western wheatgrass	*Pascopyrum smithii*
Western hackberry	*Celtis reticulata*
Wild rye	*Leymus triticoides*
Wild licorice	*Glycyrrhiza lepidota*
Wild onion	*Allium textile*

Wild rose	*Rosa woodsii*
Wolftail	*Lycurus phleoides*
Wood sorrel	*Oxalis dillenii*
Zinnia	*Zinnia elegans*

references

Adams, Robert. 1977. *Denver: A Photographic Survey of the Metropolitan Area.* Denver: Colorado Associated University Press.

Ackerman, Diane. 1993. Foreword to *By Nature's Design,* by Pat Murphy and William Neill. San Francisco: Chronicle Books.

Anderson, Edgar. 1956. Man as a maker of new plants and new plant communities. In *Man's Role in Changing the Face of the Earth,* ed. William L. Thomas. Chicago: University of Chicago Press.

Appleton, Jay. 1994. *How I Made the World: Shaping a View of Landscape.* Elloughton, U.K.: University of Hull Press.

Appleyard, Donald, Kevin Lynch, and John R. Myer. 1964. *The View from the Road.* Cambridge: MIT Press.

Aston, Michael. 1985. *Interpreting the Landscape.* London: Batesford.

Beveridge, Charles E. 1995. Regionalism in Frederick Law Olmsted's social thought and landscape practice. In *Regional Garden Design in the United States,* ed. Therese O'Malley and Marc Treib. Washington, D.C.: Dumbarton Oaks Research Library and Collection.

Billout, Guy. 1997. "Oasis." *Atlantic,* April, 103.

Bonand, Steve. 1992. Yesterday and tomorrow. *Xeriscape Colorado! Newsletter* (summer): 1-2.

Bradley, R. S., R. G. Barry, and G. Kiladis. 1982. Climatic fluctuations of the western United States during the period of instrumental records. Amherst, Mass.: University of Massachusetts, Department of Geology and Geography, Contribution 42.

Brandegee, T. S. 1876. The flora of southwest Colorado. *Bulletin of the Geological and Geographical Survey of the Territories* 2(3).

Branson, Farrel A., and Lynn M. Shown. 1989. Contrasts of vegetation, soils, microclimates, and geomorphic processes between north- and south-facing slopes on Green Mountain near Denver, Colorado. Denver: U.S. Geological Survey Water Resources Investigations Report 89-4094.

Brown, Brenda. 1991. Avant-gardism and landscape architecture. *Landscape Journal* 10(2):134-54.

Campbell, Joseph, with Bill Moyers. 1988. *The Power of Myth.* Ed. Betty Sue Flowers. New York: Doubleday.

Campbell, Joseph, and Henry Morton Robinson. 1944. *A Skeleton Key to Finnegans Wake.* New York: Harcourt, Brace.

Chronic, Halka. 1980. *Roadside Geology of Colorado.* Missoula, Mont.: Mountain Press.

City and County of Denver, Colorado. 1989. *Denver Comprehensive Plan Summary.* Denver: Denver Planning Office.

City of Boulder Open Space Department. N.d. Stop the Russian-olive invasion. Monograph. City of Boulder.

Clark, S. V., P. J. Webber, V. Komarakova, and W. A. Weber. 1980. Map of mixed prairie grassland vegetation, Rocky Flats, Colorado. Boulder: Institute of Arctic and Alpine Research Occasional Paper 35.

Clements, F. E. [1916] 1928. Plant succession: An analysis of the development of vegetation. Publication 242. Washington, D.C.: Carnegie Institution of Washington. (Reprinted in book form in 1928 by Wilson, New York.)

Colorado Natural History Museum. 1996. The New West. Exhibit at Colorado History Museum, Denver. August 1996.

Colorado Scientific Society. 1884. *The Artesian Wells of Denver.* Denver: Colorado Scientific Society.

Cooper, David J. 1987. First annual report: Chatfield Arboretum Wetland Creation Project. Golden, Colo.: Colorado School of Mines. Prepared for State of Colorado Department of Transportation.

———. 1990. Fourth annual report: Chatfield Arboretum Wetland Creation Project. Golden, Colo.: Colorado School of Mines. Prepared for State of Colorado Department of Transportation.

Cousineau, Phil, ed. 1990. *The Hero's Journey: The World of Joseph Campbell.* San Francisco: Harper San Francisco.

Covich, Alan, Becky Rudman, Skip Smith, Pat Kennedy, David Cooper, Kurt Fausch, and Ken Wilson. 1994. Literature review on the range of natural variation in the Colorado Front Range and adjacent grasslands. Fort Collins: Arapaho/Roosevelt National Forest Report.

Crowe, Sylvia, and Mary Mitchell. 1988. *The Pattern of Landscape.* Chichester, U.K.: Packard.

Davidson, James Dale, and Lord William Rees-Moog. 1991. *The Great Reckoning.* New York: Summit Books.

Dawson, Patrick, Anne Palmer Donohoe, and David S. Jackson. 1993. Boom time in the Rockies. *Time,* 6 September, 20-26.

DeBoer, Saco R. 1948. *Around the Seasons in Denver Parks and Gardens.* Denver: Smith-Brooks.

———. 1972. Plans, parks, and people. *Green Thumb* 29(5):143-225.

Denver Department of Parks and Recreation. 1997a. Workbook, Denver Commons Park work session number 4. Denver: Civitas.

———. 1997b. Workbook, Denver Commons Park work session number 6. Denver: Civitas.

———. 1997c. Workbook, Denver Commons Park work session number 7. Denver: Civitas.

Denver Municipal Facts. 1909. 1(7): cover.

Denver Regional Council of Governments (DRCOG). 1992. *2020: A Long-Range Growth Forecast for the Denver Region.* Denver: DRCOG.

———. 1995. *2015: Interim Regional Transportation Plan.* Denver: DRCOG.

Denver Water. 1994. Comprehensive annual financial report. Denver: Denver Water.

Dorsett, Lyle W. 1977. *The Queen City: A History of Denver.* Boulder: Pruett.

Dube, Richard L. 1994. Natural inspirations. *American Horticulturist* 73:23-27.

Duncan, James. 1992. Elite landscapes as cultural (re)productions: The case of Shaughnessy Heights. In *Inventing Places: Studies in Cultural Geography,* ed. Kay Anderson and Fay Gayle. Melbourne: Longman Cheshire.

Eisley, Loren. 1959. *The Immense Journey.* New York: Vintage Books.

Frampton, Kenneth. 1987. *Modern Architecture: A Critical History.* London: Thames and Hudson.

Francis, Mark, and Randolph T. Hester Jr. 1990. *The Meaning of Gardens.* Cambridge: MIT Press.

Goetzmann, William H., and William N. Goetzmann. 1986. *The West of the Imagination.* New York: Norton.

Goldstein, Barbara. 1983. Harlequin Plaza. *Landscape Architecture* 73(4):56-59.

Green Thumb Report: Will there be enough water for our gardens? 1971. *Green Thumb* 29(4):134-38.

Hadley, K. S., and T. T. Veblen. 1993. Stand response to western spruce budworm and Douglas-fir bark beetle outbreaks, Colorado Front Range. *Canadian Journal of Forestry Research* 23:479-91.

Hansen, Wallace R., John Chronic, and John Matelock. 1978. Climatography of the Front Range urban corridor and vicinity, Colorado. U.S. Geological Survey Professional Paper 1019. Washington: U.S. Government Printing Office.

Helphand, Kenneth. 1997. Defiant gardens. *Journal of Garden History* 17(2):101-21.

Helphand, Kenneth I., and Ellen Manchester. 1991. *Colorado: Visions of an American Landscape.* Niwot, Colo.: Roberts Rinehart.

Hillier, Donald E., Paul A. Schneider Jr., and E. Carter Hutchinson. 1983. Depth to water table (1976-1977) in the Greater Denver area Front Range urban corridor, Colorado. Misc. Investigations Series, Map 1-856-K. Denver: U.S. Geological Survey.

Horn, H. S. 1974. The ecology of secondary succession. *Annual Review of Ecological Systematics* 5:25-37.

Hough, Michael. 1990. *Out of Place: Restoring Identity to Regional Landscape.* New Haven: Yale University Press.

Ipsen, Diane. 1995. Reading our landscape of trees. *Mountain, Plain, and Garden* 51(1):5-7.

Johnson, Mark W. 1983. Harlequin visit. *Landscape Architecture* 73(6):29.

Joyce, James. [1939] 1960. Finnegans wake. New York: Viking Press.

Kaplan, Rachel, and Stephen Kaplan. 1990. Restorative experience: The healing power of nearby nature. In *The Meaning of Gardens,* ed. Mark Francis and Randolph T. Hester. Cambridge: MIT Press.

Kelaidis, Panayoti. 1990. The Tethyan garden. *Mountain, Plain, and Garden* 47(2):4-8.

———. 1995. The rock alpine garden. *Mountain, Plain, and Garden* 52(1):18-21.

Kingsolver, Barbara. 1988. *The Bean Trees.* New York: Harper Perennial.

Knopf, Fritz L. 1986. Changing landscapes and the cosmopolitanism of the eastern Colorado avifauna. *Wildlife Society Bulletin* 14(2):132-42.

Leonard, Stephen J., and Thomas J. Noel. 1990. *Denver: Mining Camp to Metropolis.* Niwot, Colo.: University Press of Colorado.

Leopold, Aldo. 1949. *A Sand County Almanac.* Oxford: Oxford University Press.

Lessinger, Jack. 1991. *Penturbia: Where the Real Estate Will Boom after the Crash of Suburbia.* Seattle: SocioEconomics.

Lewis, Charles A. 1990. Gardening as a healing process. In *The Meaning of Gardens,* ed. Mark Francis and Randolph T. Hester. Cambridge: MIT Press.

———. 1996. *Green Nature/Human Nature: The Meaning of Plants in Our Lives.* Urbana: University of Illinois Press.

Los Angeles Times. 1992. Warning sign on nuclear dump, 15 October.

Lynch, Kevin. 1960. *The Image of the City.* Cambridge: MIT Press.

Mandelbrot, Benoit B. 1983. *The Fractal Geometry of Nature.* New York: W. H. Freeman and Company.

Marcus, Clare Cooper. 1985. *Design Guidelines: A Bridge between Research and Decision Making.* Berkeley, Calif.: Center for Environmental Design Research.

Marr, John W. 1961. *Ecosystems of the East Slope of the Front Range in Colorado.* Boulder: University of Colorado Press.

Marr, John W., and William S. Boyd. 1979. Vegetation map of the Greater Denver area, Front Range urban corridor, Colorado. Miscellaneous Investigations Series, Map I-856-I. Reston, Va.: U.S. Geological Survey.

Marsh, W. M. 1991. *Landscape Planning: Environmental Applications.* New York: John Wiley and Sons.

Mast, Joy Nystrom, Thomas T. Veblen, and Michael E. Hodgson. 1997. Tree invasion within a pine/grassland ecotone: An approach with historic aerial photography and GIS modelling. *Forest Ecology and Management* 93:181-94.

McCrary, Irvin J. Archives. Western History Center Collection, Denver Public Library.

McGinnies, William J. 1991. *Changes in Vegetation and Land Use in Eastern Colorado: A Photographic Study, 1904-1986.* U.S. Department of Agriculture, Agriculture Research Service, ARS-85.

Mead, Elwood. 1909. *Irrigation Institutions.* New York: Macmillan.

Meinig, Donald W. 1972. American wests: Preface to a geographical interpretation. *Annals of the Association of American Geographers* 62:159-84.

——— 1990. Foreword to *The Making of the American Landscape,* ed. Michael P. Conzen. Boston: Unwin Hyman.

Miles, J. 1979. *Vegetation Dynamics.* London: Chapman and Hall.

Milne, Bruce T. 1991. The utility of fractal geometry in landscape design. *Landscape and Urban Planning* 21(1-2):81-90.

Mollison, Bill. 1990. *Permaculture: A Designer's Manual.* Tyalgum, Australia: Tagari.

Mumford, Lewis. [1925] 1976. The fourth migration. In *Planning the Fourth Migration: The Neglected Vision of the Regional Planning Association of America,* ed. Carl Sussman. Cambridge: MIT Press.

Mutel, Cornelia Fleischer, and John C. Emerick. 1992. *From Grassland to Glacier.* Boulder: Johnson Books.

Nabhan, Gary Paul. 1985. *Gathering the Desert.* Tucson: University of Arizona Press.

———. 1989. *Enduring Seeds.* San Francisco: North Point.

Nassauer, Joan. 1995. Messy ecosystems, orderly frames. *Landscape Journal* 14(2):161-70.

Neruda, Pablo. 1983. Some thoughts on impure poetry. In *Passions and Impressions,* trans. Margaret Sayers Peden. New York: Farrar, Straus and Giroux.

Noel, Thomas J., and Barbara S. Norgren. 1987. *Denver: The City Beautiful.* Denver: Historic Denver.

Noel, T. J., P. F. Mahoney, and R. E. Stevens. 1994. *Historical Atlas of Colorado.* Norman: University of Oklahoma Press.

Nolan, Bob. 1945. Cool Water. Unichappelle Music, Los Angeles, Calif.

Obmascik, Mark. 1996. Metro area is feeling the heat. *Denver Post,* 1 September.

Olin, Laurie. 1995. Regionalism and the practice of Hanna/Olin, Ltd. In *Regional Garden Design in the United States,* ed. Therese O'Malley and Marc Treib. Washington, D.C.: Dumbarton Oaks Research Library and Collection.

Orians, Gordon. 1998. Past-president's address. *Bulletin of the Ecological Society of America* 79(1):15.

Peet, Robert K. 1981. Forest vegetation of the Colorado Front Range: Composition and dynamics. *Vegetatio* 45:3-75.

Penwardin, Elaine. 1967. *It's the Plants That Matter.* London: Allen and Unwin.

Pope, Alexander. 1731. An Epistle to the Right Honorable Richard, earl of Burlington. London: Printed for L. Gilliver.

Proffitt, Steve. 1997. Jane Jacobs: Still challenging the way we think about cities. *Los Angeles Times,* 12 October.

Quinn, John R. 1994. *Wildlife Survivors: The Flora and Fauna of Tomorrow.* Blue Ridge Summit, Pa.: TAB Books.

Ramaley, Francis. 1907. Plant zones in the Rocky Mountains of Colorado. *Science* 26:642-43.

———. 1927. *Colorado Plant Life.* Boulder: University of Colorado.

Reid, Alistair. 1996. Neruda and Borges. *New Yorker* 72:56-65.

Robinson, Nick H. 1992. *The Planting Design Handbook.* Hampshire, U.K.: Gower.

Robson, S. G. 1987. Bedrock aquifers in the Denver Basin, Colorado: A quantitative water-resources appraisal. U.S. Geological Survey Professional Paper 1257. Washington: U.S. Government Printing Office.

———. 1989. Alluvial and bedrock aquifers of the Denver Basin, Colorado. Washington: U.S. Government Printing Office.

Rodis, Barbara K., and Rice Odell. 1992. *A Dictionary of Environmental Quotations.* New York: Simon and Schuster.

Royce, Josiah. 1969. *Basic Writings.* Ed. John J. McDermott. 2 vols. Chicago: University of Chicago Press.

Stapleton Redevelopment Foundation, City and County of Denver, and Citizens Advisory Board. 1995. *Stapleton Development Plan: Integrating Jobs, Environment, and Community.* Denver.

Stegner, Wallace. 1987. *The American West as Living Space.* Ann Arbor: University of Michigan Press.

———. 1992. *Where the Bluebird Sings to the Lemonade Spring: Living and Writing in the West.* New York: Penguin Books.

Steinbeck, John. 1939. *The Grapes of Wrath.* New York: Viking.

Sunset Western Garden Book. 1988. Menlo Park, Calif.: Lane.

Thompson, R. S., C. Whitlock, P. J. Bartlein, S. P. Harrison, and W. G. Spaulding. 1993. Climatic changes in the western United States since 18,000 years before present. In *Global Climates since the Last Glacial Maximum,* ed. H. E. Wright Jr., J. E. Kutzbach, T. Webb III, W. F. Ruddiman, F. A. Street-Perrott, and P. J. Bartlein. Minneapolis: University of Minnesota Press.

Thorsheim, Robert. N.d. Vestiges: Understanding patterns of human habitational response in the Colorado Front Range. Master's thesis, University of Colorado, Denver.

Trappe, James M. 1981. Mycorrhizae and productivity of arid and semiarid rangelands. In *Advances in Food-Processing Systems for Arid and Semiarid Lands.* New York: Academic.

Tuan, Yi-Fu. 1977. *Space and Place.* Minneapolis: University of Minnesota Press.

United States Department of Agriculture and State Agricultural Colleges Cooperating Extension Service. Various years. Combined annual report of county extension workers. Denver: USDA and State Agricultural Colleges Cooperating Extension Service.

Veblen, T. T., and D. C. Lorenz. 1991. *The Colorado Front Range: A Century of Ecological Change.* Salt Lake City: University of Utah Press.

Vessel, Matthew F., and Herbert H. Wong. 1987. *Natural History of Vacant Lots.* Berkeley: University of California Press.

Virgil. 1988. *Georgics.* Ed. Richard F. Thomas. Cambridge: Cambridge University Press.

Walter, Heinrich. 1985. *Vegetation of the Earth and Ecological Systems of the Geo-sphere.* Berlin: Springer.

Walter, H., E. Harnickell, and D. Mueller-Dombois. 1975. *Climate-Diagram Maps of the Individual Continents and the Ecological Climate Regions of the Earth.* New York: Springer.

Watts, Mae Theilgaard. 1975. *Reading the Landscape of America.* New York: Macmillan.

Webb, Walter Prescott. 1931. *The Great Plains.* Waltham, Mass.: Blaisdell.

Weber, William A. 1976. *Rocky Mountain Flora.* Boulder: Colorado Associated University Press.

———. 1990. *Colorado Flora: Eastern Slope.* Niwot, Colo.: University Press of Colorado.

Wenk, William E. 1978. A plains primer for knowing the natural landscape of the Denver area. Master's thesis, University of Oregon.

Whitney, Gleaves. 1983. *Colorado Front Range: Landscape Divided.* Boulder: Johnson Books.

Worster, Donald. 1987. New west, true west: Interpreting the region's history. *Western Historical Quarterly* 18:141-56.

Zelinsky, Wilbur. 1980. North America's vernacular regions. *Annals of the Association of American Geographers* 70:1-16.

Zwinger, Ann. 1988. *Beyond the Aspen Grove.* Tucson: University of Arizona Press.

index

Ackerman, Diane, 31
agricultural quilts, 128, 183
AIDS Memorial Grove, 67
Anderson, Edgar, 77
Andropogon, 181
Anglophilia, 71
animal and plant relationships, 61–63; grazing impacts of, 124–25
Appleton, Jay, 66, 152–53
aquifers, 41–43
aridity, 14, 46–48, 110
Around the Seasons in Denver's Parks and Gardens (Walter), 48
aspect patterns: north-facing slope, 12, 38–39, 114–15, 162; south-facing slope, 38–39, 115, 163

Balzac, Honore de, 26
beauty spots, 134, 156, 163, 183
Berry, Wendell, 64
biomes, 77
biotic processes, 33–34, 53–65, 110,158, 192
bird perch plants, 123, 155, 158
Boulder: City of Boulder Open Space weed abatement program, 58–59; climate, 47, 49, 51; commercial design example, 175–79; location of study transect, 17, 19; residential design example, 141; south Boulder open space, 112, 119, 141
Boulder Creek, 177, 178
Boyd, William, 81, 82
Branson, Farrel A., and Lynn M. Shown, 38–39, 114
Brighton, 17, 24, 47, 51, 133
Buckner, David, 120–21
buffalo grass: 56–57; and blue grama lawns, 121–22
Bureau of Reclamation, 19, 58

cactus barriers, 133, 156
Campbell, Joseph, 4, 139
Central Park, 133–34
Chatfield Reservoir, 51
cheatgrass, 56
checkerboards, 128
Cherry Creek, 185, 186
Cherry Creek reservoir (Lake), 21, 47, 168, 169, 170
Cherry Creek State Park, 168
Chinooks, 50–51, 167
City Beautiful movement, 97, 182, 198
Civitas, Inc., 172, 179, 187, 189, 190
Clements, F. E., 54, 60
climate, Denver region: cloud cover, 51; frost-free periods, 48–49; precipitation, 46, 47–48; storm paths, 49–50; temperature, 47; variability, 45–46, 76; wind, 50–51
climatic processes, 33, 44–53, 110, 192
Commons Park Master Plan, 187–93
connectivity, 88
cottonwood, 83, 158, 186; ditch-stitches, 116; homestead trees, 130–31, 156; meanders, 116; road-cut stripes, 31, 38, 121–22
crack plants, 122, 155, 159, 163
Crowe, Dame Sylvia, 112, 126
"cues to care," 137
cultural and personal expressions as design motivators, 70–71
cultural processes, 34, 65–73, 110, 192

DeBoer, Saco: flowerbed plantings, 48, 49, 135; Inspiration Point design, 20, 73; parkway design, 21, 115, 191
Denver Botanic Gardens, 67, 72, 78, 80
Denver Comprehensive Plan, 7
Denver Department of Parks and Recreation, 187–88
Denver design eras: confusion, 102–4;

context, 104–5; diffusion, 99–101; enhancement, 97–99; habitation, 91–92; promotion, 94–97; survival, 92–94
Denver Front Range: change of, 10; defining, 17–18; moving to, 5; potential growth pattern, 196–200; urban corridor map series 17, 19; vegetation, 80–86
Denver Regional Council of Governments (DRCOG), 7, 17, 110, 161
Denver Water, 26, 42
Design Guidelines: A Bridge between Research and Decision Making (Marcus), 153
Design Workshop, 172
disturbance patterns: fire disturbance, 123–24; fugitive plants, 127, 129; unpalatable remains, 124–25; weed infiltrations, 125–27
ditch-stitch patterns, 116
Dorsett, Lyle, 90
Duncan, James, 70, 71, 73
Dutch elm disease, 102, 132

Ecosystems of the East Slope of the Front Range in Colorado (Marr), 80
efficient irrigation patterns, 127
Eisley, Loren, 35
Eldorado Springs, 17
elevation patterns: elevation stripes, 113–14; upper and lower treeline, 114

faith, as design motivator, 67
Federal Center, 19, 22, 58
Finnegans Wake (Joyce), 44–45
fire, suppression and repercussions, 61, 123–24
"Forest Vegetation of the Colorado Front Range" (Peet), 80
formative processes, 33–73, 75, 110
Four-Mile Historic Park, 21, 23, 184–87
fractals, 112–13, 196
Frampton, Kenneth, 28
Francis, Mark, 69
Fremont, John C., 77
Frost, Robert, 122
fugitive plants, 127, 129

geomorphic processes, 33, 35–43, 110, 192
Goetzmann, William H., and William N., 8

Golden: climate, 47, 49; development, 26–27; Golden City, 92, 93; location of study transect, 17
grazing impacts, 62, 124–25
Green, Frances (Kelley), 175, 177, 178
Green Mountain, 22, 23, 38–39
grid, 19, 127, 191
groundwater, Denver basin, 41–42

hardy pink ice plant, 79–80
Hartman, Jim, 187
haystripes, 127
healing, as design motivator, 72
hedgerows and windbreaks, 131–32
Helphand, Kenneth, 68, 133, 134, 202
Hester, Randolph, 69
High Plains, 40
hogback, 30, 37
homestead siting patterns, 93, 186
homestead trees, 130–31, 155–56
Horn, H. S., 60
Hough, Michael, 28
hydrological cycle diagrams, 44–45

Inspiration Point, 20, 73
Interstate 25 and Interstate 225 interchange design, 160–64
Interstate 70 roadcut, 35

Jacobs, Jane, 147
Jefferson County Government Center, 166, 172–75
Johnson, Lady Bird, 137
Johnson, Mark, 179–83, 185, 188
Johnson, Todd, 172–74
Jones and Jones, 187–88, 189
Joyce, James, 44
juniper belts, 134, 143, 147

Kahn, Louis, 173
Kaplan, Rachel, and Steve, 71
Kelaidis, Panayoti, 78–80
Kessler, George, 180, 191
Kingsolver, Barbara, 64

Lamm, Richard, 5
Land and Water Fund of the Rockies (LAW Fund), 175–79
Leopold, Aldo, 13
Lewis, Charles, 72
Long, Stephen, 77
Los Angeles, 5, 9, 70
Lowry Air Force Base, 180, 183
Lynch, Kevin, 28

MacArthur, General Douglas, 3, 8
mail patches, 136
Mandelbrot, Benoit, 112
Marcus, Clare Cooper, 153–54
Marr, John, 80–81, 111, 113, 119
Marsh, William, 33, 75, 110
Mast, Joy, 115
McGinnies, William, 86, 124–25
Mead, Elwood, 14
meadow blankets, 119
meander patterns, 116, 183
Meinig, Donald W. (D. W.), 4, 34
microclimate protection, 130
microorganisms and plant relationships, 63–65
migration, western, 4, 6, 197
Miles, John, 33, 54
Milne, Bruce, 112–13
Morrison, 17, 38, 49
Moss, Ann, 184–187
Muir, John, 67
Mumford, Lewis, 6
Municipal Facts, 97, 132, 193
mycorrhizal fungi, 64

Nabhan, Gary, 55, 64
Nassauer, Joan, 137
National Forum on Nonpoint Source Pollution, 178
Naylor, Mark, 190, 191
Neruda, Pablo, 200
"New West, True West" (Worster), 199
Nolan, Bob, 13
north-facing slope patterns, 12, 38–39, 114–15, 162
nostalgia, 201

oasis theme, in Denver, 133–34
Olin, Laurie, 27, 199
Olmsted, Frederick Law, 133–34
order, as design motivator, 68–70
Orians, Gordon, 67

pattern, definition, 31–32
pattern-based planting design: design, 157–59; evaluation, 159–60; examples, 141–64; goals and objectives, 143–47; guidelines, 153–57; knowing the site, 147–52; patterns: —of Denver region, 113–37; —general, 31–32, 109–13; processes, 33–73; program, 152–53; region, 17–18; summary, 164–65
patterns of Denver region: aspect, 114–15, 154; elevation, 113–14; pleasure needs, 133–36; presence or lack of disturbance, 123–27; production needs, 127–29; protection needs, 129–33; soil elements, 122–23; soil moisture availability, 119–22; water concentration, 115–19, 154–55
Peet, Robert, 80, 81, 82–88
Penwardin, Elaine, 138
pivot irrigation, 127, 157, 198
Plains Indians, 76, 91–92
planning and design, scales of: city, 7; planting design, 8; regional, 7; site design, 7–8
plant communities, Denver Front Range: cottonwood forest, 83; foothills ponderosa–Douglas fir forest, 85; foothills ravine forest, 84; grasslands, 84–85; mesic foothills woodland, 85; mesic montane woodlands, 85–86; mixed wet forest, 83–84; mountain ravine forest, 84; ponderosa pine shrubland, 86; shrublands, 86; xeric foothills woodland, 86
planting design, 8, 31
plant succession, 54; adaptation and stability, 60; competition, 56–60; establishment, 55–56; immigration, 55; implications, 60–61; initiation, 54–55; relationships, 61–65; use of early successional plants, 65, 155, 159
pleasure, as design motivator, 66–72
pleasure patterns: beauty spots, 134, 156, 163, 183; juniper belts, 134, 143, 147; mail

patches, 136; oasis, 133–34; property lines, 134–35; welcome patches, 135–36
Pleistocene, 76
Pope, Alexander, 28
Popov, M. G., 78
Powell, John Wesley, 46
power, as design motivator, 68
production, as design motivator, 65
production patterns: agricultural quilts, 128, 183; checkerboards, 128; efficient irrigation, 127; haystripes, 127; sunflower frames, 128; unexpected agriculture, 129; wetland pockmarks, 128
property definition, 71, 133, 134–35
protection, as design motivator, 66
protection patterns: cactus barriers, 133, 156; homestead trees, 130–31, 155–56; microclimate protection, 130; snowfence stripes, 131, 155, 162; urban reprieves, 132, 162; windbreaks and hedgerows, 131–32

Quinn, John, 88

Ramaley, Francis, 80, 81, 119
Reading the Landscape of America (Watts), 89
Red Rocks State Park, 12, 21
region, defining, 17–18
regionalism, 28
Rhizobium, 63–64
ringed reservoirs, 116, 117, 170–71
Riverfront Park system, 188, 193
road cut stripes, 121–22
Rocky Mountain Arsenal, 131; National Wildlife Refuge, 22–24, 180, 182–83
rocky reservoirs, 119, 163, 177, 192
rootedness, 108–9, 201–3
Royce, Josiah, 28, 201
Russian olive, 58–59, 80, 83

salt response plants, 122
Sand Creek, 180
scale: of patterns, 111–13; of planning and design, 7–8; of viewing landscapes, 15–16
Shapins, Jerry, 184–87
Shop Creek, 168–72
shrubbed squares, 119–20

Siberian elms, 69, 70
Skunk Creek, 177, 178
snowfence stripes, 131, 155, 162
soil element patterns: bird perch plants, 123, 155, 158; salt response plants, 122
soil formation, 36–40, 148, 173–74
soil moisture availability patterns: crack plants, 122, 155, 159, 163; road cut stripes, 121–22; rocky reservoirs, 119, 163, 177, 192; shrubbed squares, 119–20
Sons of the Pioneers, 11
south Boulder: open space, 112, 119, 141; residential design, 141–60
south-facing slope patterns, 38–39, 115, 163
South Platte River: flows, 39–40, 42; Greenway, 62; park design, 188–92; pre-1858, 39, 91–92
Space and Place (Tuan), 203
Speer, Robert, 99, 193
Stapleton Development Plan, 179–83
Stegner, Wallace: on Denver, 199; on West, 13, 73, 110, 175, 192, 201
Stein, Gertrude, 73
Steinbeck, John, 9, 142, 165
steppe vegetation, 77–80
stockyards, 22, 25
striped watercourses, 117, 189
sunflower frames, 128
sun-shade diagramming, 149–50

tamarisk, 19, 57–58
Tethyan Sea, 79
toes of slope, 117, 163
transect method for determining regional patterns, 19
Tuan, Yi-Fu, 203
2015: Interim Regional Transportation Plan, 161
unexpected agriculture, 129
United States Geological Survey (USGS) map series, 17
unpalatable remains, 124–25
upper and lower treeline, 114

vegetation: Denver Front Range communities, 83–86; diagramming, 80–83; early descriptions, 77; steppe, 77–80

Vegetation Map of the Greater Denver Area, Front Range Urban Corridor (Marr and Boyd), 81, 82
Vegetation of the Earth (Walter), 47
Victorian era design, 96, 186
Victory Gardens, 100, 128

Walter, Heinrich, 47, 48, 77–78
water concentration patterns, 157, ditch-stitches, 116; meadow blankets, 119; meanders, 116, 183; ringed reservoirs, 116, 117, 170–71; striped watercourses, 117, 189; toes of slope, 117, 163; wetland rings, 117–18, 155, 158, 192
watermark, 14, 202
waterstain: definition, 14; legibility 11–16; meaning, 202; patterns, 110, 113–36, 155, 182–83
Watts, Mae Theilgaard, 89, 129
Webb, Walter Prescott, 4, 46–47, 110
weed infiltrations, 125–27
Weinstein, Gayle, 67
welcome patches, 135–36
Wenk, William, 37, 169–71, 175
Wenk Associates, 169, 176, 181, 182
West, the: of the imagination, 8; migrating to, 4, 6, 197; as process, 73;
westering, 4
Westerly Creek, 180–82
western sense of place, 201–3
wetland pockmarks, 128
wetland rings, 117–18, 155, 158, 192
Wildlife Survivors (Quinn), 88
windbreaks and hedgerows, 131–32
Worster, Donald, 199

Xeriscape: comparison with pattern-based design, 142, 143, 145; description, 28–29; eighth step, 84; example, 103–4

Yellowstone National Park, 138

Zelinsky, Wilbur, 18
zonobiomes, 77
Zwinger, Ann, 113

about the author

JOAN WOODWARD was born in the suburbs of Columbus, Ohio, and raised in a variety of locations throughout the Midwest. She earned a Bachelor of Arts degree in botany and German at DePauw University and a Master of Landscape Architecture at the University of Colorado, Denver. She worked for many years as a park planner, natural resource specialist, and landscape architect with the National Park Service in Alaska and Denver before shifting her career toward teaching and research in landscape architecture. She has taught at Arizona State University and at the University of Colorado, Denver and now is associate professor and graduate program coordinator at California State Polytechnic University, Pomona. Her teaching and research focus is on integrating landscape interpretation, ecology, and design. She currently lives in Sierra Madre, California, with her daughter and husband.

Library of Congress Cataloging-in-Publication Data

Woodward, Joan.
Waterstained landscapes : seeing and shaping regionally distinctive places / Joan Woodward; drawings by Kiku Kurahashi.
    p. cm. —(Center books on contemporary landscape design)
Includes bibliographical references.
ISBN 0-8018-6200-0 (alk. paper)
1. Landscape architecture. 2. Landscape assessment. 3. Regional planning.
4. Landscape architecture—Colorado. 5. Landscape assessment—Colorado.
6. Regional planning—Colorado. I. Title. II. Series.
SB472.45.W66   2000
712′.09788′6—dc21   99-026764